Drew University Studies in Liturgy Series
General Editors: Kenneth E. Rowe and Robin A. Leaver

1. *Pulpit, Table, and Song: Essays in Celebration of Howard Hageman,* by Heather Murray Elkins and Edward C. Zaragoza

2. *St. James in the Streets: The Religious Processions of Loíza Aldea, Puerto Rico,* by Edward C. Zaragoza

3. *The Impact of the Liturgical Movement on American Lutheranism,* by Timothy C. J. Quill

4. *The Language of the Psalms in Worship: American Revisions of Watts's Psalter,* by Rochelle A. Stackhouse

5. *The Matter and Manner of Praise: The Controversial Evolution of Hymnody in the Church of England, 1760–1820,* by Thomas K. McCart

6. *"Bless the Lord, O My Soul": The New-York Liturgy of the Dutch Reformed Church, 1767,* by Daniel James Meeter

7. *The Eucharistic Service of the Catholic Apostolic Church and Its Influence on Reformed Liturgical Renewals of the Nineteenth Century,* by Gregg Alan Mast

8. *Moving toward Emancipatory Language: A Study of Recent Hymns,* by Robin Knowles Wallace

9. *Two Faces of Elizabethan Anglican Theology: Sacraments and Salvation in the Thought of William Perkins and Richard Hooker,* by Bryan D. Spinks

10. *The Language of Baptism: A Study of the Authorized Baptismal Liturgies of The United Church of Canada, 1925–1995,* by William S. Kervin

11. *The Reform of Baptism and Confirmation in American Lutheranism,* by Jeffrey A. Truscott

12. *"With One Heart and One Voice": A Core Repertory of Hymn Tunes Published for Use in the Methodist Episcopal Church in the United States: 1808–1878,* by Fred Kimball Graham

"With One Heart and One Voice"

A Core Repertory of Hymn Tunes Published for Use in the Methodist Episcopal Church in the United States, 1808–1878

Fred Kimball Graham

Drew University Studies in Liturgy, No. 12

The Scarecrow Press, Inc.
Lanham, Maryland • Toronto • Oxford
2004

SCARECROW PRESS, INC.

Published in the United States of America
by Scarecrow Press, Inc.
A wholly owned subsidary of The Rowman & Littlefield Publishing Group, Inc.
4501 Forbes Boulevard, Suite 200, Lanham, Maryland 20706
www.scarecrowpress.com

PO Box 317
Oxford
OX2 9RU, UK

British Library Cataloguing in Publication Information Available

Library of Congress Cataloging-in-Publication Data

Graham, Fred Kimball, 1946–
  "With one heart and one voice" : a core repertory of hymn tunes
published for use in the Methodist Episcopal Church in the United
States, 1808–1878 / Fred Kimball Graham.
      p. cm. — (Drew university studies in liturgy ; no. 12)
  Includes bibliographical references (p.   ).
  ISBN 0-8108-4983-6 (alk. paper)
  1. Methodist Church—United States—Hymns—History and criticism. 2.
Hymn tunes—History and criticism. 3. Hymns, English—United
States—19th century—History and criticism. I. Title. II. Series: Drew
studies in liturgy ; no. 12.
  ML3170 .G683 2004
  782.32'27632—dc22

                                            2003022292

To those who sang "songs from the heart" for my days . . .

Lucy Lena Maude (Pethick) Gilmer Smith (1868–1967)

Eva Winnifred (Gilmer) Kimball (1890–1966)

Lena Winnifred (Kimball) Graham (b. 1918)

Genevieve Elizabeth (Blanchard) Treffinger Stoll (1919–1997)

Melva Rae (Treffinger) Graham (b. 1947)

Jessica Blanchard Graham (b. 1975)

Aislinn Janet Graham (b. 2002)

Contents

List of Figures ix

Foreword xi

Acknowledgments xiii

Introduction xv

1. Hymn Singing in Early America 1

2. Methodist Tunes and Tunebooks of the Eighteenth and Nineteenth Centuries 5

3. The Classifications of Tunes Contained in the Core Repertory of Tunes in Tunebooks of the Methodist Episcopal Church 19

4. Interpretation and Conclusions 29

Appendixes

A. Biographies and Content of the Core Repertory 1808–1878 in Tunebooks of the Methodist Episcopal Church 37

B. Annotated Bibliography of Tunebooks Used in the Survey 139

C. Alphabetical List of Tunes 147

D. Metrical Index of Tunes 151

E. Alphabetical List of Composers 155

F. Chronological List of Tune Appearances 159

Selected Bibliography 163

About the Author 167

Figures

2.1 HELMSLEY.
Reprinted from *The Methodist Hymn-Book with Tunes* (London: Wesleyan Conference Office, 1904), no. 200.
2.2 INVITATION.
Reprinted from *The Methodist Hymn-Book* (1904), no. 345.
3.1 SILVER STREET, no. 58.
Reprinted from *New Hymn and Tunebook: An Offering of Praise* (New York: Carlton and Porter, 1866), 228.
3.2 PIETY, no. 46.
Reprinted from *NHT* (1866), 110.
3.3 PARK STREET, no. 42.
Reprinted from *NHT* (1866), 186.
3.4 SHIRLAND, no. 56.
Reprinted from *NHT* (1866), 210.
3.5 CREATION, no. 18.
Reprinted from the *Methodist Harmonist* (1833), 237.
3.6 GREENVILLE, no. 27.
Reprinted from *NHT* (1866), 387.
3.7 LISBON, no. 30.
Reprinted from *NHT* (1866), 222.
3.8 GENEVA, no. 25.
Reprinted from *Hymnal of the Methodist Episcopal Church* (New York: Nelson and Phillips, 1878), 426.
3.9 ZION, no. 76.
Reprinted from *NHT* (1866), 350.
4.1 LENOX, no. 29. as a fuging tune, from *NHT*, (1866), 290.
4.2 LENOX, no. 29. as a homophonic setting, from *Hymnal with Tunes* (New York: Nelson and Phillips, 1878), 162.

Foreword

The first hymnal companion to document and annotate the music as well as the texts of an authorized American Methodist hymnal was *The Music and Hymnody of the Methodist Hymnal*, by Carl F. Price (1881–1947).[1] The author's commentary on tunes begins: "The story of the hymn tunes has not been told so fully as the story of the hymns, save, as it has appeared incidental to the general history of music." Price and others[2] advanced Methodist hymnic commentary beyond anecdotes about familiar hymns, authors, and composers.

Robert G. McCutchan's noteworthy and influential companion,[3] *Our Hymnody: A Manual of the Methodist Hymnal*[4] [1935], was the first to document and comment on each text and each tune in an official Methodist hymnal and to trace its precursors.[5] McCutchan's careful documentation and commentary[6] distinguished folk hymns, fuging tunes, and the camp meeting choruses as significant, vital, and neglected aspects of nineteenth-century Methodist Episcopal Church (MEC) hymnody, set new standards for hymnic scholars, widened their fields of research, and inspired a second generation of scholars, including those researching the music and performance practices of the MEC[7] from post-Revolution to the Reconstruction era. The most recent contribution to these studies is Fred K. Graham's impressive thesis, prepared under the tutelage of the preeminent music historian and hymnologist Robin A. Leaver and now available in this updated and expanded edition.

In the early chapters the author compresses into short paragraphs of readable prose essential contextual information including: general developments in church music styles, performance practices, and taste; the classification of tunes included in the study; and the evolution of Methodist authorized tunebooks and hymnals. At the center of Dr. Graham's work is a carefully constructed core of seventy-six tunes he formed by tracing the frequency of their appearance in authorized tunebooks, 1808–1878. A unique approach that charts the efforts of the church's highest political forums through its publisher to compile tune collections meant to have more extended life and use than market-driven products.

Each tune in the core is presented from three perspectives: a five-part biography including the text incipit and tune nomenclature; a census including the spelling of tune variants and the authorized tunebook in which it appears; and the tune displayed in full score. Students of American music publishing will welcome the author's inclusion of clearly reproduced scores produced by three techniques of music setting: engraving, note-punching, and typesetting. Dr. Graham's careful annotations of MEC tunebooks, 1808–1878, will assist future scholars tracing the musical sources of American Wesleyan hymnals with particular regard to the ascendancy of keyboards and choirs and their relationship to the congregation and its song, as separate tune and words editions gave way to fixed tune editions with music and words on each page. This new edition is a welcome addition to the scholarly bibliography related to nineteenth-century American Methodist hymnody.

Carlton R. Young
Professor of Church Music, Emeritus
Emory University, Atlanta, GA

Notes

1. Carl F. Price, *The Music and Hymnody of the Methodist Hymnal* [1905] (New York: Abingdon Press, 1911), 169. Price annotates selected text and tunes in the hymnal jointly produced by the Methodist Episcopal Church, and Methodist Episcopal Church, South.

2. For example, Charles S. Nutter and Wilbur F. Tillett, *The Hymns and Hymn Writers of the Church: An Annotated Edition of the Methodist Hymnal* [1905] (New York: Eaton and Mains, 1911).

3. See Robin A. Leaver, "Hymnals, Hymnal Companions, and Collection Developments," *MLA Notes:*(47:331–334, December 1990).

4. Robert G. McCutchan, *Our Hymnody: A Manual of the Methodist Hymnal*, New York: Abingdon Press, 2ⁿᵈ ed. (1942). The 1935 hymnal was produced by three branches of American Methodism: the Methodist Episcopal Church; the Methodist Episcopal Church, South; and the Methodist Protestant Church.

5. Robert G. McCutchan, "The Antecedents of *The Methodist Hymnal*," *Our Hymnody* (1942), 9–12, revised and enlarged by Carlton R. Young in *Companion to the United Methodist Hymnal* [1989] (Nashville: Abingdon Press, 1993), 94–122.

6. McCutchan often included sources of tunes as well as musical scores. For example, in *Our Hymnody*, pp. 237–38, the fuging tune LENOX is printed in original and "modernized" versions.

7. For example, these unpublished Ph.D. dissertations: Double E. Hill, "A Study of Tastes in American Church Music as Reflected in the Music of the Methodist Episcopal Church to 1900," University of Illinois, 1962, UMI #63-3270; and Terry L. Baldridge, "Evolving Tastes in Hymntunes of the Methodist Episcopal Church in the Nineteenth Century," University of Kansas, 1982, UMI #4929.

Acknowledgments

It takes an entire supportive community to birth a doctoral thesis that matures into a scholarly book. Many persons and institutions have assisted and supported the long involvement in my researching and writing the following pages.

Thanks to my parents, Alfred Walton Graham and Lena Winnifred Kimball Graham, who ensured that hymns were a regular part of my early education and spiritual formation. Thanks to the keyboard teachers and vocal mentors at the University of Toronto and the Berliner Kirchenmusikschule who underlined the breath that supports all hymns. Thanks to the leaders of the program in Liturgical Theology, Drew University, Madison, NJ, and to members of faculty: Bard Thompson, Howard Hageman, Kenneth Rowe, Charles Rice, and Heather Elkins, who steered me into the treasures of Methodism. Special thanks to the staff of the Methodist Library, Drew University, for their generous support of time and provision of access to archival materials. In the fiery days of thesis writing and formatting, Yasuko and Paul Grosjean offered timely and invaluable support.

A very special word of thanks to Robin A. Leaver of Westminster Choir College of Rider University, Princeton, NJ, for sharing a vast knowledge of the history and evolution of the subject area, as well as carefully challenging and refining the work at many stages.

As the research neared its end in 1991, I was especially fortunate to gain the generous assistance of Dr. Nicholas Temperley, University of Illinois, who enabled me to pinpoint origins and dates for nearly one-third of the repertory examined in the survey. His research was only published later in the landmark series *The Hymn Tune Index: A Census of English-Language Hymn Tunes in Printed Sources from 1535 to 1820*. For his willingness to share historical details ahead of publication, I remain indebted.

Inspirational published works were *The Core Repertory of Early American Psalmody* by Richard Crawford, and two dissertations by American scholars: "Evolving Tastes in Hymntunes of the Methodist Episcopal Church in the Nineteenth Century" by Terry L. Baldridge, and "A Study in Tastes in American Church Music as Reflected in the Music of the Methodist Episcopal Church to 1900" by Double E. Hill. Their explorations and conclusions greatly facilitated the following text.

My family supported me with the freedom to embark on the voyage of study and research, and my heart is full of gratitude to Melva, to Jessica, and to Adrian.

In the preparation of this volume, the assistance of Victoria College in the University of Toronto is acknowledged, along with the excellent and enthusiastic labors of graduate student Christopher M. Cook. The editing efforts of Melva Treffinger Graham excelled in every way; I am eternally grateful. Without such expertise and patience, the project would never have come to term. In a spirit of generosity and friendship, Carlton R. Young of Nashville has assisted by reading the manuscript and writing the foreword; I am delighted to have his support in my project. Finally, to Nicole Averill, Jessica McCleary, Melissa Ray and other excellent staff at Scarecrow Press, my praise and sincere gratitude.

Introduction

Few things can be more pleasing to the Lord, than a congregation, with one heart and one voice, praising his holy name.

So wrote Bishops Coke and Asbury in the Methodist *Discipline* (1797, 124f.), giving context to the title of my book. How did Methodists finally agree on tunes that allowed them to sing heartily with one voice?

The following pages explore the melodies which were officially sanctioned for public worship of Methodists singing "with one heart and one voice" in the first century of the denomination's life in the United States. A list of tunes representing the core repertory has been assembled by noting the repeated occurrence of a tune in successive official or semiofficial tunebooks in use between 1808 and 1878. The operative assumption was that repeat printings indicate a love and a demand for the tune, which was probably important to the singers' repertory.

This study is concerned only with tunebooks which related to the official hymnbooks of the denomination; it does not concern itself with presenting a full account of what was sung by Methodists during this period. Many are the unofficial hymn collections that were used at camp meetings, revivals, and in Sunday schools. This vast literature is beyond the scope of this study and presents great opportunity for future research. The present analysis confines itself to the narrower study of what was officially sanctioned by the denomination.

It was my decision that tunes found in any seven of the eleven official or semiofficial tunebooks of the period should be named to the core repertory of seventy-six tunes. It must be underscored that frequency of printing does not establish for certain the frequency of usage of these tunes but is a reliable guide to what was thought to be "useful." Frequency of printing was established as a research tool in the hymnological work of Karl Kroeger and Richard Crawford.

The dates above have been chosen to frame the period between the appearance of James Evans' *David's Companion* in 1808 (the first tunebook approved by the General Conference) and the publication of the *Methodist Hymnal with Tunes*, 1878, the first official hymn and tune book. It was adopted after more than half a century of matching tunes with texts, by reshaping old tunes or composing new ones. Its successor was not published in the United States until 1905, which leads to the observation that the core repertory selected was in formal use for almost a century.

During this period, many influences came to bear on tune creation, amendment, and usage: the singing schools, shape-note publications, fuging tunes, and the "better music" movement. In the course of the following analysis, the impact of such events is measured in the development of an accepted tune style. Only passing mention is made of two other denominational developments of the period in which music played a key role, namely, camp meetings and the Sunday school movement.

The eleven tunebooks listed in the annotated bibliography (appendix B) were chosen from a list of many more. They represent those that were numerically cross-referenced with the official hymn (text) book or had the greatest influence upon later tune collections.

Chapter 1 details the state of hymn singing in America in colonial days as well as in the early period of national independence. The influence of singing schools and of the "better music" movement on the tradition of metrical psalmody and fuging tunes is traced.

Chapter 2 relates the rise of the Methodist hymn singing tradition, and the story of the publication of tunebooks as companions to the official hymn collections as the nineteenth century progressed.

Chapter 3 describes the style of each tune in detail. Chapter 4 interprets the findings of the analysis in appendix A in the light of the historical trends previously described. It becomes evident that what we term "usual" today in the tunes and tunebooks of our worship lives was in formative stages during the text and tune explosion of the mid-nineteenth century.

Appendix A provides "biographies," namely, analysis of the content, background, alterations, and partial texts of each of the seventy-six tunes. The system chosen echoes the research of two leading researchers in the field of hymnology. Richard Crawford in *The Core Repertory of Early American Psalmody* (Madison, WI, 1984) developed a style of "tune biography" which includes source, authorship, and meter of each tune, accompanied by information on the category of musical form and the substantive changes in tune profile, text relationship, and harmonic support. Crawford's pattern has been imitated in this volume. Nicholas Temperley and Charles G. Manns, in *Fuging Tunes in the Eighteenth Century* (Detroit, MI, 1983), developed a system of notating the "tune profile" by using numbers (1 for "do," 2 for "re," etc.), used later to great effect in *The Hymn Tune Index* (1998) and also adopted in this survey. In the illustrations within appendix A, an italicized numeral in the "tune profile" string indicates a pitch above or below the keynote "do" or 1. Using such a scheme, tune alterations may be traced, authors or compilers recorded, keys named, and tune placement notated. The work of the pioneers of this model of analysis is gratefully acknowledged.

The origins of many of these "simple tunes" were not well recorded in bygone days; one must make an informed guess at the date of authorship and/or the date and source of first publication of a few tunes in the core repertory. Further confusion arises in finding that differing tunes shared names, or tunes had names changed and melodies altered! Many gaps in knowledge have been filled by the publication of Nicholas Temperley's *Hymn Tune Index* (1998), as well as *Hymntune Index and Related Hymn Materials* (1998), compiled and edited by D. DeWitt Wasson. To these two authors and to their encyclopedic works, I am deeply indebted.

Chapter 1
Hymn Singing in Early America

Many of the colonists arriving on American shores from Europe in the seventeenth century sought religious freedom denied them in their homelands. An integral part of their religious life was the singing of either metrical psalms or chorales. Psalms and songs were often bound up with the bible and familiar to all people. With reference to music making in this era, Irving Lowens notes "practice of the art was by no means confined to musicians . . . it was a singing age."[1]

Hymn Styles

Metrical Psalmody

To the New World, the Pilgrims brought the *Ainsworth Psalter* (Amsterdam, 1612),[2] containing musical notation. Fluency in reading words and notation must then have been good, since "lining out,"[3] practiced in the absence of tunes in psalters, seems to have taken place well after settlement began. The Puritans arriving on American shores brought the Sternhold and Hopkins psalter (London, 1562).[4] Joseph Cotton is known to have "lined out" as early as 1647,[5] which would indicate a shortage of books or a lack of reading skills. In 1640, Puritan leaders provided the first American collection of revised psalm translations in *The Whole Booke of Psalmes faithfully translated into English Metre* (Cambridge, MA, 1640), which became known as the *Bay Psalm Book*.[6] Initially it contained no music but relied on Ravenscroft's *Whole Booke of Psalms* (London, 1621) to provide tunes. Only with the 1698 edition were tunes and musical instructions included, largely from Playford's *Brief Introduction to the Skill of Musick* (London, 1679). Whereas the psalters of Ainsworth and Sternhold and Hopkins contained fifteen and seventeen differing meters (respectively), the *Bay Psalm Book* contained only six. The main omission was the rich variety of long Genevan tunes,[7] which had many differing meters to accommodate the psalm paraphrases of Marot and other Reformed poets. This wide variety stands in contrast to the English metrical psalmody, which had only a few meters.

Fuging Tunes

The middle of the eighteenth century in England saw an expansion of the old psalm tune.

> The English fuging psalm-tune, immediate predecessor of the American fuging tune, was the end-product of a short-lived 18th-century union between metrical psalmody and contrapuntal technique. Both sections of the fuging psalm-tune—the psalm tune itself and the fuge—had long coexisted as independent entities before they briefly coalesced.[8]

At the conclusion of an opening homophonic section, an imitative section (regarded as optional at first) was added as a kind of refrain. Usually the bass voice articulated a text and short musical motif, which was then imitated in successive entries of other vocal parts. This was followed by one or two homophonic phrases repeating a text. The use of imitative writing reflected an interest in Italianate music made familiar through the compositions of Handel as well as the resurgence of opera.

The practice found its way to New England, as well, where in the 1780s writers such as Daniel Read, Timothy Swan, Lewis Edson, and others were well known as authors of fuging tunes. Such tunes were enthusiastically sung in rural areas, less so in urban centers.

The first published fuging tunes in North America appeared in *Urania* (Philadelphia, 1761), compiled by James Lyons (b. 1735). The six tunes offered may be viewed as merely a sample of what was already known.[9] The movement reached a peak with the 1770 publication of *The New England Psalm-Singer*, compiled by William Billings (1746–1800). He had been a devoted participant in singing schools (see below) and was later influenced by William Tans'ur's *Royal Melody Compleat, or New Harmony of Sion* (London, 1755). Tans'ur had understood "fuging" style to be "a quantity of notes of any number beginning in any single part" followed by canonic or free imitation. Little caution was exercised over parallel octaves or fifths, in contrast to the techniques to which the post-Handelians were solely given. By writing in the usual as well as a "liberated" style throughout the Revolutionary War period, Billings achieved popular acclaim writing music exactly suited to the needs of the song schools. Melodies were florid, and supporting parts contained some variety and interest.

Great interest has been shown in the work and compositions of Billings in recent years. While it is acknowledged that Billings may have been the first American composer of a fuging tune, Lowens notes, "He was neither the most prolific nor the most influential protagonist of the idiom."[10] The style was so much in vogue that, of 286 American tune collections published before 1810, only 31 contain no fuging tunes. Indeed, in most books 25 percent of the contents can be classified as fuging-tune style.[11]

Influences on Singing of Hymns

Singing Schools

As early as 1720, Rev. Thomas Symmes pleaded for the necessity of singing by note, rather than singing by rote. He authored *The Reasonableness of Regular Singing* (Boston, 1720) amid great opposition mounted by those who felt more at ease with the old style, the "usual way" of singing. Symmes named these opponents the Anti-Regular-Singers (hence, A.R.S.es).[12] Congregationalists in Boston took their cue from Independents in London about the same time to sing according to the rules of the gamut. They directed that singing by ear must cease, and that everyone should know how to read music in G/F clefs.[13] *The Accomplished Singer* (Boston? 1723) by Cotton Mather, a "most celebrated Puritan," is a book of instruction that supports this new approach.

Singing schools were in part a protest against excessive embellishment ("gracing") found in the practices of the "usual way" of singing and "lining out." The first singing school instruction is contained in a set of twenty psalm tunes compiled by John Tufts in *An Introduction to the Singing of Psalm Tunes* (Boston, 1721).[14] Manuals usually included tunes for hymns and metrical psalms as well as noncongregational music such as anthems.

Due in large measure to the sweeping success of singing schools, the creativity of Billings, Lyons, and their contemporaries gained widespread recognition.[15]

Advent of Shape-Note Hymnody

A challenge for the instructors at the singing schools was the teaching of notation-reading skills. John Tufts (see above) had devised a system of notation which was related to the British system of solmization (fa, sol, la, mi) but which abandoned the usual style of music printing. Of the many experiments that followed, the most notable is the devising of a differing shape of note head for each syllable: triangle for *fa*, round note for *sol*, square for *la*, and diamond-shaped for *mi*. This system appeared in *The Easy Instructor* (Philadelphia, 1801) under the names of William Little and William Smith. These shapes were adaptable to any piece of music in any key desired. The music included in the *Instructor* was decidedly church music and became a favorite method of teaching "sacred harmony," that is, part singing.[16]

In imitation of "methods," hymnals quickly included shape-notes as well, the earliest being Timothy Swan's *New England Harmony* (Boston, 1801). In the main, these were published and used in the South and retain a following to our present generation. Shape-notes became standard fare for the folk hymns of rural singers in their singing for enjoyment.[17]

Shape-notes were rejected by compilers such as Andrew Law (1749–1821) and Thomas Hastings (1784–1872), who called them "dunce notes." Hastings and his associates were keen to cultivate the European and "scientific" musical styles and learning in urban centers.

Shape-note books appear in oblong format, with the tune set in three or four parts, usually showing one verse of text under each separated vocal line. Two outstanding examples of the genre are John Wyeth's *Repository of Sacred Music* (Harrisburg, PA, 1810), and his Repository, Part Second (Harrisburg, PA, 1813).[18] The contents of these and other tune collections were borrowed freely from various existing collections, but compilers added their own distinctive tune styles.

New Trends in the Early Nineteenth Century

Lowell Mason and the "Better Music" Movement

Even as the folk hymns of the singing schools enjoyed success in the South and Midwest, another movement arose in the Northeast. The music of Billings, Read, and their contemporaries was set aside in favor of "correct" or "scientific" European music. The leaders in this "better music" movement took European tunes as models, and frequently arranged melodies from famous composers for congregational singing.

A leading figure in this reform was Lowell Mason (1792–1872). Born in Massachusetts, Mason took part in singing schools as a youth, and studied music-harmony lessons while leading the life of a businessman in Savannah, Georgia. After returning to Boston, he became president of the Boston Handel and Haydn Society and compiled over eighty volumes of music. The introduction of music instruction into Boston schools was one of his great pioneering efforts.[19]

He championed the raising of standards in church music, which for him meant mixing the elements of secular (choral and symphonic) music with the musical needs of church music. His vast output of over 1,600 hymn and psalm tunes[20] was influenced by the English collection of William Gardiner, *Sacred Melodies*, which appeared in two volumes in 1812 and 1815. From this source come tunes such as PARK STREET (tune no. 42 in this study) and LYONS (no. 35), both introduced to America by Mason.

Thomas Hastings, who collaborated in publishing ventures with Mason, was a leading contemporary and also a prolific writer of hymn tunes and some 600 hymn texts. Both men advocated simplicity and dignity in tunes in a time when the shape and embellishment of Handelian-style tunes were still favored. Both arranged many orchestral and oratorio melodies for hymnic use of the congregation. The aforementioned PARK STREET tune originated in a dance form by the composer Marc-Antoine Venua (1786–1872).

The principal musical elements in Mason's church music publications appear to be (i) diatonic melodies; (ii) simple rhythms with mild (or no) syncopations; (iii) accompaniment in chordal style; (iv) symmetrical phrases with repeated structures; (v) syllabic underlay of text; and (vi) simply stated direct texts.[21]

In this maelstrom of shape-notes, fuging tunes, "better music," and urban–rural dichotomy, American Methodists began to create their own repertory of favored tunes at the beginning of the nineteenth century.

Notes

1. Irving Lowens, *Music and Musicians in Early America* (New York: W. W. Norton, 1964), 17.

2. Henry Ainsworth, an English separatist minister residing in Amsterdam, compiled thirty-nine tunes from English and Genevan sources. It remained in use for almost a century. See the study by Waldo S. Pratt, *The Music of the Pilgrims* (Boston: Oliver Ditson, 1921; reprint, New York: AMS Press, 1966). See also the critical edition of the psalter in *Early Psalmody in America*, Series I: "The Ainsworth Psalter," Carlton S. Smith, ed. (New York: C. F. Peters, 1938).

3. To "line out," a minister or clerk would read or sing the metrical psalm line by line, whereupon the congregation would echo it. The practice, known as the "usual way" of singing led to many alterations (and differing versions) in the tune. The result was described by Thomas Walter in *The Grounds and Rules of Music Explained, or An Introduction to the Art of Singing by Note* (Boston, 1721) as a "horrid Medley of confused and disorderly Noises"; quoted in Gilbert Chase, *America's Music*, 2nd ed. rev. (New York: McGraw Hill, 1966), 26. See also Nicholas Temperley, "The Old Way of Singing," *Journal of the American Musicological Society* 34, no. 3 (Fall 1981).

4. On the origins of the Sternhold and Hopkins psalter, see Robin A. Leaver, *Goostly Psalmes and Spirituall Songes: English and Dutch Metrical Psalms from Coverdale to Utenhove, 1535–1566* (Oxford: Clarendon Press, 1991).

5. Lowens, *Music and Musicians*, 18.

6. See R. G. Appel, *The Music of the Bay Psalm Book, 9th Edition* (1698) (New York, 1975). Also Irving Lowens, "The Bay Psalm Book in 17th-Century New England," in *Music and Musicians in Early America.* Also Zoltan Haraszti, *The Enigma of the Bay Psalm Book* (Chicago, 1956).

7. Lowens, *Music and Musicians,* 29. For discussion of the evolution of the Genevan tune, see Erik Routley, *The Music of Christian Hymns* (Chicago: GIA Publications, 1981), 28–34.

8. Lowens, *Music and Musicians,* 241.

9. Lowens, *Music and Musicians,* 245.

10. Lowens, *Music and Musicians,* 248. See also Nicholas Temperley and Charles G. Manns, *Fuging Tunes in the Eighteenth Century* (Detroit, MI: Information Coordinators, 1983).

11. Lowens, *Music and Musicians,* 248.

12. Lowens, *Music and Musicians,* 19.

13. Robert Stevenson, *Protestant Church Music in America* (New York: W. W. Norton, 1966), 21.

14. See the facsimile reprint of the 5th ed. Philadelphia: Printed for *Musical Americana* by Albert Saifer, 1954. For further details on Tufts' *Introduction*, see Lowens, 39–57.

15. Stevenson, *Protestant Church Music,* 30.

16. Routley, *The Music of Christian Hymns*, 125ff.

17. For an overview, see Richard J. Stanislaw, *A Checklist of Four-Shape Shape-Note Tunebooks* (New York: Institute for Studies in American Music, Brooklyn College, 1978).

18. Wyeth, *Repository*, Part Second is reprinted by Da Capo Press (New York, 1964), I. Lowens, ed.

19. See Carol A. Pemberton, *Lowell Mason: His Life and Work* (Ann Arbor, MI: UMI Research Press, 1985).

20. See Henry L. Mason, *Hymn Tunes of Lowell Mason: A Bibliography* (Cambridge, MA: University Press, 1944).

21. Carol A. Pemberton, *Lowell Mason: A Bio-Bibliography* (New York: Greenwood Press, 1988), 31.

Chapter 2
Methodist Tunes and Tunebooks of the Eighteenth and Nineteenth Centuries

The Rise of Methodist Hymnody[1]

Soon after John Wesley arrived in America in 1735 as a young missionary-priest, he realized that those to whom he preached needed printed hymn texts similar to those the Methodist groups in England had been using already. With the help of an associate of Benjamin Franklin, he succeeded in publishing the first hymn collection printed in America, *A Collection of Hymns and Psalms*.[2] This first hymnal for use in Anglicanism made its appearance at Charleston, South Carolina, in 1737. Thus began Wesley's considerable influence in the selection of tunes and texts for public worship found in subsequent publications following his return to England.

Wesley's journal, begun on the trip to America and continued for the duration of his life, reveals that he disliked the slow dragging songs that he thought too lazy. Nicholas Temperley points out that the slow style of singing may be explained in part due to some compilers treating a semibreve as a unit of absolute duration (four seconds).[3] The absence of an accompanying rhythmic beat made forward pulse and movement almost impossible.

Wesley disliked the florid, repetitious, occasionally fugal music he regularly heard in Anglican worship. The psalm fuging tunes (see chapter 1) had been adopted enthusiastically particularly in the country, and Wesley disapproved of the tendency towards sentimentalism.[4] In the north of England where choirs had begun to chant the psalms and the liturgy, touring singing masters touted the use of fuging tunes. The pioneers of this style, Watts, East, and Everet, were all local singing masters in rural England.[5] This "exclusively Anglican development"[6] was for Wesley an insult to God's word, due to the unintelligibility of the text when the voices overlapped. The hearty melodies of the Moravians heard on-board the ship *Simmons* on the voyage to America in 1735 had appealed greatly to Wesley. He found their balladlike tunes simple and direct, and he was stirred by the textual reflections on faith.

With regard to anthems, Wesley seemed less bothered by the complex musical structure. At least one of them, "Out of the Deep" (probably in the setting by Dr. Croft), had a profound impact on his own spirituality. "Vital Spark of Heavenly Flame"[7] was another anthem he enjoyed repeatedly throughout his life.

His greatest love was promoting congregational hymn singing; he wanted all to join in a heartfelt and spontaneous act of worship. This demanded provision of a simple style of music to proclaim a message of "certainty and safety."[8] The "plain truth for plain people" demonstrated in his sermons found a complement in plain music.

In 1742 Wesley oversaw the publication of *A Collection of Tunes Set to Music as They Are Commonly Sung at the Foundery* (referred to as *FC*). This booklet gives forty tunes (with no harmonies), with text for one stanza underlaid. Its appearance was significant in establishing tunes for new meters of poetry, and it represented a departure from the traditional psalter music of the day. The use of two or more notes for each syllable in many of these tunes caused Louis Benson to describe them as "old Methodist" tunes. An example, seen at **Figure 2.1**, is HELMSLEY.[9]

The importance of this publication can hardly be overstated. It demonstrates the first steps towards securing tunes in new meters to fit the expanding metrical breadth of the hymn poetry of Charles Wesley.[10]

Twenty years later (1761) Wesley published *Sacred Melody*, the second part of *Select Hymns with Tunes Annext*,[11] giving the tune and some text; the book also contained the first appearance of Wesley's famous "Directions" for the singing of hymns.[12] The revised and harmonized contents of 120 tunes for 128 hymns appeared under the title *Sacred Harmony; or A Choice Collection of Psalms and Hymns Set to Music in Two and Three Parts for the Voice, Harpsichord, and Organ* (London, 1780).[13]

Figure 2.1 - HELMSLEY

Through ongoing publication of hymns and tunes "Wesley continued to shape the hymn singing of Methodists on both sides of the Atlantic throughout the eighteenth and early nineteenth centuries."[14] The succeeding landmark was named *A Collection of Hymns for the Use of the People Called Methodists* (London, 1780), and by its fifth edition (1786) it carried a suggested tune name at the top of each hymn. The tunes were to be found in *Sacred Harmony*, first published in 1780.[15]

Wesley struck up a friendship with a bassoonist named John Frederic Lampe (1703–1751), whom James Lightwood calls the "first Methodist composer."[16] Lampe composed tunes with figured bass for twenty-four Wesley texts in *Hymns on the Great Festivals* (1786).[17] Like most of Lampe's tunes, INVITATION (see **Figure 2.2**) is carefully shaped, the peak of each phrase rising in pitch nine beats after the preceding peak. The original ornamentation in this Long Meter tune is understood by leading hymnologist Erik Routley (1917–1982) to be for accompaniment instruments rather than voices.[18] We are well aware that Primitive Methodists even as late as the twentieth century retained "shakes" and decorations in their vocal performance.

Such graceful late English Baroque contributions to the tune repertoire survive the lifetime of Wesley in spirit if not in consummate style, as in the instance of NEW SABBATH (appendix A, no. 39).

Figure 2.2 - INVITATION

Methodist Hymnbooks in the United States

The first official Methodist hymnbook in the United States was adopted at the organizing Conference at Christmas in Baltimore, 1784. The *Collection of Psalms and Hymns for the Lord's Day*[19] contained 118 metrical psalms and hymns (no tunes) selected by Wesley from his much larger *Collection of Psalms and Hymns* (London, 1741). Together with *The Sunday Service of the Methodists in North America*, a modest revision of the *Book of Common Prayer*, they were adopted as the newly formed church's official liturgy and hymnody.[20] Neither liturgy nor hymnal enjoyed a wide appeal, however, and they were used only until 1792.[21]

Wesley had published *A Pocket Hymnbook, for the Use of Christians of All Denominations* (London, 1787) to counter a popular "pirated" edition published by Robert Spence of York in 1781. The "pocket hymnals" of both Spence and Wesley were widely circulated on both sides of the Atlantic. Bishops Coke and Asbury issued a reprint under the title *A Pocket Hymn-Book Designed as a Constant Companion for the Pious: Collected from Various Authors* (Philadelphia, 1790). This became the second official hymnbook[22] of the Methodist Episcopal Church, and the basis for succeeding generations of hymn and tune collections.[23] The preface to the book offers an explanation by Bishops Asbury and Coke:

> The Hymn-Books, which have already been published amongst us, are excellent. The Select Hymns, the double[24] collection of Hymns and Psalms, and the Redemption Hymns display great spirituality, as well as purity of diction. The large Congregational Hymn-Book is admirable indeed, but it is too expensive for the poor, who have little time and less money. The Pocket Hymnbook lately sent abroad in these States is a most valuable performance for those who are deeply spiritual, but it is better suited to European Methodists, among whom all the before-mentioned books have been thoroughly circulated for many years.[25]

The *Pocket Hymn-Book* contained texts but frequently cited tune names at the head of a hymn to assist in finding the appropriate tune.

It was not until 1808 that official action was undertaken to sanction a book of tunes for the Methodist Episcopal Church, and only in 1857 did tunes appear in the same (unofficial) book with texts. An official collection featuring both texts and tunes was not published until 1878.

The First Methodist Tunebook in America

Those who attended the General Conference of 1808 heard Ezekiel Cooper read to the conference a proposal from Brother James Evans, of New York, for publishing a music book as a standard for the use of the Methodist churches throughout the United States.[26]

James Evans (1800–1880) arrived in New York from Manchester, England, to take up musical duties at John Street Church. He was known as an exceptional tenor singer, performer on cello and flute, and as a promoter of "better" sacred music.

The conference Committee of Review acknowledged that improvement and uniformity in singing was desirable, but considered it improper to "take Mr. Evans's, or any other man's music-book under our patronage."[27] However, to their societies they were prepared to recommend such a book, if published.

Shortly thereafter Evans published *David's Companion* (1808).[28] On the title page, it is clearly stated that the book contains "hymn and psalm tunes adapted to the words and measures in the *Methodist Pocket Hymn-book*." In his preface, Evans makes note of the sanction given by the General Conference, even though it could not be considered an "official" book.

The second edition (1811) was entitled *David's Companion, or The Methodist Standard*. The title page of this edition points to its being aligned with the "Large Hymnbook" (i.e., Mr. Wesley's 1780 volume *A Collection of Hymns for the Use of the People Called Methodists*), which was growing in popularity in America after being imported from England. The eighteenth London edition was used as the basis for reprinting at Baltimore in 1814.[29]

When Nathan Bangs, representing Evans at the 1812 General Conference, asked for support for a tunebook, the committee both declined to support a move to make the 1811 edition official and withdrew previously given sanction (which had undoubtedly served Evans well) for *David's Companion*. Methodists continued to use the resources nonetheless, so that a reprint edition was published in 1817, and a supplement in 1820[30] under the title *Wesleyan Selection, Being a Supplement to David's Companion.*

WESLEYAN SELECTION,

BEING

A Supplement to David's Companion;

CONSISTING OF

ANTHEMS AND HYMN TUNES,

FROM SEVERAL AUTHORS,

AND USED BY THE

WESLEYAN SACRED MUSIC SOCIETY,

BELONGING TO THE

Methodist Episcopal Church in John-street,

NEW-YORK.

TEACHING AND ADMONISHING ONE ANOTHER IN PSALMS, AND HYMNS, AND SPIRITUAL SONGS, SINGING WITH GRACE IN YOUR HEARTS TO THE LORD.—Col. iii. 16.

New-York:

PRINTED BY ABRAHAM PAUL, CORNER OF WATER-STREET AND BURLING-SLIP.

1820.

The First Authorized Tunebook

By May of 1820, the Methodist General Conference was ready to authorize a collection of tunes.

> The Committee on the Book Concern [was] instructed to inquire into the expediency of adopting measures for the compilation and publication of a tune-book which may be recommended to our societies and congregations at large.[31]

The tunebook was copyrighted in January 1822 and published as *The Methodist Harmonist.*[32] Each tune in this resource is underlaid with one stanza of a hymn and includes a hymn number from the official hymnal where additional stanzas were to be found. Owing to the popular reception of this tunebook, reprints were issued in 1823, 1825, 1827, and 1831.

The Second Tunebook Authorized by General Conference

The General Conference of 1832 requested preparation and publication of a revised and improved tunebook. *The Methodist Harmonist* (1833)[33] retained all tunes found in the 1822 tunebook but added some anthems and new tunes.

THE

METHODIST HARMONIST,

CONTAINING

A COLLECTION OF TUNES

FROM THE

BEST AUTHORS, EMBRACING EVERY VARIETY OF METRE,

AND ADAPTED TO THE WORSHIP OF THE

METHODIST EPISCOPAL CHURCH.

———

TO WHICH IS ADDED

A SELECTION OF ANTHEMS, PIECES, AND SENTENCES,

FOR PARTICULAR OCCASIONS.

————————————

NEW EDITION—REVISED AND GREATLY ENLARGED.

————————————

NEW-YORK,

PUBLISHED BY B. WAUGH AND T. MASON, FOR THE METHODIST EPISCOPAL CHURCH, AT THE CONFERENCE OFFICE,
NO. 200 MULBERRY-STREET.

———
J. COLLORD, PRINTER.
1833.

Subsequent Tunebooks

Since the General Conference of 1820 had passed a motion stating that "the book-agents shall have liberty to publish any new work not before published by us which shall be approved and recommended by the Book Committee at New-York,"[34] the book agents were free to compile and publish tunebooks as taste and demand seemed to require. The first effort in this direction resulted in *The Harmonist* of 1837,[35] which was larger than previous publications. Its success lasted more than a decade, and reprints were issued in 1842 and 1845.

THE

HARMONIST:

BEING

A COLLECTION OF TUNES FROM THE MOST APPROVED AUTHORS

ADAPTED TO

EVERY VARIETY OF METRE IN THE METHODIST HYMN-BOOK.

AND, FOR PARTICULAR OCCASIONS,

A SELECTION OF ANTHEMS, PIECES, AND SENTENCES.

————

NEW EDITION, IN PATENT NOTES—REVISED AND GREATLY ENLARGED.

NEW-YORK:

PUBLISHED BY G. LANE & P. P. SANDFORD,
FOR THE METHODIST EPISCOPAL CHURCH, AT THE CONFERENCE OFFICE, 200 MULBERRY-STREET.

JAMES COLLORD, PRINTER.

1842.

The second effort led to the production of *Sacred Harmony* (1848),[36] which was published in both round-note and shape-note editions. Some voices of dissatisfaction had been heard regarding the 1837 *Harmonist*, and the compilers were dedicated not just to preventing the use of non-Methodist materials but also to meeting the needs of their constituency. When accusations were heard of the new book's being merely old songs between new covers, lively discussion ensued:

> It seems to have been taken for granted by some, at least, that the forthcoming work is only a revision of "The Harmonist" with additions, emendations, corrections, etc. . . . The new book will not be in any sense a "revised" "Harmonist." It is to be a "new book" of music, yet not absolutely a book of "new music." It will, however contain many "original tunes . . . " old standard tunes as it seemed necessary to republish have been adopted from "The Harmonist."[37]

SACRED HARMONY:

A COLLECTION OF MUSIC,

ADAPTED TO THE GREATEST VARIETY OF METRES NOW IN USE:

And, for Special Occasions,

A CHOICE SELECTION OF SENTENCES, ANTHEMS, MOTETS, AND CHANTS.

Harmonized, and Arranged with an Accompaniment for the Organ or Piano Forte,

BY SAMUEL JACKSON.

WITH AN IMPROVED SYSTEM OF ELEMENTARY INSTRUCTION.

New-York:

PUBLISHED BY GEORGE LANE & CHARLES B. TIPPETT, 200 MULBERRY-STREET.

JOSEPH LONGKING, PRINTER.

1848.

The editor, Samuel Jackson (1818–1885), was active as an editor and as a composer for organ and choir in New York. His committee stressed in the new publication that taste had made great advances, and that the tunes of the great European masters to be included would be well appreciated. In spite of articles, advertisements, and encouragement, the reception of this book was not at all favorable, and its use lasted less than a year. During that time, the General Conference met and instigated revision of the official hymnbook. Both the failure of *Sacred Harmony* and the appearance of a new hymnbook led to the preparation of yet another tunebook.

THE
DEVOTIONAL HARMONIST:
A COLLECTION OF SACRED MUSIC,
COMPRISING A LARGE VARIETY OF
NEW AND ORIGINAL TUNES, SENTENCES, ANTHEMS, ETC.
In addition to many of the most Popular Tunes in common use.
PRESENTING A GREATER NUMBER OF METRES THAN ANY BOOK HERETOFORE PUBLISHED.
TO WHICH IS PREFIXED
A Progressive System of Elementary Instruction for Schools and Private Tuition.
EDITED BY CHARLES DINGLEY,
TEACHER OF MUSIC, EDITOR OF THE FAMILY MINSTREL, SUNDAY-SCHOOL HARMONIST, ETC., ETC.
New-York:
PUBLISHED BY GEORGE LANE AND LEVI SCOTT, 200 MULBERRY-STREET
JOSEPH LONGKING, PRINTER.
1850.

Advertisements for *The Devotional Harmonist* of 1849[38] claimed it was based largely upon *The Harmonist* (1837), and no mention was made of *Sacred Harmony* (1848). Many publishing houses were involved in providing substitute tunebooks to satisfy the public demand for variety and change. Isaac B. Woodbury (b. 1819) of Boston became a singing teacher in Vermont before studying for a time in Europe. He later taught singing in the city of New York and edited hymn collections and manuals for music instruction. He compiled two tunebooks that became very popular although they were "unofficial."

One of them was published by the official Methodist Book Concern (Carlton and Porter), even though it was not compiled by one of their own committees. In compiling *The Lute of Zion* (1853).[39] Woodbury was assisted by Dr. Hiram Mattison (1811–1868), an elder in the Methodist Episcopal Church who was the editor of a dozen religious booklets, and pastor at Trinity Church, Jersey City.

A COLLECTION OF SACRED MUSIC,
DESIGNED FOR THE USE OF
THE METHODIST EPISCOPAL CHURCH
CONSISTING OF A CHOICE COLLECTION OF NEW TUNES FROM THE BEST FOREIGN AND AMERICAN COMPOSERS, WITH MOST
OF THE OLD TUNES IN COMMON USE; TOGETHER WITH A CONCISE ELEMENTARY COURSE, SIMPLIFIED
AND ADAPTED TO THE CAPACITIES OF BEGINNERS, &c. &c.

BY I. B. WOODBURY,
AUTHOR OF "THE DULCIMER," "LIBER MUSICUS," "COTTAGE GLEES," "CULTIVATION OF THE VOICE," "CHORUS GLEE BOOK," ETC. ETC.
ASSISTED BY REV. H. MATTISON, A.M.,
PASTOR OF THE JOHN STREET METHODIST EPISCOPAL CHURCH, NEW YORK.

NEW YORK:
CARLTON & PHILLIPS, 200 MULBERRY STREET.—F. J. HUNTINGTON, 23 PARK ROW.

The 1853 collection and *The New Lute of Zion* (1856)[40] enjoyed wide circulation. Even though they were "unofficial," their widespread use had an influence on the later tunebooks of the Methodist Episcopal Church.

THE

NEW LUTE OF ZION

A Collection of Sacred Music,

DESIGNED FOR THE USE OF CONGREGATIONS GENERALLY,

BUT MORE ESPECIALLY

THE METHODIST EPISCOPAL CHURCH.

BY I. B. WOODBURY,

EDITOR OF "MUSICAL PIONEER," AND AUTHOR OF "CYTHARA," "LIBER MUSICUS," "SONG CROWN," ETC., ETC.

NEW YORK:

CARLTON AND PORTER, 200 MULBERRY STREET.

SOLD BY F. J. HUNTINGTON, 7 BEEKMAN ST.; AND MASON BROTHERS, 108 & 110 DUANE ST.

Semiofficial Hymnals with Tunes

When the public demand for a book containing both hymn texts and appropriate tunes became evident, the book agents issued a new style of publication in 1857.[41] Its shape changed from the oblong shape opening on the short side that had remained constant from the time of the early "Harmonists" through to *The New Lute of Zion*. The new format opening on the long side had a tune underlaid with one verse at the top of each page; subsequent verses and alternative texts for that tune filled the remainder of the page.

HYMNS

FOR THE USE OF

THE METHODIST EPISCOPAL CHURCH

WITH

TUNES FOR CONGREGATIONAL WORSHIP.

I will sing with the Spirit, and I will sing with the understanding also.—1 Cor. xiv, 15.

FORTIETH THOUSAND.

New York:

PUBLISHED BY CARLTON & PORTER,

200 MULBERRY-STREET.

Recognition is accorded the Woodbury publications in the provision of bracketed numbers beside all tunes found also in those two collections. A unique remark occurs in the preface to this hymnal:

It will be observed that we have used several tunes in the minor key. The reason for this is that no compositions are better adapted for devotional purpose. . . . They were so used by our people for many years after the introduction of Methodism into this country.[42]

It may be that influences from the "better music" movement with its love for things classical and foreign are glimpsed in this recommendation. Although tunes in minor keys may well have been used, few achieved a lasting place in the repertory of the people, as later analysis will show.

In the events leading to a resource containing *both* texts and tunes, it was significant that the old and many new tunes were clearly cross-referenced with the current book of hymn texts. The publishers provided the following introduction:

In presenting this work to the Church, the publishers beg leave to say that it has been prepared with reference to what seems to be an imperative demand. Its object is, in the most quiet and satisfactory way, to promote congregational singing. They have therefore made use of all the hymns contained in our standard hymnbook, and no others, so that the introduction of this book to our pulpits and a part of our pews shall produce no inconvenience to any who do not incline to avail themselves of its benefits. As the numbers of the hymns correspond with the numbers of the same hymns in our standard book, if the preacher will announce both the hymn and the page, all will be equally accommodated.[43]

NEW

HYMN AND TUNE BOOK:

AN

Offering of Praise

FOR THE

METHODIST EPISCOPAL CHURCH.

EDITED BY

PHILIP PHILLIPS,

AUTHOR OF THE "SINGING PILGRIM," "MUSICAL LEAVES," ETC.

New York:

PUBLISHED BY CARLTON & PORTER,

200 MULBERRY STREET.

CINCINNATI AND CHICAGO: POE & HITCHCOCK.

1867.

To meet a perceived need for new tunes, and without warrant from the General Conference, the book agents soon offered more new tunes in book form. In 1866 the church's publishing branch produced the *New Hymn and Tune Book*.[44]

The editor, Philip Phillips, was a layperson who became a distinguished singer and frequently presented "song evenings" for the benefit of the church. In 1866, he became musical editor of the Methodist Book Concern, New York. The new publication contained over 200 new tunes; a special "Choir Edition" contained an additional section of anthems.

Creation of an Official Hymnal with Tunes

By 1872, calls were heard to revise the aging 1849 hymnal, but support was lacking until the next General Conference in 1876, where the following motion was presented:

> "Resolved," That a Special Committee of nine be appointed by the Chair, to consider the propriety of revising our Hymn and Tune Books, so as to adapt them more perfectly to general use in all our Churches and congregations.[45]

It is notable that reference to "Hymn and Tune Books" probably meant the "unofficial" books of 1857 and 1866.[46] Debate ensued about the size of the Special Committee, about the words "and Tune" and about the implication that earlier publications had somehow become official. Feeling against having tunes in a hymnbook ran high, but the committee was finally given authority firstly to revise the hymnal, then "to prepare a suitable Hymn and Tune Book for the use of the Church."[47]

HYMNAL

OF THE

METHODIST EPISCOPAL CHURCH.

WITH TUNES.

NEW YORK: HUNT & EATON.
CINCINNATI: CRANSTON & STOWE.

A compromise was reached, and in 1878 the new *Hymnal of the Methodist Episcopal Church*[48] was published in two versions, one without tunes, and its counterpart with tunes. This hymnal is notable for the following reasons: it was the first official hymnal of the denomination to contain tunes; it was the last hymnal of this denomination in the nineteenth century; and it was the last official publication of hymns issued solely by the Methodist Episcopal Church. Later publications involved joint efforts with other streams of Methodism.

Notes

1. See James T. Lightwood, *Methodist Music in the Eighteenth Century* (London: Epworth Press, 1927); also Louis F. Benson, *The English Hymn: Its Development and Use in Worship,* reprint ed. (Richmond: John Knox Press, 1962).

2. See Carlton Young, "John Wesley's 1737 Charlestown Collection of Psalms and Hymns," *The Hymn*, 41, no.4 (October 1990): 19–27.

3. Nicholas Temperley, "The Old Way of Singing," *Journal of the American Musicological Society* 34, no.3 (Fall 1981): 524.

4. See Nicholas Temperley, *The Music of the English Parish Church*, Vol. 1 (London: Cambridge Press, 1979), 176, 209, 211–12.

5. Temperley, *Parish*, 176.

6. Temperley, *Parish*, 212.

7. "Vital Spark" appeared first in Harwood's *A Set of hymns and psalms* (Chester, ca. 1770). The text is by Alexander Pope.

8. Routley, *The Music of Christian Hymnody* (London: London Independent Press, 1957), 97.

9. Probably a psalm setting by A. Roner, 1721; first appeared in *FC*, 28.

10. See Nelson F. Adams, "The Musical Sources for John Wesley's Tune-Books: The Genealogy of 148 Tunes" (DSM dissertation, Union Theological Seminary, 1973), 67ff.

11. *Select Hymns with Tunes Annext: Designed Chiefly for the Use of The People Called Methodists* (London, np, 1761), iv, 5–139.

12. See *The Works of John Wesley*, Vol. 7 (Oxford: Clarendon Press, 1983), 765.

13 For a comparison of *Sacred Melody* (1761) and *Sacred Harmony* (1780), see O. Beckerlegge and F. Baker, *Wesley Works* Vol. 7, 772.

14. Terry L. Baldridge, "Evolving Tastes in Hymn Tunes of the Methodist Episcopal Church in the Nineteenth Century" (Ph.D. dissertation, University of Kansas, 1982), 36.

15. The full account of Wesley's tunebooks may be found in *The Works of John Wesley*, Vol. 7 (New York: Oxford University Press, 1983), appendixes E–J, 738–787.

16. James T. Lightwood, *The Music of the Methodist Hymnbook* (London: Epworth Press, 1935), 274ff.

17. *Hymns on the Great Festivals*, [J. F. Lampe, ed.] (London: for M. Cooper, 1746). See also commentary by Robin A. Leaver in *A Facsimile of the First Edition* (Madison, NJ: Charles Wesley Society, 1996), 34–35.

18. Routley, *The Music of Christian Hymns* (Chicago: GIA Publications, 1981), 74.

19. *Collection of Psalms and Hymns for the Lord's Day.* Published by John Wesley, M.A., Late Fellow of Lincoln College, Oxford; and Charles Wesley, M.A., Late Student of Christ Church, Oxford. London: printed in the year 1784.

20. See the reprint edition: *John Wesley's Sunday Service of the Methodists in North America*, with an introduction by James F. White (Nashville: United Methodist Publishing House, 1984).

21. Robert G. McCutchan, *Our Hymnody: A Manual of the Methodist Hymnal* (New York: Methodist Book Concern, 1937), 10.

22 For an overview of authorized hymnals, see Carlton R. Young, *Companion to the United Methodist Hymnal* (Nashville: Abingdon Press, 1993), 94, 100–106.

23. McCutchan, *Our Hymnody*, 10.

24. The reference is to *A Selection of Hymns from various authors, designed as a supplement to the Methodist Pocket Hymnbook, compiled under the direction of Bishop Asbury and published by order of the General Conference* (New York, 1808). Some tune names were provided.

25. W. J. Townsend, H. B. Workman, George Eayrs, eds., *A New History of Methodism*, Vol. 2 (London: Hodder and Stoughton, 1901), 142–43, quoted in Double E. Hill, "A Study in Tastes in American Church Music as Reflected in the Music of the Methodist Episcopal Church to 1900" (Ph.D. dissertation, University of Illinois, 1962), 127.

26. Journals of the General Conference of the Methodist Episcopal Church, Vol. 1: 1796-1836 (New York: Carlton and Phillips, 1855), 74.

27. Journals, Vol. 1, 87.

28. *David's Companion, being a choice selection of hymn and psalm tunes adapted to the words and measures of the Methodist Pocket Hymnbook, containing a variety of tunes to all the metres that are now in use in the difference churches; with many new tunes, principally from Dr. Miller, Leach and other composers* (New York: J. Evans, 1808).

29. Baldridge, "Evolving Tastes," 46. McCutchan's view is that the "Large Hymnbook" was hardly known in the United States prior to the 1814 reprint, but Baldridge notes that it is unlikely that Evans would have published a companion tunebook for a hymnal that did not enjoy popular use.

30. Hill, "A Study of Tastes," 147, assumes the 1820 *Wesleyan Selection* is a supplement to the 1811 edition of *David's Companion*. With subsequent knowledge of the 1817 reprint, Baldridge, "Evolving Tastes," 47, states that the 1820 edition is instead a supplement of the 1817 version.

31. Journals, Vol. 1 (1796-1836), 186.

32. *The Methodist Harmonist* (New York: Published by N. Bangs and T. Mason for the Methodist Episcopal Church, 1822).

33. *The Methodist Harmonist* (New York: B. Waugh and T. Mason, 1833). See annotated bibliography (appendix B) for full reference.

34. Journals of the General Conference (1820), 186.

35. *The Harmonist* (New York: G. Lane and P. P. Sandford, 1837, 1842). See annotated bibliography (appendix B) for full reference.

36. *Sacred Harmony*, S. Jackson, ed. (New York: George Lane and Charles B. Tippett, 1848). See annotated bibliography (appendix B) for full reference.

37. "Church Music Again—the New Tunebook, etc.," *Christian Advocate and Journal* (New York), January 19, 1848, 9.

38. *The Devotional Harmonist*, Charles Dingley, ed. (New York: G. Lane and Levi Scott, 1849). See annotated bibliography (appendix B) for full reference.

39. *The Lute of Zion*, I. B. Woodbury, ed. (New York: F. J. Huntington and Mason Brothers, 1853). See annotated bibliography (appendix B) for full reference.

40. I. B. Woodbury, *The New Lute of Zion* (New York: Carlton and Porter, 1856). See annotated bibliography (appendix B) for full reference.

41. *Hymns for the Use of the Methodist Episcopal Church with Tunes for Congregational Worship* (New York: Carlton and Porter, 1857). See annotated bibliography (appendix B) for full reference.

42. *Hymns for the Use*, preface.

43. *Hymns for the Use*, 3.

44. *New Hymn and Tunebook: An Offering of Praise for the Methodist Episcopal Church,* Philip Phillips, ed. (New York: Carlton and Porter, 1866). See annotated bibliography (appendix B) for full reference.

45. Journal of the General Conference of the Methodist Episcopal Church, held in Baltimore, MD, May 1–31, 1876 (New York: Nelson & Phillips, 1876), 76.

46. Baldridge, "Evolving Tastes," 65.

47. Journal of the General Conference (1876), 343.

48. *Hymnal of the Methodist Episcopal Church with Tunes* (New York: Hunt and Eaton. Copyright by Nelson and Phillips, 1878). See annotated bibliography (appendix B) for full reference.

Chapter 3
The Classifications of Tunes Contained in the Core Repertory of Tunes in Tunebooks of the Methodist Episcopal Church

The Methodist Conferences officially adopted hymns, but there was no official sanction given to early tunes or tunebooks. The collections examined in this book may be considered "semiofficial" in that the officially adopted book of hymn texts made reference to tunes available in the tunebooks and hymns were often cross-referenced with these tunes. Without the evidence of personal records or public worship lists, it is impossible to assess exactly what was sung by Methodists in the period 1810–1878. By examining the contents of the tunebooks outlined in the preceding chapter, it may be discovered what was available for use and these contents may be categorized in a way to show broad groupings of materials recurring in succeeding tunebooks.

Classifications of the tunes may be described under the headings Hymn (and Psalm) Tunes, Folk Tunes, Fuging Tunes, Gospel Tunes, and Set Pieces.

Hymn Tunes

This title refers to music which accompanies strophic text, and which is syllabic (or nearly syllabic) in structure. The texture of such compositions is homophonic. In the survey that follows, three designations will be used: (a) plain tune, (b) plain tune-with-extension, and (c) antiphonal tune. Occasionally the term "antiphonal tune-with-extension" will be used.

Plain Tune

In this style of composition, all voices move in the same rhythm and are active at all times. No text repetition occurs, although motivic repetition in the tune may be seen. It is the most widely used tune form of the repertory; an example is no. 58, SILVER STREET (see **Figure 3.1**). As pointed out by Baldridge,[1] some of the sources create confusion in classification, due to the practice of printing one or more voice parts in small notes for a few measures. While such small print disappeared by 1878, it can be conjectured that earlier editors were trying to flesh out an antiphonal tune (see below) to create a plain tune. It may also be that these small notes provided assistance to the growing numbers of note readers, including keyboard players (in city churches, or at home).

Figure 3.1 - SILVER STREET

Tune-with-Extension

Crawford uses this term[2] and defines it as a tune that contains a portion of text that is either repeated to new music or stretched so that the text is not the controlling factor in the musical form. Within this category are two types, the first of which may be seen in PIETY, no. 46 (see **Figure 3.2**). Here the unusually long fourth phrase uses repeated text, and the tune is clearly designed to continue the character of a penultimate phrase but requires the repetition of text to do so. The second type is found in PARK STREET, no. 42 (see **Figure 3.3**), where there are five phrases of equal length but a repetition of text is necessary in the final phrase in order to complete the tune.

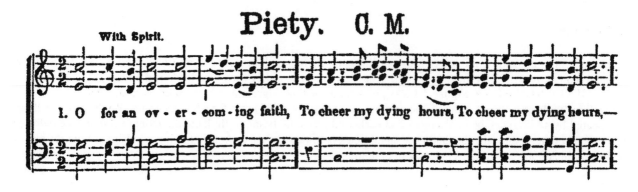

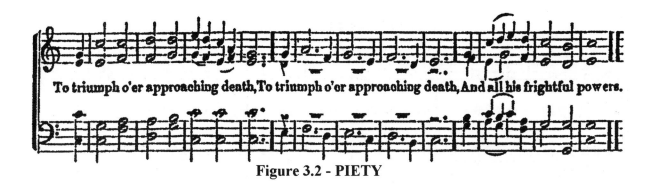

To triumph o'er approaching death, To triumph o'er approaching death, And all his frightful powers.

Figure 3.2 - PIETY

Park Street. L. M.

1. Abraham, when se-vere-ly tried, His faith by his o - bedience show'd; He with the

harsh command complied, And gave his Isaac back to God, And gave his I - saac back to God.

Figure 3.3 - PARK STREET

Antiphonal Tune

This type allows the tune to proceed during one phrase with one or two accompanying voices rather than full four-part support. SHIRLAND (see **Figure 3.4**) is one of these. In comparing this with other tunes, there seems to be no pattern dictating which voices drop out or when, though pairing of the melody with another voice is the usual practice. Occasionally one voice is left to proceed on its own. An antiphonal tune-with-extension results when text is repeated to support the irregular tune structure, and often one of the repeat phrases has a reduced number of voices. This prompts the frequent use of directions for dynamics (e.g., *piano*) according to the density of the texture. CREATION (**Figure 3.5**) demonstrates this style of antiphonal tune. Dynamic markings appear at measures 9 and 17.

Figure 3.4 - SHIRLAND

Figure 3.5 - CREATION

Folk Tunes

Substantial research has been done recently into the relation between folk melodies and nineteenth-century hymnody. George Pullen Jackson accomplished the pioneering work in this area.[3] He has identified only twenty-four from the Methodist repertoire as being influenced by folk style. He includes some that may not actually be folk tunes but demonstrate clearly the folk influence.[4] The usual standards of assessment are the shape of the melody, the melodic intervals, the range, and the type of scale used. GREENVILLE (see **Figure 3.6**) is such a tune, containing a limited range, *aaba* form, and almost exclusively stepwise intervallic motion.

Figure 3.6 - GREENVILLE

Fuging Tunes

Most fuging tunes of the Methodist repertory include successive entries of the vocal parts using melodic or rhythmic imitation and identical text. This results in the text overlap and repetition, to which John Wesley had so strenuously objected. In the extensive treatment this topic has recently received, writers such as Irving Lowens and Nicholas Temperley have discounted the earlier assumption that William Billings was the American inventor of the style.[5] That it was an Anglican development is discussed in depth in Temperley's *The Music of the English Parish Church.*[6] There are several styles of fuging tune: Plain fuging tune[7] such as LISBON (see **Figure 3.7**), extended plain fuging tune,[8] antiphonal fuging tune,[9] and reverse fuging tune[10] such as GENEVA (see **Figure 3.8**).

Figure 3.7 - LISBON

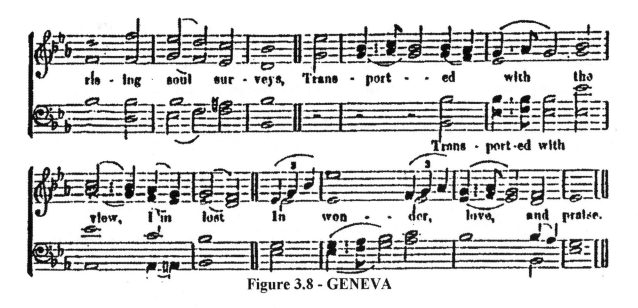

Figure 3.8 - GENEVA

Gospel Tunes

This category of tune was associated with the religious movement that occurred in the 1870s.[11] The limit of 1878 in this study precludes listing important gospel tunes that reached a refined level later in the century. It is clear, however, that the revival tune (a rural phenomenon) and the "better music" movement (an urban phenomenon) meet in the gospel tune style. It found a ready home in praise meetings and in Sunday school gatherings. Lowell Mason's influence was felt once again, in that his student William B. Bradbury (1816–1868) was a leading composer of music for the Sunday school. Among his musical settings are those for "Jesus Loves Me" (CHINA) and "Just as I am, without one plea."[12] Notable characteristics are the simple harmonies, plain melodic lines with rhythmic rather than ornamental interest, and use of compound meter (frequently duple meter). The blandness of the compositions of the "better music" movement was increasingly offset by rhythmic patterns (dotted rhythms, responsive effects, etc.) borrowed from the old revival tunes. ZION (no. 76) is an example of such a gospel tune (see **Figure 3.9**).

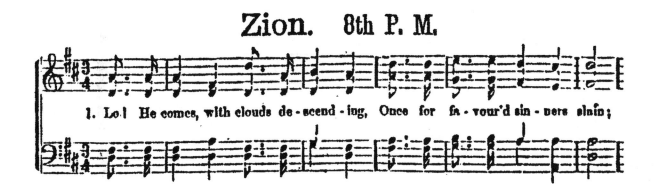

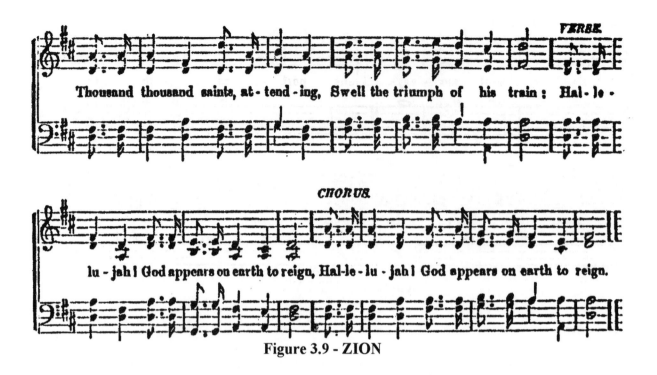

Figure 3.9 - ZION

Set Pieces

From the time of the earliest publications, it has been difficult to differentiate between a set piece and an anthem. In the early 1800s, Andrew Law's standard was based on the difference between poetry (set piece) and prose (anthem).[13] However, Crawford deems several stanzas that are through-composed but less elaborate than a prose-text setting a set piece. More recent studies by Karl Kroeger[14] recognize the degree of complexity as the standard for naming a composition a set piece or an anthem. The one unmistakable trait is that all such pieces have one permanent text. In the analysis following, such compositions are encountered, for example in FOREST (no. 23) and SCOTLAND (no. 55).

Notes

1. Terry L. Baldridge, "Evolving Tastes in Hymntunes of the Methodist Episcopal Church in the Nineteenth Century" (Ph.D. dissertation, University of Kansas, 1982), 124.

2. Richard A. Crawford, *Andrew Law, American Psalmodist* (Evanston, IL: Northwestern University Press, 1968), 14, note.

3. George Pullen Jackson, *White Spirituals in the Southern Uplands* (Chapel Hill: University of North Carolina Press, 1933); *Spiritual Folk-Songs in Early America* (New York: J. J. Augustin, 1937); *Down-East Spirituals and Others,* 2nd ed. (New York: J. J. Augustin, 1953); *White and Negro Spirituals* (New York: J. J. Augustin, 1943); *Another Sheaf of White Spirituals* (Gainesville: University of Florida Press, 1952).

4. See Dorothy D. Horn, *Sing to Me of Heaven* (Gainesville: University of Florida Press, 1970), for a discussion of BENEVENTO, CHINA, and MEAR.

5. See Irving Lowens, "The Origins of the American Fuging Tune," *Journal of the American Musicological Society* 6 (Spring 1953): 43–52, reprinted in *Music and Musicians in Early America* (New York: W. W. Norton, 1964); also Nicholas Temperley and Charles G. Manns, *Fuging Tunes in the Eighteenth Century*, Detroit Studies in Music Bibliography No. 49 (Detroit: Information Coordinators, 1983).

6. Nicholas Temperley, *The Music of the English Parish Church*, Vol. 1 (Cambridge: Cambridge University Press, 1979), 212f.

7. The "plain fuging tune" opens with a homophonic section, which reaches a definite cadence. The imitative section follows with each voice proclaiming the same text.

8. An "extended plain fuging tune" may contain more than one imitative section, with a homophonic section separating such sections.

9. An "antiphonal fuging tune" occurs when it is indicated that a section of the fugue is to be sung by a small group (women, one voice, etc.).

10. In "reverse fuging tunes" the order of the imitative and homophonic sections is changed. The fugue comes first, and the tune ends in homophony.

11. See William J. Reynolds, *A Survey of Christian Hymnody* (New York: Holt, Rinehart and Winston, 1963), 104.

12. See Harry Eskew and Hugh T. McElrath, *Sing with Understanding: An Introduction to Christian Hymnology* (Nashville, TN: Broadman Press, 1980), 176f.

13. See Crawford, *Andrew Law, American Psalmodist*, 15.

14. Karl Kroeger, "The Worcester Collection of Sacred Harmony and Sacred Music in America, 1786–1803" (Ph.D. dissertation, Brown University, 1976).

Chapter 4
Interpretation and Conclusions

Evolution of the Tunebooks

John Wesley's *Foundery Collection* provided forty-two tunes comprising selections from English and German sources and from the metrical psalters, as well as one adaptation of a march by Handel, and a few original works.[1] Two of Wesley's choices survive the succession of tunebooks and appear in the core repertory list: AMSTERDAM (no. 2) and ST. MICHAEL'S (no. 53). As American Methodism expanded, the number and variety of tunes grew rapidly, and with the American publication of *David's Companion* (New York, 1808) the newer KENTUCKY was offered alongside Tans'ur's ST. MARTIN'S (GAINSBOROUGH). The greatest variety is seen in the *New Hymn and Tunebook* (New York, 1866) containing 642 tunes; the *Hymn and Tunebook* (New York, 1878) reduced the number of tunes to 430.

Throughout most of the period under study, meter is the guiding principle for the sequence of tune publication, and tunes are published in groups according to their meter. For example, in *The Harmonist* (1837), the first seventy-one pages contain only Common Meter tunes; after this begin the Long Meter tunes. The pattern continues with Short Meter, Particular Meters, and so on. At the top of each tune is a hymn number, to assist the user to find the complete text in the official hymn collection of the day. By far the largest number of tunes is classified as Common Meter, Long Meter, or Short Meter settings. The percentage of these three meters decreases steadily over the century from 63 percent of the collection of 1822, to only 50 percent of the 1878 collection. The exception to this statement is found in the 1853 *Lute of Zion*, in which 71 percent of the tunes fall into these metrical categories. Their dominant presence demonstrates an attachment that the old psalm tune style enjoyed, as well as a penchant for the flow of the style of the old psalm texts.

On the other hand, the list of other meters (e.g., 87.87, or 668 D, etc.) grows tremendously, comprising only 16 percent of the 1822 *Methodist Harmonist* but occupying 47 percent of the contents of the 1878 volume. This reflects the activity of authors of texts emulating the model of Charles Wesley's crafting of new metrical shapes.

Hymns for the Use of the Methodist Episcopal Church (New York, 1857) was the first publication of tunes in random order rather than in metrical groupings. The 1866 *New Hymn and Tunebook* reverted to the older style, but the 1878 *Hymn and Tunebook* abandoned a metrical layout and adopted instead seasons, themes, and ritual character in the sequence used in the hymnbook. This is reflected in the index of the hymn and tune books, where the metrical index, once a primary resource, becomes clearly secondary to thematic lists. Whereas the format of earlier books had been governed by melodic and metrical considerations, the later books lifted up the textual-verbal content first and suggested an appropriate tune as a secondary consideration.

The shape of the early tunebooks was that of the "open-ender," an oblong format in which the short side formed the spine. In 1857, however, *Hymns for the Use* (see above) adopted the layout of spine on the long side (as we know hymnals today). Tunes were provided opposite texts in this new format. Although the "unofficial" tunebooks had previously contained some cross references to texts and tunes, they were relegated to "companion" status until need and appeal were demonstrated (1857, 1866) in paving the way for their "official" combination in 1878.

Origins of the Compositions

Examination of the chronology of the compositional dates of tunes (see appendix F) in the period under discussion shows the following results:

    16th century: 3 tunes
    17th century: 1 tune
    18th century: 41 tunes
    19th century: 30 tunes
    Unidentified: 1 tune

The heritage of the eighteenth century appears to be a dominant presence in the tune availability for Methodists of the middle of the nineteenth century. Within the core list itself, twelve of the fifteen tunes which appeared in at least ten of the eleven sources are found to originate in the eighteenth century; the exceptions in this group are DUNDEE, EATON, OLD HUNDREDTH, and LUTHER'S HYMN (numbers 21, 22, 41, and 33 respectively).

Frequency of Appearance and Place of Origin

The following tunes, all of European origin, and all in the major mode, appeared in all sources:

    AMSTERDAM, no. 2
    MEAR, no. 10
    OLD HUNDREDTH, no. 41

Tunes that appeared in ten of the eleven sources are:

    AYLESBURY, no. 5
    DUNDEE, no. 21
    EATON, no. 22
    LENOX, no. 29
    LUTHER'S HYMN, no. 33
    LUTON, no. 34
    PLEYEL'S HYMN, no. 47
    ST. THOMAS, no. 54
    SHIRLAND, no. 56
    THATCHER, no. 62
    TRURO, no. 65
    WATCHMAN, no. 69

Of these, LENOX (no. 29) is of American origin, and all others are from Europe or Britain. Of the fifteen tunes that appear most frequently, AYLESBURY (no. 5) is the only one in minor mode. Indeed, it is one of only four minor-mode tunes in the entire core list. The recommendations of the various compilers that Methodists use minor-mode tunes "for devotional purposes" (see quote from the preface of 1857, chapter 2) seem to have had little impact.

According to the review by Robin A. Leaver of Richard Crawford's *Core Repertory*,[2] the top ten tunes published in the period leading up to 1810 were OLD HUNDREDTH, WELLS, ST. MARTIN'S, LITTLE MARLBOROUGH, AYLESBURY, MEAR, HANOVER/PSALM 149, WINDSOR, PSALM 34, and BANGOR. Of this list, the first eight form part of the Methodist repertory named as central to the period 1808–1878.

Leaver also points out that, of the top ten tunes included in Crawford's survey as American compositions (prior to 1810), fully eight are fuging tunes.[3] In sharp contrast, it may be seen that of the seventy-six tunes in the core repertory of 1808–1878, BRIDGEWATER (no. 9), GENEVA (no. 25: a reverse fuging tune), LENOX (no. 29), and LISBON (no. 30) are the only four fuging tunes to survive. LENOX is the only one in the top fifteen which is a fuging tune.

Meter

The largest percentage of the core repertory is classed under Common Meter (twenty-two tunes), of which only one is in the minor mode. Of the twenty-two tunes, fifteen are known to be of European origin, six of American, and one remains unidentified.

Eighteen tunes appear in Long Meter, of which only one is in minor mode. Eleven of these are derived from European sources, six from American, and one is as yet unidentified.

Eleven tunes appear in Short Meter, of which two are in minor mode. Eight are from European or British sources, three from American sources.

The meters 88.88.88, 886 D, and 77.77 are linked to three tunes each.

Particular Meter tunes appear in increasing numbers, especially those with extensions, as choruslike repeats become appended to tunes. Some of them are flexible in metrical structure, accommodating themselves to other meters through addition of a note, or addition of a melisma for one syllable. The 1853 *Lute of Zion* even offers instructions regarding alteration of a tune to fit a different text meter (see details in appendix A, NUREMBURG, tune 40d). Examples may also be seen in no. 33 (LUTHER'S HYMN: 87.87.888 *or* 87.87.887) and no. 67 (WARSAW: 66.66.88 *or* 66.86.86).

Influence of Singing Schools and Shape Notes

Singing schools had been started in order to improve congregational singing in the mid-eighteenth century, and they flourished particularly at the end of the century under famous singing masters such as William Billings. Formal singing instruction was commended in the 1792 *Discipline*; Methodist publications urged people to "appoint meetings for the purpose."[4] Instruction materials were largely from the psalm and hymn repertoire, and tunebook publishers quickly picked up the pattern of printing "A Brief Introduction to the Science of Music," or "The Music Teacher," in the first few pages of the tunebook.

After the introduction of the systems of shape-notes (four-shape, eight-shape)[5] the instructional sections of tunebooks also featured directions for learning the system, and the tunes printed also used the shape-notes. In the tunebooks of this survey we find use of shape-note notation up to and including the 1837 *Harmonist*. The 1848 *Sacred Harmonist* was published in two versions: one uses only conventional round notation, the other the shape-note system. It may be deduced that the "better music" movement had made yet another "correction" by banishing both the practice of "social" singing (which relied on shape notes) and the use of the popular fuging tunes. At least in urban centers, keyboard accompaniment was becoming standard, hence the close score offered in the 1848 collection, and the increasing use of two rather than four staves in succeeding books.

The "Better Music" Movement

The followers of the "better music" movement, led by Lowell Mason, discouraged the use of fuging tunes, folk tunes, and revival tunes. They advocated plain tunes of narrow range, with limited harmonic and rhythmic variety.[6] Chiefly concerned with tunes, they turned enthusiastically to European composers for melodies to arrange. Thomas Hastings, a collaborator of Mason, admitted to preferring music which cited a European source, and even to using European-sounding pseudonyms himself to ensure the success of his music. In light of this trend, the music of Pleyel, Beethoven, Palestrina, and Mozart, arranged for congregational use, made inroads on the repertory of Methodists.

The "old Methodist style" tunes were not displaced quickly or easily. The wide range and melodic shapes of ANTI-GUA (no. 3), BRATTLE STREET (no. 8), CHRISTMAS (no. 14), MAJESTY (no. 36), and PLYMOUTH DOCK (no. 48) attest to a mixture of composers and sources from various periods.

For other old tunes, however, the proponents of "better music" had other ideas. One was "smoothing out" the melody line, which can be seen in the evolution of tunes like SWANWICK or AMSTERDAM, detailed in the analysis at nos. 2 and 61 in appendix A. In the former, an interval of a third is filled with a passing note, and the triplets of phrase 3 disappear altogether after 1857. In the latter, the sixteenth notes or "graces" are removed to create a rhythmically plain, angular melody.

As early as 1837, the preface in tunebooks made apology for the inclusion of fuging tunes. Even though the General Conferences had described them as suitable for "private, not public worship," the publishers knew the people enjoyed using fuging tunes. Hence, in the 1849 tunebook, the fuging tunes are gathered in their own section, separate from other tunes. In the 1878 collection, they are found under the heading "Occasional Music," indicating the minimal level of approval for use in public worship.

Prefaces also presented apologies to "scientific" musicians for including certain styles of composition. Publishers were increasingly influenced to adopt standards of "correct" music, and the "correct" simplified tunes and harmonies gradually dominated the content of tunebooks.

In some of the tunebooks surveyed, this meant an increase in the number of anthems, to the delight of the "better music" proponents. The 1848 source demonstrates this trend clearly. Congregations were not always delighted, however, at having singing wrested away from them. In May 1864, the General Conference received a Memorial of Choristers:

> The place which music has ever held in the Church, and the part it has performed in the success of Methodism, establishes its importance. While some denominations of Christians, by artistic skill unattainable by the masses, have excited admiration, it has been the purpose of the Methodist Church that music should be the medium and instrument of fervent spiritual devotions, adapted to all . . . we need music of an elevated and devotional character . . . producing a oneness of taste and practice. Then shall we accomplish the prophetic desire: "Let the people praise thee, O God; let *all* the people praise thee!"[7]

It was subsequently resolved that "singing is the part of public worship in which the whole congregation can unite, and therefore the assignment of this service to a select few, practically to the exclusion of the congregation, is at variance with the spirit of divine worship, and subversive of its purposes."[8]

The *Sacred Harmony* of 1848 provides music on two staves to assist players of organ or pianoforte, as advertised in cover materials appearing on page 141. Much later, in 1864, the General Conference resolved that

> The human voice is the standard of perfection in music; and as accompaniment, not supersedure, of the vocal powers is the object of instrumental music in sacred worship and as the modern organ, in its genera, combines in one instrument the excellence for such purposes, we therefore recommend the organ as the most suitable instrument.[9]

This was official acknowledgment that instrumental leadership was replacing the precentor or cantor and the paid quartet.

Hymn Tunes in the Late Nineteenth Century

Folk Tunes

In the core repertory, only GREENVILLE, arranged in 1818 and appearing first in the *Boston Handel and Haydn Collection* (Boston, 1823), has the characteristics of folk tune: a limited range, stepwise approach to the tonic at cadences, *aaba* form. Yet there are folk influences to be observed in many older melodies, e.g., AYLESBURY, with its modal flavor, arched phrases, and few leaps.[10]

Gospel Tunes

Methodists were very active in the religious movement at the end of the century known as the Second Great Awakening, during which the gospel song was in its early stages of development. It bloomed in the final quarter of the century and is therefore scarcely represented in this survey. In its style it combines the dotted rhythms and refrains of the revival tunes emerging from "praise meetings" (which sprang up after the 1850s) with the "correct" harmonies and melodic shape of the "better music" movement.[11]

One of the composers who flourished in this style was William Bradbury (1816–1868), who published many collections for the Sunday school movement that expanded quickly after 1850. In recognition of the changing needs, *The Lute of Zion* (1853) includes a section for "Sabbath School." Demand grew, and the 1864 General Conference resolved that

> a selection of hymns for Sunday-school purposes be embodied in the Church Hymn-Book, and engrossed in the general index.[12]

In the 1866 source may be found a section for "Sunday Schools" and thirty-four gospel tunes, of which nineteen come from Bradbury. The 1878 collection contains twelve.

Adapted Fuging Tunes

As described above, the debates of the Conferences and the influence of the "better music" musicians combined to suppress the popular fuging tune style. It is worth noting that BRIDGEWATER, LENOX, and LISBON appear in the 1866 source in fuging style, but that by 1878, all three have been rearranged to appear in the usual "hymn style" of composition without the imitative entries. The reverse fuging tune GENEVA retains its original shape in the 1878 source. Along with GREENFIELD (not in this repertory), LENOX was the most published fuging tune in the United States and outlived all others in its homophonic form (see **Figures 4.1** and **4.2**).

Figure 4.1 - LENOX

THE CHRISTIAN—JUSTIFICATION AND ADOPTION.

LENOX.   H. M.   Lewis Edson.

Figure 4.2 - LENOX

Summary

The core repertory of the period 1810–1878 in Methodist circles is dominated by "plain tunes" which seem to suit Methodists best. This would have delighted Bishops Coke and Asbury who had recommended in 1798, "We must surely be sensible of the necessity of confining ourselves to simple tunes."

Old psalm-style tunes (OLD HUNDREDTH, DUNDEE) were retained, and new tunes of similar character (EATON) were introduced. Over 57 percent of those tunes originated in the previous century, but over 31 percent were compositions of the nineteenth century. It should be noted that with the appearance of the 1878 hymnal, English Victorian parish hymn tunes, parallel in style to the plain tunes, made their first appearance. Joseph Barnby is represented by two, John Dykes by seven, and Arthur Sullivan by five tunes, joining the ranks of Mason and Hastings to give clear direction to the provisions of the 1905 and 1935 tune and text books.[13]

Considering the rapid rise of the Sunday school, and its effects upon architecture, churchgoing, and spiritual formation, it is surprising that none of its songs entered into the core repertory, and only a very few exist in the final hymn and tune book included in this survey. The Methodist practice from the beginnings of the Sunday school movement was to use a separate Sunday school hymnal. The duality of staid public worship patterns alongside the informal style of Sunday school is not revealed in the contents of the later collections, and certainly not in the core repertory.

Although the proposals of the "better music" leaders were accepted with regard to shape of tune, there was rejection of the "scientific" model espoused in the 1848 *Sacred Harmony*. Discussions of "better music" and the available options seemed to provoke a great interest in the original intent and style of composers, and a kind of "restoration" of note values, and of harmony. Most importantly, there was heard the demand to restore the music of the people to the people.

By the end of the century, organs and choirs became more or less standard in Methodist churches. Hymnals contained tunes tied to a text. Hymn singing by congregations continued to be a distinguishing mark of Methodists' attempts to sing God's praises "with one heart and one voice."

Notes

1. Nelson F. Adams, "The Musical Sources for John Wesley's Tunebooks: the Genealogy of 148 Tunes" (S.M.D. dissertation, Union Theological Seminary, New York, 1973), 70ff.

2. Robin A. Leaver, in "News of Hymnody," no. 17 (January 1986), reviewing *The Core Repertory of Early American Psalmody*, 5ff.

3. Leaver, "News," 7.

4. See "Singing—Social Meetings" in *Zion's Herald and Wesleyan Journal*, January 17, 1849, 10.

5. See Henry W. Foote, *Three Centuries of American Hymnody* (Cambridge: Harvard University Press, 1940; reprint, Camden, CT: 1961).

6. See Henry L. Mason, *Hymn Tunes of Lowell Mason: A Bibliography* (Cambridge, MA: 1944); also Pemberton, *Lowell Mason: His Life and Work* (Ann Arbor, MI: 1985).

7. Erastus Wentworth, "Methodists and Music," *Methodist Quarterly Review* 47 (New York: July 1865) 375–78.

8. Wentworth, "Methodists and Music," Resolution 2.

9. Wentworth, "Methodists and Music," 8.

10. Terry L. Baldridge, "Evolving Tastes in Hymn Tunes of the Methodist Episcopal Church in the Nineteenth Century" (Ph.D. dissertation, University of Kansas, 1982), 144.

11. William J. Reynolds, *A Survey of Christian Hymnody* (New York: Holt, Rinehart, and Winston, 1963), 104.

12. Wentworth, "Methodists and Music."

13. Details proffered by Carlton R. Young in correspondence, June 2003. He also points out that despite their growing popularity after 1900, African American spirituals made no appearance in hymnals of the Methodist Church until 1966.

Appendix A
Biographies and Content of the Core Repertory 1808-1878 in Tunebooks of the Methodist Episcopal Church

Tune Biographies[1]

a. First publication and/or first U.S. publication;[2] original text if relevant.
b. Category of musical form (see * below), textual meter (CM, LM, 886 D, etc.), major/minor mode.
c. Characteristics of the tune, or voicing.
d. Comparison of the settings examined in this study.
e. Text incipit found in each collection.

Additional References:
Resources where further tune information is available.

Tune Census

The eleven items related to each tune have been described in the following format:

Numerical tune profile line by line						Source/date of profile
(Italicized numbers indicate pitches outside the principal octave)						Meter
Date of tunebook	numerical profile	editor and book title	tune name	first letter of opening words	arranger/ composer	key and location of melody line

*Nomenclature:

Plain tune:	setting of text without sectional or textual repetition
Tune-with-extension:	repeats words or sections of the tune
Antiphonal tune:	at least one voice rests in at least one phrase of the fuging tune at least one section has imitative vocal entries that produce text overlap
Through-composed:	a) anthem (prose text) b) set piece (verse text)

1. **ALFRETON** by William Beastall (fl. early 19th c.)

a. First appearances were in *Musical Primer*, Harrisburg, ca. 1814, and *New York Selection of Sacred Music*, 1818.[3]

b. This tune is a Long Meter "plain tune" in the major mode; it has duple meter.

c. The tune is very regular, mixing half, quarter, and dotted half notes. It shows some influence of the "old Methodist" tunes with its eight slurred pairs (one syllable for two notes).

d. The tune pitches remain the same in all examples. The rhythm of the cadence of phrase 3 varies in 1837 and 1848; in these versions the rhythm is ♩♩♩ and contrasts with all other versions that use ♩♩♩ for the identical pitches.

e. Texts used:

22/33/37/49	OTTWAS	O thou, to whose all-searching sight
48	OHDTFM	O happy day that fixed my choice
53/56	TLICTH	The Lord is come; the heavens
57	SOGIJL	Servants of God in joyful lays
66	EDOLDI	Eternal depth of love divine

Additional references:
1. Temperley, *HTI*, no. 14890
2. Wasson, *HI*, no. 00564

ALFRETON   NHT: 1866

1. 1543656321
2. 3565878765
3. 58565544332
4. 567856321   Meter: LM

1808	X						
1822	1543656321	BANGNMH	ALFRETON	OTTWAS	Beastall	F	3/4
1833	1543656321	BANGNMH	ALFRETON	OTTWAS	Beastall	F	3/4
1837	1543656321	LANEG-H	ALFRETON	OTTWAS	Beastall	F	3/4
1848	1543656321	JACKSSH	ALFRETON	OHDTFM	Beastall	F	3/4
1849	1543656321	DINGCDH	ALFRETON	OTTWAS	Beastall	F	3/4
1853	1543656321	WOODILZ	ALFRETON	TLICTH	Beastall	F	1/4
1856	1543656321	WOODINLZ	ALFRETON	TLICTH	Beastall	F	1/4
1857	1543656321	=====HU	ALFRETON	SOGIJL	Beastall	F	2/4
1866	1543656321	PHILPNHT	ALFRETON	EDOLDI	Beastall	F	1/4
1878	X						

2. **AMSTERDAM** by Johann Georg Hille (fl. early 18th century)

a. First published in *The Foundery Collection*, London, 1742. It was first published in the United States by Josiah Flagg in *A Collection of the Best Psalm Tunes*, Boston, 1764, or Thomas Walter, *The Grounds and Rules of Musick* [8th ed.], Boston, 1764. There it had the text "Rise my soul" as written by Robert Seagrave.[4]

b. AMSTERDAM is a PM (Particular Meter) tune-with-extension in duple time, in the major mode.

c. Crawford suggests that the tune indicates the influence of secular musical techniques on Wesleyan Methodism. The notation is remarkable for this century, with quarters, eighths, and even sixteenth notes as decorations. The form, *aaba*, would indicate an instrumental origin for this tune.

d. In all appearances to 1833 as well as 1848, the tune begins 151232; it is progressively simplified to 15132 in 1837 and 1849, and further to 1512 in all sources from 1853 through 1878. In 1853 and 1856 the texture in measure 5 is thinned to two parts for four measures. A similar style occurs in 1857 in measure 5.

e. Texts used:

08/22/33	OAGOLT	O Almighty God of love thy holy arm
37/48	GGAAHT	Glorious God accept a heart
49/53/56/57/66/78	RMSAST	Rise my soul, and stretch thy wings

Additional references:
1. Crawford, *Core Repertory*, no. 4
2. McCutchan, *Our Hymnody*, no. 524
3. Temperley, *HTI*, no. 1648c
4. Wasson, *HI*, no. 01130

AMSTERDAM

HWT: 1878

1. 15123234
2. 565432
3. 15123234
4. 565432
5. 56565432
6. 3234321232
7. 15123234
8. 5654321

Meter: 76.76.77.76

1808	1512323234		AMSTERDAM	OAGOLT		G	1/2
1822	1512323234	BANGNMH	AMSTERDAM	OAGOLT		G	2/3
1833	1512323234	BANGNMH	AMSTERDAM	OAGOLT		G	2/3
1837	1513232345	LANEG-H	AMSTERDAM	GGAAHT	Nares	G	3/4
1848	1512323234	JACKSSH	AMSTERDAM	GGAAHT	Nares	G	3/4
1849	1513232345	DINGCDH	AMSTERDAM	RMSAST	Nares	G	3/4
1853	1512323456	WOODILZ	AMSTERDAM	RMSAST		G	1/4
1856	1512323456	WOODINLZ	AMSTERDAM	RMSAST		G	1/4
1857	1512323456	=====HU	AMSTERDAM	RMSAST		G	2/4
1866	1512323456	PHILPNHT	AMSTERDAM	RMSAST	NaresJ	G	1/4
1878	1512323456	NELSHWT	AMSTERDAM	RMSAST	NaresJ	G	1/4

Hymn 113.   AMSTERDAM.   7. 6. 7. 6. 7. 7. 7. 6.

O Al-migh-ty God of Love, Thy ho-ly arm dis-play; Send me succour from a-bove, In this my e-vil day:

Arm my weakness with thy pow'r, Woman's Seed, appear with-in! Be my safeguard and my tower, Against the face of sin

3. ANTIGUA

a. First published in Stephen Addington, *A Collection of Psalm Tunes for Publick Worship*, 8th ed., London, 1788. Its first appearance in the United States was in Amos Pilsbury, *The United States' Sacred Harmony*, Boston, 1799.[5]

b. This tune is a Long Meter "plain tune" in duple time in the major mode.

c. This is an "old Methodist" style tune, which covers a broad range of one octave and a fourth, and contains several melismatic passages.

d. All tune versions contain identical notation and slurred passages (melismas). The one rhythmic variant occurs in 1833 at the close of the third section, where the resolution of the tonic six-four is presented as ♩♪ values, whereas all other examples are presented as a ♪♩ sequence.

e. Texts used:

22/33/37	JMATHI	Jesus, my all, to heaven is gone
48	HDTMCM	How do thy mercies close me
53/56	GGAWZS	Great God, attend while Zion sings
57	GIORAD	God is our refuge and defence

Additional references:
1. Temperley, *HTI*, no. 4939
2. Wasson, *HI*, no. 01331

ANTIGUA   HU: 1857

1. 5823854321
2. 58782328543215
3. 5823866234287
4. 587823862878   Meter: LM

1808	X					
1822	5823854321	BANGNMH	ANTIGUA	JMATHI	C	3/4
1833	5823854321	BANGNMH	ANTIGUA	JMATHI	C	3/4

1837	5823854321	LANEG-H	ANTIGUA	JMATHI		C	3/4
1848	5823854321	JACKSSH	ANTIGUA	HDTMCM	Wells	C	3/4
1849	X						
1853	5823854321	WOODILZ	ANTIGUA	GGAWZS	English	C	3/4
1856	5823854321	WOODINLZ	ANTIGUA	GGAWZS	English	C	3/4
1857	5823854321	=====HU	ANTIGUA	GIORAD	English	C	2/4
1866	X						
1878	X						

4. **ARLINGTON** (ARNE) attrib. to Thomas Arne (1710–1778)

a. Appears in Harrison's *Sacred Harmony*, Vol. 1, 1784, in England. First appearance in the United States was in *The Chorister's Companion*, 2nd ed., New Haven, 1788.[6] It is adapted from the minuet of the overture to Arne's opera *Artaxerxes*. Other names for this tune are TRIUMPH and ARTAXERXES.[7]

b. This is a Common Meter "plain tune" in triple time (3/2), in the major mode.

c. The style of this hymn tune derives from simplification of the instrumental line into the basic pattern of ♪♪♩♩. The rhythmic pattern of the first half of the tune is imitated in the second half.

d. The setting barely changes through the period under study. The melody's closing gesture reads 1 134321 in the earliest tunebooks but becomes simplified to read 1 24321 in the 1853 and successive sources.

e. Text used:

22/33/37	OJSBIS	On Jordan's stormy banks I stand

Additional references:
1. Temperley, *HTI*, no. 4443
2. Wasson, *HI*, no. 01444

53	TITDTL	This is the day the Lord hath made
56	JUBTGA	Jesus, united by thy grace
57/66	AIASOT	Am I a soldier of the cross
78	JTARLT	Jesus, thou all-redeeming Lord
	OGOSTT	O God our strength
	ATODTC	A thousand oracles divine

ARLINGTON (ARNE)   HWT: 1878

1. 13332111
2. 2354332
3. 43336555
4. 124321   Meter: CM

1808	X						
1822	1333211123	BANGNMH	ARLINGTON	OJSBIS	Arne	G	3/4
1833	1333211123	BANGNMH	ARLINGTON	OJSBIS	Arne	G	3/4
1837	1333211123	LANEG-H	ARLINGTON	OJSBIS	Arne	G	3/4
1848	X						
1849							
1853	1333211123	WOODILZ	ARLINGTON	TITDTL	Arne	E	1/4
1856	1333211123	WOODINLZ	ARLINGTON	JUBTGA	Arne	G	3/4
1857	1333211123	=====HU	ARLINGTON	AIASOT	Arne	G	2/4
1866	1333211123	PHILPNHT	ARLINGTON	AIASOT	ArneT	G	1/4
1878	1333211123	NELSHWT	ARLINGTON	JTARLT	ArneT	G	1/4
				OGOSTT			
				ATODTC			

HYMN 546.   ARLINGTON. C. M.   Dr. Arne.   3

1 On Jordan's stor-my banks I stand, And cast a wish-ful eye, To Canaan's fair and hap-py land, Where my pos-ses-sions lie.

2. O the transport-ing, rapt'rous scene That ri-ses to my sight! Sweet fields ar-ray'd in liv-ing green, And ri-vers of de-light!

5. AYLESBURY

a. First published in this form in James Green, *A Book of Psalm-Tunes*, 5th ed., London, 1724. It was first published in the United States in Thomas Johnston, [untitled collection], Boston, 1755, ca. 1760. Printed 130 times prior to 1810.[8] In England it was sung to the Short Meter text of Watts for Psalm 23. Other names used for this tune were EXETER, GAINSBOROUGH, ST. PHILIPS, and WIRKSWORTH.

b. AYLESBURY is a duple time plain tune in minor mode which appears with great frequency. This Short Meter tune was printed with more than a dozen texts and was sung to Watts' Psalm 23 as early as Williams Collection (1769) and as late as the end of the period examined in this study.

c. It has one principal melodic gesture and a dominant dactylic characteristic; the fourth phrase is almost identical to the opening phrase. The melody usually follows a natural minor scale, except for the version in 1878.

d. There is great variety in keys of the settings: a minor, e minor, and the most frequent, g minor. Rhythm is standard throughout. The dominant pedal point presented in 1837 recurs only in the 1878 setting. The latter appears in the section "Occasional Pieces and Chants," where a note directs the reader to a text much earlier in the collection. By far the most florid (with passing note sevenths, and chromatic alterations) is the setting of the 1848 book in a mature Baroque style.

The 1878 version, found in the section "Occasional Pieces and Chants," includes a raised leading tone and raised second degree, which alters the effect of both tune and harmony, the latter being oriented towards b minor instead of a modal tonality.[9]

e. Texts Used:

08	ACTKIH	A charge to keep I have
22/33/37	AAIBTD	And am I born to die?
48	AMTBDT	And must this body die, this well
53/56	OTWATL	O thou who art the Light
57	ACIYDM	And can I yet delay my little all
66	BWAPTJ	Behold! With awful pomp the judge
78	AHSFMB	Ah, how shall fallen man be just

Additional references:
1. Crawford, *Core Repertory*, no. 7
2. Temperley, *HTI*, no. 848b, d
3. Wasson, *HI*, no. 01923

AYLESBURY (minor)   HWT: 1878

1. 154321
2. 576545
3. 32153432
4. 254321   Meter: SM (6686)

1808	1543215765		AYLESBURY	ACTKIH	Miller	g	3/4
1822	1543215765	BANGNMH	AYLESBURY	AAIBTD	Green	a	3/4
1833	1543215765	BANGNMH	AYLESBURY	AAIBTD	Green	a	3/4
1837	1543215765	LANEG-H	AYLESBURY	AAIBTD	Green	e	3/4
1848	1543215765	JACKSSH	AYLESBURY	AMTBDT	Green	g	3/4
1849	X						
1853	1543215765	WOODILZ	AYLESBURY	OTWATL	Green	g	3/4
1856	1543215765	WOODINLZ	AYLESBURY	OTWATL	Green	g	3/4
1857	1543215765	=====HU	AYLESBURY	ACIYDM	Green	g	2/4
1866	1543215765	PHILPNHT	AYLESBURY	BWAPTJ	GreeneM	g	1/4
1878	1543215765	NELSHWT	AYLESBURY	AHSFMB	GreenJ	g	1/4

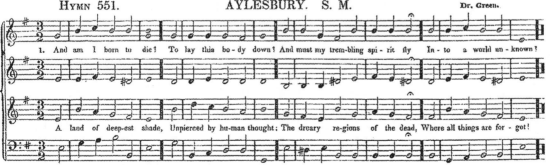

6. **BANISTER** (ROMAINE, DUNKIRK) by C. W. Banister (1768–1831)

a. First published in Charles William Banister, *Twelve Psalm & Hymn Tunes*, London, 1792. Its first appearance in the

United States was in Andrew Law, *The Art of Singing, I: The Musical Primer*, Cambridge, 1803.[10]

b. This is an antiphonal tune-with-extension in 7676 (doubled) meter in the major mode.[11]

c. The tune has a broad range of an octave and a fourth. It is supported by four-part harmony for twelve measures, before breaking into an imitative section, the text of which is repeated in the final homophonic phrase.

d. Only the 1833 source uses ¢ as a time signature; all others use 4/4. In the imitative fourth phrase of the 1833 version, the line above the tune is marked "Trebles" for two measures, then "Tenor." The topmost line remains undesignated. The same markings appear in the 1837 source, but within the topmost staff of music.

In 1848, the point of imitation for the entry of the second voice shows a minor change; whereas the original motif reads 5111, the second entry reads 17111. The 1849 version reclaims the exact imitation.

The 1853 and 1856 sources make only one rhythmic change, in dividing equally the final note of phrase 4 and the beginning of phrase 5 into two half-note values, replacing the ♩. pattern. At the imitative section in these sources, there is a further melodic change: the tune profile reads 51112 321, whereas all others read 51113 2 1.

e. Texts used:

33	OLHGTF	O Lord, how great's the favour
37/48/49	FGIMFI	From Greenland's icy mountains
53/56	WSTVOS	When shall the voice of singing
66	TTOGAS	To thee, our God and Saviour

Additional references:
1. Temperley, *HTI*, no. 5997
2. Wasson, *HI*, nos. 08724 and 33559

BANISTER (ROMAINE, DUNKIRK)   NHT: 1866

1. 511534333221171
2. 511534323456545
3. 543513433321654332
4. 511132112333543
x 3455586555432171   Meter: 76.76 D

1808	X						
1822	X						
1833	5115343332	BANGSMH	BANISTER	OLHGTF	Banister	G	3/4
1837	5115343332	LANEG-H	BANISTER	FGIMFI	Banister	G	3/4
1848	5115343332	JACKSSH	BANISTER	FGIMFI	Banister	G	3/4
1849	5115343332	DINGCDH	BANNISTER	FGIMFI	Banister	G	3/4
1853	5115343332	WOODILZ	ROMAINE	WSTVOS	Banister	G	1/4
1856	5115343332	WOODINLZ	ROMAINE	WSTVOS	Banister	G	1/4
1857	X						
1866	5115343332	PHILNHT	BANISTER	TTOGAS		G	1/4
1878	X						

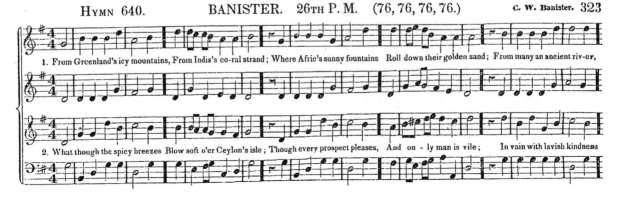

HYMN 640.   BANISTER.   26TH P. M.   (76, 76, 76, 76.)   C. W. Banister. 323

1. From Greenland's icy mountains, From India's co-ral strand; Where Afric's sunny fountains Roll down their golden sand; From many an ancient riv-er,

2. What though the spicy breezes Blow soft o'er Ceylon's isle; Though every prospect pleases, And on - ly man is vile; In vain with lavish kindness

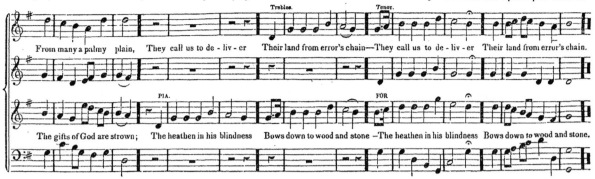

7. **BENEVENTO** by Samuel Webbe (1740–1816)

a. First published in John Whitaker, *The Seraph*, Vol. 2, London, ca. 1819.[12]

b. This is a "plain tune," except for 1833, in which the second half is repeated, creating a plain tune extended. It uses duple time in the major mode and a meter of 77.77 (doubled).

c. This tune, spanning an octave, is characterized by the repetition of pitches as phrases commence. The first half ends firmly in the home key, before the tune shifts into the area of the dominant key briefly to imitate the opening motif.

d. The melody remains the same in all sources, as does the harmony. The only variant is the repeat of text and music stipulated in the 1833 source.

e. Texts used:

33/37	JIOCLH	Jesus is our common Lord; He is
48	STWWYD	Sinners, turn; why will ye die?
49/53/56/57/78	WWCCTS	While with ceaseless course the sun
66	STWGIN	Sinners, turn while God is near.

Additional references:
1. Temperley, *HTI*, no. 16570
2. Wasson, *HI*, no. 02507

BENEVENTO   HWT: 1878

1. 1111321
2. 2222432
3. 3332555
4. 67833421
5. 5555765
6. 2222432
7. 3332555
8. 67833421   Meter: 77.77 D

1808	X						
1822	X						
1833	1111321222	BANGNMH	BENEVENTO	JIOCLH	Webbe	F	3/4
1837	1111321222	LANEG-H	BENEVENTO	JIOCLH	Webbe	F	3/4
1848	1111321222	JACKSSH	BENEVENTO	STWWYD	Webbe	F	3/4
1849	1111321222	DINGCDH	BENEVENTO	WWCCTS	Webbe	F	3/4
1853	1111321222	WOODILZ	BENEVENTO	WWCCTS	Webbe	E♭	1/4
1856	1111321222	WOODINLZ	BENEVENTO	WWCCTS	Webbe	E♭	1/4
1857	1111321222	=====HU	BENEVENTO	WWCCTS	Webbe	E♭	1/4

| 1866 | 1111321222 | PHILPNHT | BENEVENTO | STWGIN | WebbeS | E♭ | 1/4 |
| 1878 | 1111321222 | NELSHWT | BENEVENTO | WWCCTS | WebbeS | E | 1/4 |

8. BRATTLE STREET (DEVOTION) by Ignace Pleyel (1757–1831)

a. First published in Thomas Costellow, *Sunday's Amusement*, London, ca. 1805, and based on the second movement of Pleyel's *Symphonie Concertante* of 1786. First appeared in the United States in O[liver] Shaw, A[mos] Albee, and H[erman] Mann, *The Columbian Sacred Harmonist, or Collection of Grammatical Music*, Dedham, 1808.[13]

b. This is a "plain tune" which includes antiphonal sections in the earliest sources. It is in the major mode in duple time and has a meter of Common Meter (doubled).

c. Though this tune was composed later than the "old Methodist tunes," the use of a whole octave, of varied rhythms, and of *abcb* shape leads to the inevitable comparison with the older style.

d. The melody remains constant throughout with the following exceptions:

i)

Source	Measure(s)	Melody notes	Rhythm
1833	4; 8	358 864	
1837	4; 8	38 64	
1853/56/57	4; 8	358 864	
1866	4; 8	358 864	

ii) The melody of the third phrase in the 1866 source is altered substantively:

1857 third-phrase tune: 223446531323445665
1866 third-phrase tune: 2234346531323588728765432

iii) The upbeat to each phrase in the three earliest sources is a full quarter (♩), whereas all later sources show an eighth-note upbeat (♪).

e. Texts Used:

22/33	OJSOGG	O joyful sound of gospel grace
37	MSOLWS	My span of life will soon be done
53/56/57	WTISPP	While Thee I seek, Protecting Power
66	LOMLOM	Lord of my life, O may thy praise

Additional references:
1. Temperley, *HTI*, no. 8465a
2. Wasson, *HI*, no. 03146

BRATTLE STREET (DEVOTION)

NHT: 1866

1. 55853442
2. 212315332
3. 55853442
4. 4358864321
5. 22343465313
6. 588728765432
7. 55853442
8. 4358864321

Meter: CMD

1808	X						
1822	5585344221	BANGNMH	DEVOTION	OJSOGG	Pleyel	E♭	3/4
1833	5585344221	BANGNMH	DEVOTION	OJSOGG	Pleyel	E♭	3/4
1837	5585344221	LANEG-H	DEVOTION	MSOLWS	Pleyel	E♭	3/4
1848	X						
1849	X						
1853	5585344221	WOODILZ	BRATTLE ST	WTISPP	Pleyel	E♭	3/4
1856	5585344221	WOODINLZ	BRATTLE ST	WTISPP	Pleyel	E♭	3/4
1857	5585344221	=====HU	BRATTLE ST	WTISPP	Pleyel	E♭	2/4
1866	5585344221	PHILPNHT	BRATTLE ST	LOMLOM		D	1/4
1878	X						

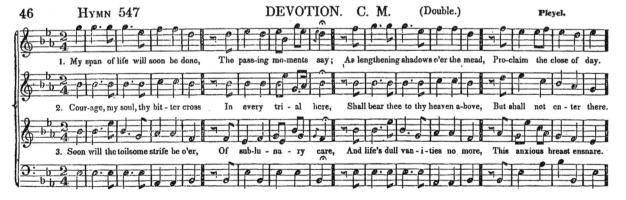

O that my heart might dwell a - loof, From all creat - ed things, And learn that wisdom from a - bove, Whence true contentment springs!

The sigh-ing ones that hum-bly seek In sorrowing paths be - low, Shall in e - ter - ni - ty re - joice, Where endless comforts flow.

Courage, my soul, on God re - ly, De - liverance soon will come, A thousand ways has Pro-vi - dence To bring be - lievers home.

9. **BRIDGEWATER** by Lewis Edson (1748–1820)

a. First published in *The Chorister's Companion, or Church Music Revised*, New Haven, 1782.[14]

b. BRIDGEWATER is a Long Meter fuging tune in major mode. In early publications it was linked most frequently with "My soul, thy great Creator" (twenty-eight verses). Its textless printing in the 1801 collection of the composer's son highlights its independence from any given text.

c. It follows the standard fuging tune form, setting a single four-line stanza with a fugue on the third line of text. This tune is unusual in later versions in the use of 3/2 to the end of the fugue, followed by homophony in 2/2 to the closing cadence.

d. The early sources show the tune in duple time (2/2) throughout. The rhythm ♩♪♪♪♪♪♪♪ lends itself more naturally, however, to a triple accentuation. In all sources after 1853, the first three phrases are in 3/2 time, followed by the final phrase in 2/2. The tune has a narrow scope, utilizing pitches between 7 and 4 only (a diminished fifth).

e. Texts used:

08	SWOYWS	Say which of you would see the Lord
22/33/37	GOMLWG	God of my life, whose gracious power
53/56/57/78	GGAWZS	Great God, attend while Zion sings
66	SOGIJL	Servants of God, in joyful lays

Additional references:
1. Crawford, *Core Repertory*, no. 12
2. Nicholas Temperley and Charles G. Manns, *Fuging Tunes in the Eighteenth Century*, no. 187
3. Temperley, *HTI*, no. 4274
4. Wasson, *HI*, no. 03239

BRIDGEWATER   HWT: 1878

1. 13122171
2. 321432132
3. 5111133332111
   612223111
4. 322214321   Meter: LM

1808	1312217132		BRIDGEWATER	SWOYWS	C	3/4
1822	1312217132	BANGNMH	BRIDGEWATER	GOMLWG	C	3/4
1833	1312217132	BANGNMH	BRIDGEWATER	GOMLWG	C	3/4
1837	1312217132	LANEG-H	BRIDGEWATER	GOMLWG Edson	C	3/4
1848	X					
1849	X					

1853	1312217132	WOODILZ	BRIDGEWATER	GGAWZS	Edson	B♭	3/4
1856	1312217132	WOODINLZ	BRIDGEWATER	GGAWZS	Edson	B♭	3/4
1857	1312217132	=====HU	BRIDGEWATER	GGAWZS	Edson	B♭	2/4
1866	1312217132	PHILPNHT	BRIDGEWATER	SOGIJL	EdsonJ	B♭	1/4
1878	1312217132	NELSHWT	BRIDGEWATER	GGAWZS	EdsonL	B♭	1/4

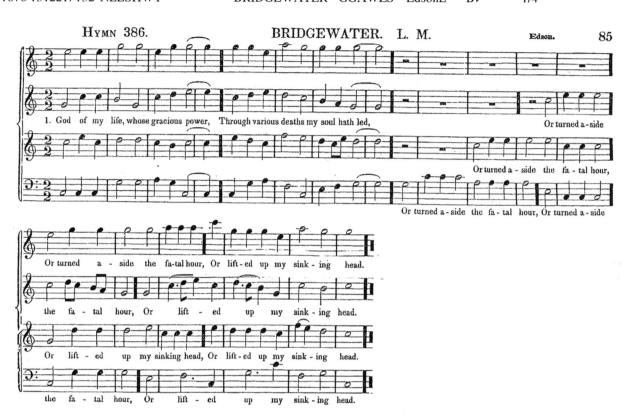

10. BRIGHTON

a. The tune is from Lowell Mason, 1823.

b. This is a "plain tune" using six lines of Long Meter in the major mode in duple time.

c. The tune opens with two balanced phrases ending in a feminine cadence; phrase 3 echoes phrase 1, but phrase 4 presents a new idea, and in early sources a raised subdominant to lead to the ending on the dominant. There are seventeen instances of slurred pairs of notes in the tune, which spans a whole octave.

d. The 1833 and 1837 sources share the characteristic of a reduced texture (three parts only) in phrases 1 and 3, hence the designation "plain antiphonal tune."[15] The first phrase gains a tenor part in sources 1848 and following. The bass part in early sources demonstrates interesting activity (see measure 7), which is missing from later sources. By 1848, the bass line is straightforward, depending on primary harmonies only.

An interesting feature of the tune is a raised fourth degree in the melody at measure 13. The 1853 source allows this note to remain a B-flat, which is copied in all subsequent sources. Another influence of the 1853 source is to alter the rhythm of the final note of phrase 3 and the first of phrase 4 to a half-note value; this alteration survives in all subsequent sources. The 1866 version contains one printing error, a B-flat instead of a C (dominant) in the bass of the penultimate chord.

e. Texts used:

33/37/48/49/57/66	OLDWHT	O love divine, what hast thou done!
53	BWWGPG	Blest who with generous pity glows

Additional reference:
Wasson, *HI*, no. 03260

BRIGHTON   NHT: 1866

1. 334532234
2. 2334587654332
3. 3334532234
4. 23345678765
5. 222354323345
6. 55886421321   Meter: 888 D

1808	X					
1822	X					
1833	3345322342	BANGNMH	BRIGHTON	OLDWHT	F	3/4
1837	3345322342	LANEG-H	BRIGHTON	OLDWHT	F	3/4
1848	3345322342	JACKSSH	BRIGHTON	OLDWHT	F	3/4
1849	3345322342	DINGCDH	BRIGHTON	OLDWHT	F	3/4
1853	3345322342	WOODILZ	BRIGHTON	BWWGPG	English F	1/4
1856	3345322342	WOODINLZ	BRIGHTON	OLDWHT	English F	2/4
1857	3345322342	=====HU	BRIGHTON	OLDWHT	English F	2/4
1866	3345322342	PHILNHT	BRIGHTON	OLDWHT	F	2/4
1878	X					

HYMN 187.   BRIGHTON.   1ST P. M.   6 LINES 8's.   143

1. O love divine, what hast thou done! Th'immortal God hath died for me! The Father's co - e - ter - nal Son Bore all my sins up - on the tree.

2. Behold Him, all ye that pass by,   The bleeding Prince of life and peace! Come see, ye worms, your Maker die, And say, Was ev - er grief like his!

Th'im-mor-tal God for me hath died: My Lord, my Love is cru - ci - fied.

Come, feel with me his blood ap - plied: My Lord, my Love is cru - ci - fied.

11. **BURNHAM** (ANTICIPATION) by Thomas Clark (1775–1859)

a. First published in *A Sett of Psalm and Hymn Tunes*, London, 1805. The first American publication is James Evans, *David's Companion, or The Methodist Standard*, New York, [1810].[16]

b. This is an antiphonal tune-with-extension using 66.66.88 meter in the major mode. It is in duple time.

c. The tune is shaped in four three-measure phrases followed by three four-measure phrases as extension. The text of the fifth line is used in repetition for imitative entries before entering the final phrase and text in full four-part homophony. The range of the tune is a tenth. In all sources except 1866, the tenor is omitted from phrase 3, creating the antiphonal effect.

d. The tune changes only slightly in the course of the study. In early sources up to 1848, phrases 2 and 3 read 58654345, 8762. In all later·sources they read 58654345, 78762. In only the 1848 source, the third phrase ends with a feminine ending 28 87. In contrast, other versions use the ending 28 7.

The harmonic support for the fifth phrase in both 1833 and 1837 (a countertenor E) receives correction in subsequent sources to a C-sharp.

e. Texts used:

22/33/37/56/57	YRSHTP	Ye ransomed sinners hear, the prisoners
48	YMAMRY	Young men and maidens raise your
66	BITNMO	Baptized into thy name, Mysterious One

Additional references:
1. Temperley, *HTI*, no. 10890
2. Wasson, *HI*, no. 01327

BURNHAM (ANTICIPATION)   NHT: 1866

1. 13586278
2. 58654345.
3. 7876287
4. 78654321
5. 5555675888
   6666786222
6. 78232878   Meter: 66.66.88

1808	X						
1822	1358627858	BANGNMH	BURNHAM	YRSHTP	Clark	D	3/4
1833	1358627858	BANGNMH	BURNHAM	YRSHTP	Clark	D	3/4
1837	1358627858	LANEG-H	BURNHAM	YRSHTP	ClarkT	D	3/4
1848	1358627858	JACKSSH	BURNHAM	YMAMRY	Clark	D	3/4
1849	X						
1853	X						
1856	1358627858	WOODINLZ	BURNHAM	YRSHTP		D	3/4
1857	1358627858	=====HU	BURNHAM	YRSHTP		D	2/4
1866	1358627858	PHILPNHT	BURNHAM	BITNMO	ClarkT	D	1/4
1878	X						

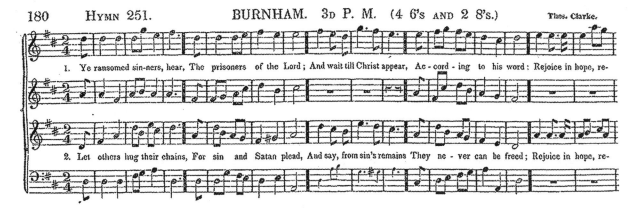

180   HYMN 251.   BURNHAM. 3D P. M. (4 6's AND 2 8's.)   Thos. Clarke.

1. Ye ransomed sin-ners, hear, The prisoners of the Lord; And wait till Christ appear, Ac-cord-ing to his word: Rejoice in hope, re-

2. Let others hug their chains, For sin and Satan plead, And say, from sin's remains They ne-ver can be freed; Rejoice in hope, re-

12. **CAMBRIDGE** (RANDALL) by John Randall (1717–1799)

a. Probable first publication by Stephen Addington, *A Collection of Psalm Tunes for Publick Worship*, 6th ed., London, 1786. The first appearance in the United States is Nehemiah Shumway, *The American Harmony*, 2nd ed., Philadelphia, 1801.[17]

b. This is a tune-with-extension using duple time in the major mode. In some sources it is an antiphonal tune-with-extension. The text meter is Common Meter.

c. For the initial three phrases, the tune is restricted to the range of a diminished fifth and moves in regular half notes and quarter notes. In the antiphonal segments of section four, the range of the tune increases to a minor seventh. The tune ends in four-part setting as at the opening.

d. After the third phrase, the fourth line of text enters in a unison line. However, in 1833 and 1837 the tune is accompanied at the interval of a third, with two other voices silent, adding the antiphonal characteristic. Unlike a fuging tune, there is no text overlap even though the voices enter separately.

 The earliest sources in the study use a time signature of ◯ . All others indicate 2/2.

e. Texts used:

22/33/37	TWULTR	Talk with us, Lord, thyself reveal
53/56	STTLAN	Sing to the Lord a new made song
57	CYTLTS	Come, ye that love the Saviour's
66	AGTTDL	All glory to the dying Lamb
78	SOTJSW	Salvation! O the joyful sound

Additional references:
1. Temperley, *HTI*, no. 4665a, b
2. Wasson, *HI*, no. 03633

CAMBRIDGE (RANDALL)   HWT: 1878

1. 13321432
2. 1342171
3. 13321432
4. 121*765*
 343217
 2342171   Meter: CM

1808	X						
1822	1332143213	BANGNMH	RANDALL	TWULTR	Randall	B♭	3/4
1833	1332143213	BANGNMH	RANDALL	TWULTR	Randall	B♭	3/4

1837	1332143213	LANEG-H	RANDALL	TWULTR	Randall	B♭	3/4
1848	X						
1849	X						
1853	1332143213	WOODILZ	CAMBRIDGE	STTLAN	Randall	B♭	1/4
1856	1332143213	WOODINLZ	CAMBRIDGE	STTLAN	Clark	B♭	1/4
1857	1332143213	=====HU	CAMBRIDGE	CYTLTS	Randall	B♭	1/4
1866	1332143213	PHILPNHT	CAMBRIDGE	AGTTDL	Randall	B♭	1/4
1878	1332143213	NELSHWT	CAMBRIDGE	SOTJSW	Randall	B♭	1/4

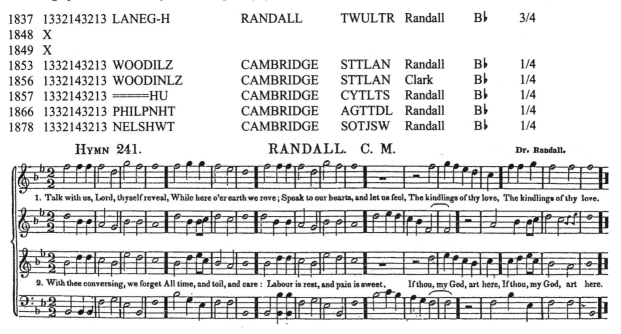

HYMN 241. RANDALL. C. M. Dr. Randall.

1. Talk with us, Lord, thyself reveal, While here o'er earth we rove; Speak to our hearts, and let us feel, The kindlings of thy love, The kindlings of thy love.

2. With thee conversing, we forget All time, and toil, and care : Labour is rest, and pain is sweet, If thou, my God, art here, If thou, my God, art here.

13. **CHINA** by Timothy Swan (1758–1842)

a. The composer considered this his best tune, which first appeared in *New England Harmony*, Northampton, 1801.[18]

b. This is a Common Meter tune in the major mode. This plain tune is in triple (3/4) time.

c. The shape of the "rude tune"[19] and the harmonic arrangements are the work of a composer of limited skills. The range of an octave for a tune is not unusual; however, the use of wide leaps as seen in CHINA is awkward. The tune is fashioned in four phrases of regular length. The 1853 and 1856 sources present a second ending that reads 543 to replace the triplet rise to the tonic of 567 8.

The frequent appearance of triplet groups is a reminder of the ornate Handelian style, which had largely disappeared by the beginning of the nineteenth century.

d. The tune profile (322113*663*) of the earliest versions is softened to 32211236653 in the 1857 version. The melodic triplet ♩ ♪♪♪ (measure 9) of early versions is changed in 1849 to the rhythm ♩ ♫ ♩ but the triplet is restored in succeeding publications. The absence of the fourth degree of the scale lends it a folk or modal character. The 1853 and 1856 text, "Why do we mourn departing friends," is replaced by "Why do we mourn for dying friends" in later sources.

e. Texts used:

22/33/37/49	TWAENA	Thee we adore, Eternal Name
53/56/57/66/78	WDWMFD	Why do we mourn for dying friends?

Additional references:
1. G. P. Jackson, *Down-East Spirituals*, no. 112
2. Temperley, *HTI*, no. 8729a
3. Wasson, *HI*, no. 04212

CHINA   HWT: 1878

1. 322113*663*
2. *5556671*
3. 2231613213212
4. *3513165671*

Meter: CM

1808	X						
1822	322113663	BANGNMH	CHINA	TWAENA	Swan	C	3/4
1833	322113663	BANGNMH	CHINA	TWAENA	Swan	C	3/4
1837	322113663	LANEG-H	CHINA	TWAENA	Swan	C	3/4
1848	X						
1849	3221123663	DINGCDH	CHINA	TWAENA	Swan	C	3/4
1853	3221123663	WOODILZ	CHINA	WDWMDF	Swan	C	1/4
1856	3221123663	WOODINLZ	CHINA	WDWMDF	Swan	C	1/4
1857	3221123663	=====HU	CHINA	WDWMFD	Swan	C	2/4
1866	3221123663	PHILPNHT	CHINA	WDWMFD	SwanT	C	1/4
1878	3221136635	NELSHWT	CHINA	WDWMFD	SwanT	B♭	1/4

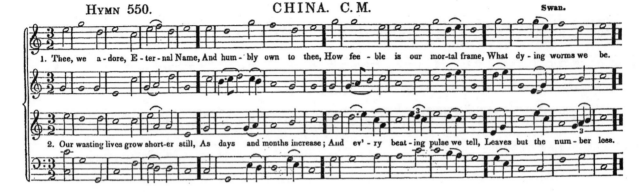

HYMN 550.   CHINA. C. M.   Swan.

1. Thee, we a-dore, E-ter-nal Name, And hum-bly own to thee, How fee-ble is our mor-tal frame, What dy-ing worms we be.

2. Our wasting lives grow short-er still, As days and months increase; And ev'-ry beat-ing pulse we tell, Leaves but the num-ber less.

14. CHRISTMAS

a. First published in Samuel Arnold, *The Psalms of David*, London, 1791. First published in the United States by Andrew Law, *The Musical Magazine*, no. 3, Cheshire, 1794.[20]

b. CHRISTMAS is a major mode tune in duple time, a tune-with-extension as favored by British Methodists. It was sung to many different Common Meter texts, almost all relating to the birth of Jesus.

c. This tune, based on an aria from Handel's opera *Siroe* of 1728, was set for three voice parts with the melody in the treble. Law's setting, in an arrangement considered progressive for the time, keeps the melody on top, adding a fourth voice—a kind of second treble—below the melody. Parenthetically, some other compilers shifted the melody to the tenor and added the notation "Altered from Madan." The appoggiaturas in the melody are typical of the "Methodist" style, as are the repetitions of text to new music (measures 5–10) and of both text and music (measures 15–20).

d. The tune mixes stepwise motion with leaps, as seen in the final two phrases: 6543 65 *2* 5 8 321. Only the 1857 and 1878 sources retain four vocal lines throughout in support of the tune, while others omit a vocal part in the fourth phrase. The text is repeated for the fifth phrase (the extension), which ends in an authentic cadence that contrasts with the tonic pedal point of the fourth phrase.

e. Texts used:

22/33/37/57/78	WSWTFB	While shepherds watched their flocks
48	SRLUYE	Shepherds, rejoice! lift up your eyes
53/56	AMSSEN	Awake my soul, stretch every nerve
66	LEMEAA	Let every mortal ear attend

Additional references:
1. Crawford, *Core Repertory*, no. 21
2. Temperley, *HTI*, no. 5649
3. Wasson, *HI*, no. 04425

CHRISTMAS

HWT: 1878

1. 3458765123
2. 345554332
3. 7825444323
4. 87654365 258321

Meter: CM

1808	X						
1822	3458765123	BANGNMH	CHRISTMAS	WSWTFB	Handel	E♭	3/4
1833	3458765123	BANGNMH	CHRISTMAS	WSWTFB	Handel	E♭	3/4
1837	3458765123	LANEG-H	CHRISTMAS	WSWTFB	Handel	E♭	3/4
1848	3458765123	JACKSSH	CHRISTMAS	SRLUYE	Handel	E♭	3/4
1849	X						
1853	3458765123	WOODILZ	CHRISTMAS	AMSSEN	Handel	D	1/4
1856	3458765123	WOODINLZ	CHRISTMAS	AMSSEN	Handel	D	1/4
1857	3458765123	=====HU	CHRISTMAS	WSWTFB	Handel	D	2/4
1866	3458765123	PHILPNHT	CHRISTMAS	LEMEAA	Handel	E♭	1/4
1878	3458765123	NELSHWT	CHRISTMAS	WSWTFB	Handel	D	1/4

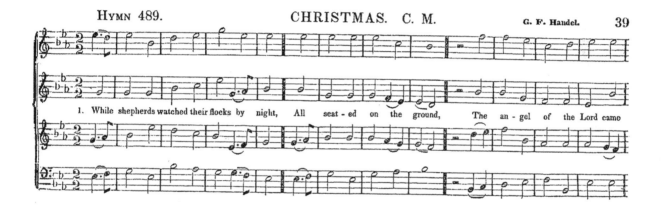

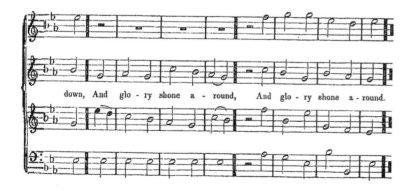

15. **COLCHESTER** by William Tans'ur (1706–1783)

a. The source may be Henry Purcell (1659–1695). It was first published in William Tans'ur, *A Compleat Melody*, London, 1735, to accompany the text "Yield unto God, the mighty Lord." First published in the United States in Thomas Walter, *The Grounds and Rules of Musick*, [7th ed.], Boston, [1759].[21] As noted below, it is attributed to Williams in the sources of this survey.

b. This major mode Common Meter tune in triple time frequently appeared without text; in addition to those below, it appeared with "My never ceasing songs shall show" (Watts, Ps. 89).

c. COLCHESTER is made from the simplest materials, emphasizing the major scale found in part or whole in every phrase, supported almost wholly by the tonic triad.

d. The 1833 and 1837 sources use shape notes and include a grace (measure 8) in the melody, which after 1848 becomes a regular melody note. In all appearances before 1853, the tune ends with 7832878; after 1853 the ending becomes 78232878.

Harmonic treatment shows considerable variety: the 1833 and 1837 sources use a bass line of variety and intervallic interest. The 1848 source presents the alto and tenor parts above the melody that is printed within all four parts on two staves. Harmonically, this is the richest of all settings, using secondary dominants in measures 3 and 10.

From 1853 through 1857, primary harmonies only are used with the addition of an apparent "pedal" to begin the third phrase. That device disappears in 1866 when one of the secondary dominants appears in the third phrase.

e. Texts used:

33/37	LITMTS	Lord, in the morning thou shalt hear
48	CDDFHA	Celestial Dove, descend from high
53/56	OTAJST	O 'twas a joyful sound to hear
57	DTWTHH	Deepen the wound thy hands have made
66	NENIYW	Now, even now, I yield with all

Additional references:
1. Crawford, *Core Repertory*, no. 22
2. Temperley, *HTI*, no.1393a, c
3. Wasson, *HI*, no. 04756

COLCHESTER

NHT: 1866

1. 8876543215
2. 5678278
3. 5432158765
4. 78232878

Meter: CM

Year							
1808	X						
1822	X						
1833	8876543215	BANGNMH	COLCHESTER	LITMTS	William	D	3/4
1837	8876543215	LANEG-H	COLCHESTER	LITMTS	William	D	3/4
1848	8876543215	JACKSSH	COLCHESTER	CDDFHA	William	D	3/4
1849	X						
1853	8876543215	WOODILZ	COLCHESTER	OTAJST	William	C	1/4
1856	8876543215	WOODINLZ	COLCHESTER	OTAJST	William	C	1/4
1857	8876543215	=====HU	COLCHESTER	DTWTHH	William	D	2/4
1866	8876543215	PHILPNHT	COLCHESTER	NENIYW		C	1/4
1878	X						

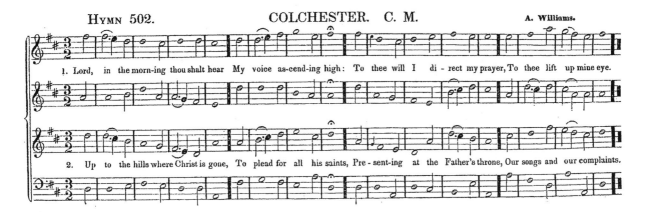

HYMN 502.   COLCHESTER.   C. M.   A. Williams.

1. Lord, in the morn-ing thou shalt hear My voice as-cend-ing high: To thee will I di - rect my prayer, To thee lift up mine eye.

2. Up to the hills where Christ is gone, To plead for all his saints, Pre - sent-ing at the Father's throne, Our songs and our complaints.

16. COME YE DISCONSOLATE (ALMA, CONSOLATION, GILFORD, MERCY SEAT) by Samuel Webbe (1740–1816)

a. First published in J. Challenger, *A Collection of Motetts*, London, 1792. First appearance in the United States is Thomas Hastings and Lowell Mason, *Spiritual Songs for Social Worship*, 1831.[22]

b. This is a plain tune (or plain antiphonal tune) in the major mode, variously noted as using 4 Sevens, Long Meter, 11.10.11.10, or 87.87.77 meter.

c. Substantive changes are detailed below.

d. The tune is entitled ALMA in 1822, 1833, and 1849; only in 1837 is it called GILFORD. Two variants in the tune exist in 1857, one called ALMA and the other called COME YE DISCONSOLATE. This latter title is used in 1866 and 1878.

The 1837 GILFORD is related to the 1857 and ALMA versions (see below). Some alterations in tune are due to changes in text used, but there is no apparent reason for title changes. Changes in tune profile and harmonic setting are as follows:

1822/33	ALMA ¢ 4 Sevens 5316543456785 324686445 87653587653 53388664321 Two parts given, bass very simple.
1837	GILFORD 2/2 Long Meter 5316545678 5334565445 787653828765 345388643211 Four parts given throughout, harmonic structure varied.
1849	ALMA 2/2 87.87.77 5316543456785 334686545(rpt) 87653587653 53388664321 Four parts throughout, less active harmonic structure.
1853/56	COME YE DISCON 4/4 11.10 doubled 5316554567855 3334465445: 8765438287653 53388643211 Directions given for "solo," "duet," "chorus." Soprano in large notes for two phrases, soprano and alto for two more phrases that are repeated in full four-part writing at "chorus" to end.
1857	COME YE DISCON 4/4 PM (11.10.11.10) 5316554567855 3334465445: 8765438287653 53388643211 Soprano in large notes with accompaniment in small notes used for two phrases. Tune and parts in full notation for the remainder, with directions: "First time, Duet—Second time, Chorus."

1857   ALMA 2/2   PM   4 Sevens
                       5316543456785 334686545 87653587653 5*3388664321*
                       Four parts given throughout, harmonic support simple.

1866   COME YE DISCON 4/4   PM (11.10.11.10)
                       5316554567855 3334465445: 87654382876553 5*3388643211*
                       Set out as in 1857 "COME YE"

1878   COME YE DISCON 2/2   11.10.11.10
                       5316554567855 3334465445 87654382876543 5*3388643221*
                       Four parts given throughout, harmonic support simple.

e. Texts used:
22/33   JLOMSL   Jesus, lover of my soul
37   JTWSBS   Jesus, thy wandering sheep behold!
49   CTCHMS   Come to Calvary's holy mountain
53/56/57/66/78   CYDWYL   Come, ye disconsolate, where'er ye languish

Additional reference:
Wasson, *HI*, no. 05277 (CONSOLATION)

COME YE DISCONSOLATE (ALMA, CONSOLATION, GILFORD, MERCY SEAT) HWT: 1878

1. 5316554567855
2. 3334465445
3. 87654382876543
4. 5*3388643221*   Meter: 11.10 D

Year							
1808	X						
1822	53165434567	BANGNMH	ALMA	JLOMSL		D	1/2
1833	53165434567	BANGNMH	ALMA	JLOMSL		D	3/4
1837	531654567U1	LANEG-H	GILFORD	JTWSBS	Bridgewater	D	3/4
1848	X						
1849	5316543567	DINGCDH	ALMA	CTCHMS	Webbe	D	3/4
1853	5316554567	WOODILZ	COME YE DI	CYDWYL	Webbe	D	1/4
1856	5316554567	WOODINLZ	COME YE DI	CYDWYL	Webbe	D	1/4
1857	5316554567	=====HU	COME YE DI	CYDWYL	Webbe	D	1/4
1866	5316554567	PHILPNHT	COME YE DI	CYDWYL	WebbeS	D	1/4
1878	5316554567	NELSHWT	COME YE DI	CYDWYL	WebbeS	D	1/4

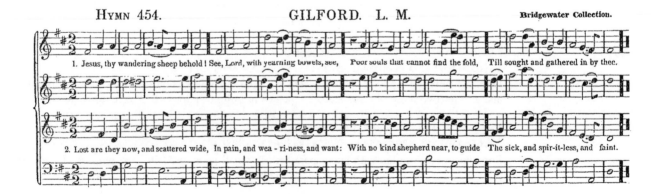

HYMN 454.   GILFORD. L. M.   Bridgewater Collection.

1. Jesus, thy wandering sheep behold ! See, Lord, with yearning bowels, see,   Poor souls that cannot find the fold,   Till sought and gathered in by thee.

2. Lost are they now, and scattered wide, In pain, and wea-ri-ness, and want: With no kind shepherd near, to guide   The sick, and spir-it-less, and faint.

17. **CRANBROOK** arr. by Thomas Clark (1775–1859)

a. First published in Thomas Clark, *A Sett of Psalm and Hymn Tunes* [Set I], London, [1805]. The first appearance in the United States was Andrew Law, *The Art of Singing*, 5th ed., Philadelphia, 1811.[23]

b. This is an antiphonal tune-with-extension in the major mode for Short Meter texts.

c. The range of the tune is a tenth, including a mixture of note values and several pairs of slurred notes in the opening section. The two imitative sections show pairs of voices entering without textual overlap, and each section ends in a four-part homophonic passage.

d. The tune remains the same throughout the study, except for minor changes in note values at upbeats to phrases, e.g., the conjunction of phrases 1 and 2, where in 1849 the melodic rhythm ♩♪ appears, whereas the rhythm ♩♩ appears in 1853.

e. Texts used:
22/33/37	CYTLTL Come, ye that love the Lord
49/53/56/66	GTACSH Grace! 'tis a charming sound

Additional references:
1. Temperley, *HTI*, no. 10893
2. Wasson, *HI*, no. 14224 (Ilkley Moor)

CRANBROOK   NHT: 1866

1. 85654321
2. 58765654332
3. 55675678
4. *22872245*
5. 588878*233323*
   *322*878   Meter: SM

1808	X					
1822	8565432158 BANGNMH	CRANBROOK	CYTLTL	Clark	D	3/4
1833	8565432158 BANGNMH	CRANBROOK	CYTLTL	Clark	D	3/4
1837	8565432158 LANEG-H	CRANBROOK	CYTLTL	ClarkT	D	3/4
1848	X					
1849	8565432158 DINGCDH	CRANBROOK	GTACSH	ClarkT	D	3/4
1853	8565432158 WOODILZ	CRANBROOK	GTACSH	ClarkT	C	3/4
1856	8565432158 WOODINLZ	CRANBROOK	GTACSH	ClarkT	C	3/4
1857	X					
1866	8565432158 PHILPNHT	CRANBROOK	GTACSH		C	1/4
1878	X					

HYMN 252.   CRANBROOK. S. M.   Thomas Clark.   131

18. **CREATION** adapted from Franz Josef Haydn (1732–1809)

a. Often set to "Awake my soul and with the sun," it is an adaptation of "The heavens are telling" from Haydn's *Creation*, 1798. Isaac B. Woodbury may have been the arranger.[24] The earliest version is found in Samuel Webbe, *A Collection of Tunes chiefly from the works of Handel, Corelli, Purcell, Haydn &c.*, London, ca. 1806. It was adapted by Gardiner in *Sacred Melodies from Haydn, Mozart and Beethoven*, Vol. 1, London, 1812. The first U.S. appearance was a variant version in Arthur Clifton, *An Original Collection of Psalm Tunes*, Baltimore, [1819].[25]

b. This "plain tune" in the major mode was treated with antiphonal effects. In all appearances to 1866, the meter was 6 Eights; in 1878 the meter changes to Long Meter (8 Eights) through repetition of the opening phrases.

c. The range is one octave, set usually in C major, excepting the final appearance, which is in A major.

d. The second measure of the melody receives differing treatments as follows: *5112176531* (1833, 1837) compared with *5112231* (all other sources). In sources up to 1856, the paired (antiphonal) entries are maintained in accordance with the original composition. An instrumental trill on high G (as in the original score) is suggested (*ad lib*) in 1848 and 1853. The 1857, 1866, and 1878 sources choose a dominant "pedal" as basis for the paired entries, creating a four-part texture.

e. Texts used:

33	FATDBT	From all that dwell below the skies
37	WSMWSB	Where shall my wandering soul begin
48/53	IPMMWM	I'll praise my maker with my breath
49	ETWCDA	Expand thy wings, celestial dove
56/57	ATAPTH	All things are possible to him
66	LGIHLU	Lo! God is here, let us adore
78	TSFOHW	The spacious firmament on high

Additional references:
1. Temperley, *HTI*, no. 11690c, f
2. Wasson, *HI*, no. 05493

CREATION

HWT: 1878

1. 51122316217
2. 5671234332171
3. 55511223
4. 23453234234532
5. 55511223
6. 234532342171

Meter: LM

1808	X							
1822	X							
1833	5112176531	BANGNMH	CREATION	FATDBT	Haydn	C	3/4
1837	5112176531	LANEG-H	CREATION	WSMWSB	Haydn	C	3/4
1848	5112231621	JACKSSH	CREATION	IPMMWI	Haydn	C	3/6
1849	5112176531	DINGCDH	CREATION	ETWCDA	Haydn	C	3/4
1853	5112231621	WOODILZ	CREATION	IPMMWI	Haydn	C	3/4
1856	5112231621	WOODINLZ	CREATION	ATAPTH	Haydn	C	2/4
1857	5112231621	=====HU	CREATION	ATAPTH	HaydnF	C	2/4
1866	5112231621	PHILPNHT	CREATION	LGIHLU	HaydnM	C	1/4
1878	5112231621	NELSHWT	CREATION	TSFOHW	HaydnF	A	1/4

19. **DEVIZES** by Isaac Tucker (1761–1825)

a. First published in Stephen Addington, *A Collection of Psalm Tunes for Publick Worship*, 11th ed., London, 1792. First appearance in the United States in Timothy Olmstead, *The Musical Olio*,Northampton, 1805. [26]

b. DEVIZES is a Common Meter tune-with-extension which receives antiphonal treatment in most sources. It is set in the major mode in duple (2/2) time.

c. Using a range of a seventh, the tune contains five phrases, the last two being similar in text and melody but not in setting. The fourth phrase creates an antiphonal effect, with the soprano and alto lines forming a duet of parallel thirds. In 1857 and 1866, this duet floats over a simple tonic-dominant line; in 1878 the duet is doubled at the tenor-bass level. In each case, the tune ends in four-part harmony.

d. The tune shows some evolution in shape over the period in the study. Note the shaping of phrase three:

1808/22/33/37	555443217 15123
1853/56/57/66	2354432171 345654323
1878	5554432171 345654323

e. Texts used:

08/22/33/37/57	HTSTJJ	Happy the souls to Jesus joined
53/56	CLUJOC	Come, let us join our cheerful
66	INATOM	I'm not ashamed to own my Lord
78	HHECOG	How happy every child of grace

Additional references:
1. Temperley, *HTI*, no. 5978
2. Wasson, *HI*, no. 06525

DEVIZES   HWT: 1878

1. 1123432171
2. 23542312
3. 5554432171
4. 345654323
   345654321   Meter: CM

1808	1123432171		DEVIZES	HTSTJJ	Rippon	A	3/4
1822	1123432171	BANGNMH	DEVIZES	HTSTJJ	Cuzens	A	3/4
1833	1123432171	BANGNMH	DEVIZES	HTSTJJ	Cuzens	A	3/4
1837	1123432171	LANEG-H	DEVIZES	HTSTJJ	Cuzens	A	3/4
1848	X						
1849	X						
1853	1123432171	WOODILZ	DEVIZES	CLUJOC	Tucker	G	1/4
1856	1123432171	WOODINLZ	DEVIZES	CLUJOC	Tucker	G	1/4
1857	1123432171	=====HU	DEVIZES	HTSTJJ	TuckerI	G	1/4
1866	1123432171	PHILPNHT	DEVIZES	INATOM	TuckerI	G	1/4
1878	1123432171	NELSHWT	DEVIZES	HHECOG	Tucker	G	1/4

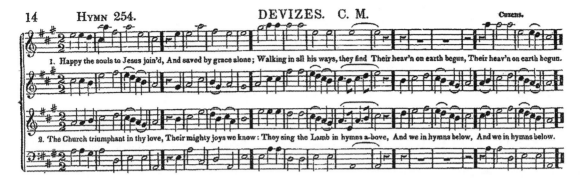

14   HYMN 254.   DEVIZES. C. M.   Cuzens.

1. Happy the souls to Jesus join'd, And saved by grace alone; Walking in all his ways, they find Their heav'n on earth begun, Their heav'n on earth begun.

2. The Church triumphant in thy love, Their mighty joys we know: They sing the Lamb in hymns a-bove, And we in hymns below, And we in hymns below.

20. DUKE STREET (NEWRY) by John Warrington Hatton (ca.1710–1793)

a. First published in Henry Boyd's *Select Collection of Psalm and Hymn Tunes*, Glasgow, 1793, named as "Addison's 19th Psalm." In William Dixon's *Euphonia*, Liverpool, ca. 1807, it is named DUKE STREET. First use in the United States was O[liver] Shaw, A[mos] Albee, and H[erman] Mann, *The Columbian Harmonist, or Collection of Grammatical Music*, Dedham, 1808.[27]

b. This "plain tune" in the major mode in duple time is set to text with Long Meter.

c. The contour of each phrase of the tune contains an arch; the rhythm follows a simple pattern, each phrase commencing with the ♩ ♪ ♪ rhythm. The supporting harmonies are limited to primary chords of I/IV and V, and each phrase excepting the final finishes with a half close.

d. In the 1822, 1833, and 1837 sources, this could be considered a plain antiphonal tune due to the omission of the tenor part for a phrase. In addition, it is noted that the 1822 and 1833 sources show a repeat sign for phrases 3 and 4, hence an antiphonal tune-with-extension. The only tune variant occurs at the end of phrase 3, which in most sources reads 6543 32 but in the 1878 source is presented as 6543 2.

e. Texts used:

22/33/37/49	JFWABF	Jesus, from whom all blessings flow
53/56	TIHGTS	Though I have grieved thy spirit
57/66	FATDBT	From all that dwell below the skies
78	CLUTOL	Come, let us tune our loftiest song
	OLOHWG	O Lord of hosts, whose glory fills
	GGBWPE	Great God! beneath whose piercing eye

Additional references:
1. Temperley, *HTI*, no. 6143
2. Wasson, *HI*, no. 07171

DUKE STREET (NEWRY)   HWT: 1878

1. 1345678765
2. 55565432
3. 332135865432
4. 56784321   Meter: LM

1808 X

1822 1345678765	BANGNMH	NEWRY	JFWABF		F	3/4
1833 1345678765	BANGNMH	NEWRY	JFWABF		F	3/4
1837 1345678765	LANEG-H	NEWRY	JFWABF	Hatton	F	3/4

1848 X

1849	1345678765	DINGCDH	NEWRY	JFWABF	Hatton	F	3/4	
1853	1345678765	WOODILZ	DUKE STR	TIHGTS	Hatton	F	3/4	
1856	1345678765	WOODINLZ	DUKE STR	TIHGTS	Hatton	F	3/4	
1857	1345678765	=====HU	DUKE STR	FATDBT	Hatton	F	2/4	
1866	1345678765	PHILPNHT	DUKE STR	FATDBT	Hatton	F	1/4	
1878	1345678765	NELSHWT	DUKE STR	CLUTOL	Hatton	E♭	1/4	

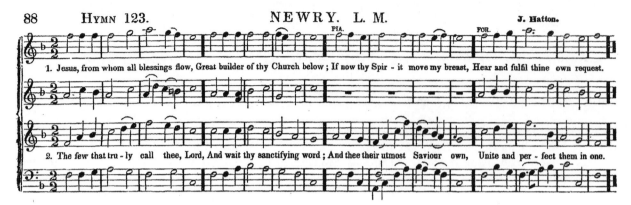

21. **DUNDEE** (FRENCH TUNE)

a. This is one of twelve common tunes (contrasting with "proper tunes," which are attached to certain lyrics) in the *CL Psalmes of David in Prose and Meeter with their whole usuall Notes and Tunes*, published by Andro Hart, ed., Edinburgh, 1615. In that collection it is entitled FRENCH TUNE.[28] It was dubbed DUNDY by Thomas Ravenscroft in his psalter of 1621. First published in the United States in Andrew Law, *The Rudiments of Music*, Cheshire, 1783.[29]

b. DUNDEE is a Common Meter "plain tune" in the major mode in duple time.

c. This tune of four phrases falls into two halves, the first of which begins and ends on the tonic. The range is that of a ninth, with the upper range occurring at the opening of phrase 3, whence the tune descends to the closing tonic.

d. The 1833 source (where the tune is named NORWICH) is very similar to the 1837 source with two exceptions: (a) the dotted rhythm of the penultimate measure is changed to equal values in the later version; (b) the third note of the tune is raised a semitone. This same melodic alteration is evident in 1848, but not in other sources. In these three sources, the melody ends thus: 3214321. With the 1849 source, two endings are given:
> 1. 3214321 annotated "Last line as usually sung."[30]
> 2. 321171 annotated "Last line as originally written."

Both endings are given in both 1853 and 1856. By 1857 the earlier version has been smoothed out as 321421, a profile copied in the 1866 source. The 1878 source, however, reverts to the ending 321171.

e. Texts used:

22/33/37/49/57	JGSOTS	Jesus, great Shepherd of the sheep
48	WSISTW	When shall I see the welcome hour
53/56	LNDNFR	Let not despair nor fell revenge
66	TADWSC	That awful day will surely come
78	OTWWWD	O thou, who when we did complain
	TKOHHT	The King of heaven his table
	OTWOVT	O thou whose own vast temple

Additional references:
1. Temperley, *HTI*, no. 327a, b
2. Wasson, *HI*, no. 07198

DUNDEE (FRENCH TUNE)   HWT: 1878

1. 13451234
2. 321171
3. 58765545
4. 321171   Meter: CM

1808 X

Year	Motif						
1822	1345123432	BANGNMH	NORWICH	JGSOTS		G	3/4
1833	1345123432	BANGNMH	NORWICH	JGSOTS		G	3/4
1837	1345123432	LANEG-H	DUNDEE	JGSOTS		F	3/4
1848	134512343	JACKSSH	DUNDEE	WSISTW		F	3/4
1849	134512343	DINGCDH	DUNDEE	JGSOTS	Scotch	F	3/4
1853	134512343	WOODILZ	DUNDEE	LNDNFR	Scottish	F	1/4
1856	134512343	WOODINLZ	DUNDEE	LNDNFR	Scottish	F	1/4
1857	1345123432	=====HU	DUNDEE	JGSOTS	Scottish	F	2/4
1866	1345123432	PHILPNHT	DUNDEE	TADWSC	Franc G.	F	1/4
1878	1345123432	NELSHWT	DUNDEE	OTWWWD	Franc G.	E♭	1/4
		TKOHHT			Franc G.	E♭	1/4
		OTWOVT			Franc G.	E♭	1/4

HYMN 393.   DUNDEE. C. M.

1. Jesus, great Shepherd of the sheep, To thee for help we fly : Thy lit - tle flock in safe - ty keep, For, O, the wolf is nigh !

3. Us in - to thy pro-tec - tion take, And gather with thy arm ; Un-less the fold we first forsake, The wolf can nev - er harm.

22. **EATON** by Zerubbabel Wyvill (1763–1837)

a. First appeared in Thomas Walker, *Second Appendix to Dr. Rippon's Selection of Tunes*, [London, 1802]. In the United States, it first appeared in Samuel Holyoke, *The Vocal Companion*, Exeter, 1807. The variant found in the 1833 source appeared in *Tunes Adapted to Psalms and Hymns for . . . the Chapel of Ease in Worthing*, [London,1815], and for the United States, in Samuel Dyer, *A New Selection of Sacred Music*, Baltimore, 1817. [31]

b. EATON is a Long Meter tune (six lines) set in the major mode in duple time.

c. This tune has great variety in its rich contours. There are passages of stepwise motion, as well as large leaps up and down (e.g., up an octave in phrase 5 down a sixth in phrase 6). Especially noteworthy is the ornament in measure 6, 5434 3, which figures in all examples to 1866.

d. The 1833 source presents antiphonal sections: at phrase 3 a duet for soprano and alto; at phrase 4 a trio for bass, alto, and soprano. The ending is in full four-part harmony. The opening note is a full quarter note. The 1837 source differs in only one respect, namely that the duet is for soprano and tenor, the trio for bass, tenor, and soprano.

In the 1848 source, the opening note has been reduced from whole note to ◦ (half) value. The third phrase is a duet for soprano and alto, followed immediately by four-part harmony in phrase 4. The opening tune motif reads 112354321. In the 1849 source, the opening motif reads 11234321. In this version, the duet/trio combination has disappeared, but the extension (phrase 5) shows the tune leading off with a harmonic accompaniment following a beat later. Sources 1853 and 1856 copy the 1849 version.

In the 1857 and 1866 sources, antiphonal and imitative writing have disappeared in favor of regular homophonic writing, and the harmony is heavily dependent on the tonic chord. Only the two cadential measures which close phrases 2 and 4 do not include the tonic chord. In the 1878 source, the melody remains the same, but the harmonic underpinnings are greatly enriched, demanding greater versatility on the part of the performers.

e. Texts used:

22/33	.SOTGWH	Sinners, obey the gospel word
37	THLOGW	Thou hidden love of God, whose height
48	CSBWAT	Creator, Spirit, by whose aid
49/53/56/66	BTSOTL	Behold! the servant of the Lord
57	ACIBTI	And can it be that I should gain
78	JTTOHW	Jesus to thee our hearts we lift

Additional references:
1. Temperley, *HTI*, no. 9147b
2. Wasson, *HI*, no. 07378

EATON   HWT: 1878

1. 112354321
2. 23458765
3. 55435543
4. 56658432
5. 1865431865   Meter: 88.88.88
6. 7123454321

1808 X

1822	1123432123	BANGNMH	EATON	SOTGWH	Wyvill	E	3/4
1833	1123543212	BANGNMH	EATON	SOTGWH	Wyvill	E	3/4
1837	1123433212	LANEG-H	EATON	THLOGW	Wyvill	F	3/4
1848	1123543212	JACKSSH	EATON	CSBWAT	Wyvil	E	3/4
1849	1123432123	DINGCDH	EATON	BTSOTL	Wyvil	F	3/4
1853	1123432123	WOODILZ	EATON	BTSOTL	Wyvil	F	3/4
1856	1123432123	WOODINLZ	EATON	BTSOTL	Wyvil	F	3/4
1857	1123432123	=====HU	EATON	ACIBTI	Wyvil	F	2/4
1866	1123432123	PHILPNHT	EATON	BTSOTL	WyvillZ	F	1/4
1878	1123543212	NELSHWT	EATON	JTTOHW	WyvillZ	E	1/4

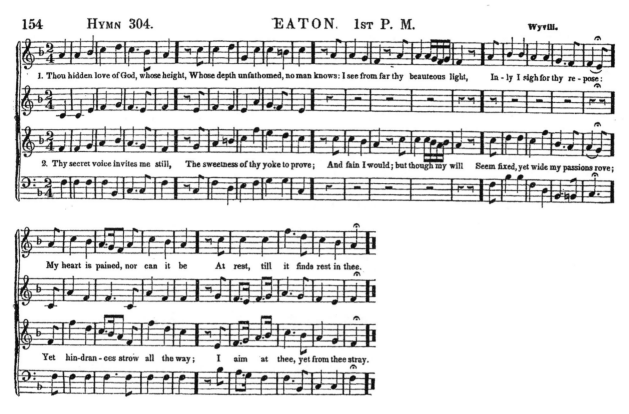

154   HYMN 304.   EATON. 1ST P. M.   Wyvill.

1. Thou hidden love of God, whose height, Whose depth unfathomed, no man knows: I see from far thy beauteous light, In - ly I sigh for thy re - pose:

2. Thy secret voice invites me still, The sweetness of thy yoke to prove; And fain I would; but though my will Seem fixed, yet wide my passions rove;

My heart is pained, nor can it be   At rest, till it finds rest in thee.

Yet hin-dran - ces strow all the way;   I aim at thee, yet from thee stray.

23. **FOREST** by Lucius Chapin (1760–1842)

a. First published in *David's Harp*, Baltimore, 1813.[32]

b. FOREST is a Long Meter "plain tune" in the major mode using triple (3/2) time, except in 1822 and 1833, where the ¢ signature is used.

c. When triple meter is used, the tune acquires an isorhythm within each measure: ♩ ♩ ♩ ♩ The motif of phrase 3 is related to that of phrase 2. Phrases 1 and 4 also have similar melodic shapes, making it easy for the singer to learn.

d. The tune itself remains the same throughout the study. As mentioned above, the time signature changes between 1833 and 1837. The supporting harmonies are closely linked to the tonic and dominant; in one version the tonic chord appears twenty-three times in eight measures.

e. Texts used:

22/33/37/56/57/66	OTMLOS	O that my load of sin were gone
53	GTGWSG	Glory to God, whose sovereign grace

Additional references:
1. Temperley, *HTI*, no. 14403
2. Wasson, *HI*, no. 25558 (Rockbridge)

FOREST   NHT: 1866
1. 16511321
2. 1353123
3. 131353131
4. 21651321   Meter: LM

1808 X						
1822 8658832113	BANGNMH	FOREST	OTMLOS		C	2/3
1833 1651132113	BANGNMH	FOREST	OTMLOS		C	2/3
1837 1651132113	LANEG-H	FOREST	OTMLOS		Bb	3/4
1848 X						
1849 X						
1853 8658832113	WOODILZ	FOREST/ROCKBRIDG	GTGWSG	Chapin	Bb	3/4
1856 1651132113	WOODINLZ	FOREST	OTMLOS	Chapin	Bb	1/4
1857 1651132113	=====HU	FOREST	OTMLOS	Chapin	Bb	2/4
1866 1651132113	PHILPNHT	FOREST	OTMLOS		Bb	1/4
1878 X						

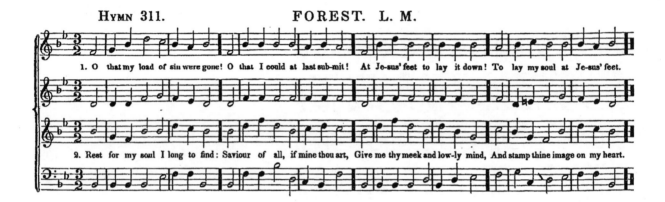

24. **GANGES** (GORHAM) by S. Chandler (fl. late 18th c.)

a. Hughes states that the tune first appeared in *The American Musical Miscellany* [1798] as a setting for a poem, "The Indian Philosopher."[33] Temperley ascribes the first appearance to Joel Read, *The New England Selection*, Boston, 1808.[34] Oliver Shaw, Amos Albee, and Herman Mann arranged the tune in four parts in *The Columbian Sacred Harmonist*, 1808.

b. Usually GANGES is a "plain tune," except in the 1822, 1833, and 1856 sources, where an extension is provided by a repeat of the second half. It is in the major mode and uses meter 886 (doubled).

c. The earliest sources use the title GORHAM; after 1837, all sources use GANGES. The tune spans a tenth in range and starts uniquely on the second of two or four beats. The missing beat is not recovered elsewhere until 1866.

d. Time signatures are usually in duple form (◯, 2/4, or 4/4). The 1866 source uses a 3/2 signature, producing the characteristic ♩ ♩ ♩ rhythm of many tunes of the period that suits it more than duple time. The melody is unchanging throughout, and the harmonic support uses basic chords.

e. Texts used:

22/33/37/78	COMPID	Come on, my partners in distress
56	OLOGFS	O Lamb of God, for sinners slain
57	TGMGUW	Thou great mysterious God, unknown
66	IDOFAU	If death our friends and us divide

Additional references:
1. Temperley, *HTI*, no. 8879b
2. Wasson, *HI*, no. 09499

GANGES (GORHAM)   HWT: 1878

1. 13331555
2. 58565632
3. 136578
4. 58883282
5. *38565632*
6. 136578   Meter: 886 D

1808	X				
1822	1333255558 BANGNMH	GORHAM	COMPID	E	2/3
1833	1333255558 BANGNMH	GORHAM	COMPID	E	2/3
1837	1333255558 LANEG-H	GORHAM	COMPID	D	3/4
1848	X				
1849	X				
1853	X				
1856	1333155558 WOODINLZ	GANGES	OLOGFS	D	3/4
1857	1333155558 =====HU	GANGES	TGMGUW	D	1/4
1866	1333255558 PHILPNHT	GANGES	IDOFAU Chandler	D	1/4
1878	1333155558 NELSHWT	GANGES	COMPID Chandler	C	1/4

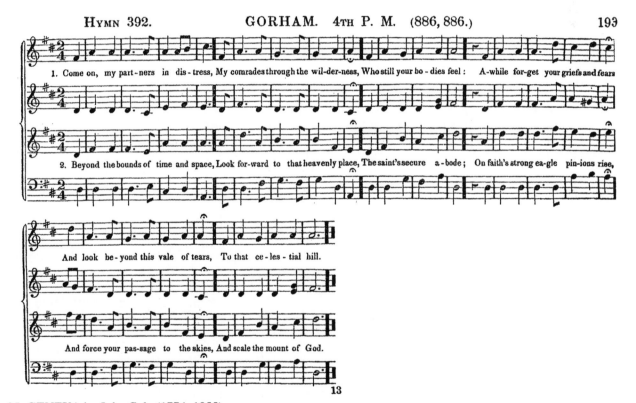

HYMN 392.   GORHAM. 4TH P. M.   (886, 886.)   193

1. Come on, my part-ners in dis-tress, My comrades through the wil-der-ness, Who still your bo-dies feel : A-while for-get your griefs and fears

2. Beyond the bounds of time and space, Look for-ward to that heavenly place, The saint's secure a-bode ; On faith's strong ea-gle pin-ions rise,

And look be-yond this vale of tears, To that ce-les-tial hill.

And force your pas-sage to the skies, And scale the mount of God.

13

25. **GENEVA** by John Cole (1774–1855)

a. First published in the United States in Elias Mann, *The Northampton Collection of Sacred Harmony*, Northampton, 1797.[35]

b. GENEVA is a Common Meter tune in the major mode. It is a reverse fuging tune which uses triple (3/2) time.

c. The tune spans a ninth in range. Slurs or melismas are used to begin almost all measures, giving prominence to the downbeat syllable of text. Normally, fugal entries would follow a homophonic section; in this tune, the imitative entries occur at the beginning of the tune, allowing soprano, then alto, then tenor and bass entries. Phrase 2 following is in four-part homophonic style. Phrase 3 is constructed antiphonally, followed by a four-part ending passage.

d. The text overlap typical of fugal entries is common to all versions of this tune. All sources to 1849 show antiphonal effects in phrases 2, 3, and 4. In two instances, the silent part is the tenor, in one instance the alto. Sources after 1853 show the fugal beginning, and the duet-style opening of phrase 3; otherwise all parts are active in these versions.

e. Texts used:

33/37/48	LTRGTA	Let the redeemed give thanks and praise
48	MGMPAM	My God, my portion and my love
53/56/78	WATMOM	When all thy mercies, O my God

Additional references:
1. Temperley and Manns, *Fuging Tunes*, no. 50
2. Temperley, *HTI*, no. 7393
3. Wasson, *HI*, no. 09637

GENEVA

HWT: 1878

1. 1123345878
2. 5628765
3. 8565543435654332
4. 135823434321

Meter: CM

1808	X						
1822	X						
1833	1123345878	BANGNMH	GENEVA	LTRGTA	Cole J	F	3/4
1837	1123345878	LANGEG-H	GENEVA	LTRGTA	Cole J	F	3/4
1848	1123345878	JACKSSH	GENEVA	MGMPAM	Cole J	E♭	3/4
1849	1123345878	DINGCDH	GENEVA	LTRGTA	Cole J	F	3/4
1853	1123345878	WOODILZ	GENEVA	WATMOM	Cole J	E♭	3/4
1856	1123345878	WOODINLZ	GENEVA	WATMOM	Cole J	E♭	3/4
1857	X						
1866	X						
1878	1123345878	NELSHWT	GENEVA	WATMOM	Cole J	E♭	1/4

26. GOD OF ABRAHAM

a. This variant was first published in John Beaumont, *The New Harmonic Magazine*, London, 1801, and in the United States in J[ames] Evans, *David's Companion*, New York, 1808.[36]

b. This "plain tune" in the major mode has the meter 66.84 (doubled). In this study it appears with only one text.

c. A rest usually separates the eight phrases of the tune, and the tune uses a tonic pitch to end the first half as well as the whole tune. The tune uses only seven pitches, with either a tonic or a dominant harmony ending every phrase.

d. The 1833 source demonstrates the most adventuresome setting. The tune is on the middle of three staves and includes ornaments such as a grace at the end of phrase 2 and a trill on the halfway cadence, as well as at the close. Whereas later sources show a pedal point (usually a dominant pitch) for four measures in the second half, 1833 honors the tradition of contrary motion and gives an interesting descending bass line. The 1833 source also provides for a repeat of the second half and states dynamic preferences: "2nd time PIA[NO]." The 1808, 1822, and 1833 settings also give double pitches (tonic and dominant) for the opening note. Subsequent settings are straightforward and virtually identical.

e. Text used:
08/22/33/37/49/56/57   TGOAPW   The God of Abraham praise

Additional reference:
Temperley, *HTI*, no. 8435

GOD OF ABRAHAM   HU: 1857

1. 131271
2. 23454332
3. 232345432
4. 34321
5. 1712345
6. 4322234
7. 323712345
8. 64321   Meter: 66.84 D

1808	1312712345		GOD OF ABRAH	TGOAPW	Beaumont	A	1/3
1822	1312712345	BANGNMH	GOD OF ABRAH	TGOAPW		A	2/3
1833	1312712345	BANGNMH	GOD OF ABRAH	TGOAPW		A	2/3
1837	1312712345	LANEG-H	GOD OF ABRAH	TGOAPW		A	3/4
1848 X							
1849	1312712345	DINGCDH	GOD OF ABRAH	TGOAPW		A	3/4
1853 X							
1856	1312712345	WOODINLZ	GOD OF ABRAH	TGOAPW		A	2/4
1857	1312712345	=====HU	GOD OF ABRAH	TGOAPW		A	2/4
1866 X							

1878 [text appears, but only with tune LEONI]

HYMN 270.   GOD OF ABRAHAM.   21ST P. M.   (66, 84, 66, 84.)   311

1. The God of Abrah'm praise, Who reigns enthroned above: Ancient of ever-last-ing days, And God of love: JEHOVAH, GREAT I AM!

2. The God of Abrah'm praise, At whose supreme command From earth I rise—and seek the joys At his right hand: I   all on earth forsake,

By earth and heaven confessed; I bow and bless the sacred name, For ever blest.

Its wisdom, fame, and power; And him my only portion make, My shield and tower.

27. GREENVILLE (ABSENCE) by Jean-Jacques Rousseau (1712–1778)

a. McCutchan states that this tune is also known as ROUSSEAU or ROUSSEAU'S DREAM,[37] and Temperley (*HTI*, IV/751) gives its first publication as Thomas Walker, *Second Supplement to Walker's Companion*, London, 1819. Although the titles above do not appear in this study, the tune originates in the opera *Le Devin du Village*, composed by Rousseau and performed at Fontainebleau in 1752. Hill states that J. B. Cramer evolved a tune from the original for publication (with variations) about 1818.[38] This melody is also known as "Go tell Aunt Tabbie" (or "Rhody") and is one of the tunes associated with NETTLETON.[39]

For hymn use, the tune is altered considerably from the original. It may have been in use in England in the early 1800s, and it appeared in the United States in the *Handel and Haydn Collection of Church Music*, Boston, 1823.

b. This tune in the major mode is a "plain tune" except in the 1853 and 1856 sources, where it may be called a "plain antiphonal tune" due to the two-part writing for the center section. The meter is 87.87 (doubled).

c. The tune has a simple, folk-song quality about it and is composed in four sections, with sections 1, 2, and 4 being identical. The range is only a sixth (except for 1833), all pitches above the keynote.

d. The 1833 source may lie closest to the original composition as it was actually performed. The dotted rhythms hint at a dance style and "notes inégales" of the French school. This is the only instance where the tune outline of phrase 3 is 334556653 334556865. The rise to 8, broadening the range, is exceptional.

The 1837 source has no "graces," but the harmonic structure of both these early sources is varied and interesting. By contrast, the remaining sources depend almost solely on tonic and dominant harmonies. The 1853 and 1856 sources present the third section of the piece in parallel thirds for soprano and alto, sketching suggested harmonies in small notation only in the bass clef.

e. Texts used:

33/37	OTGHGA	O to grace, how great a debtor
53/56	HTODJH	Hail! thou once despised Jesus

57	GTTAFF	Glory to th'almighty Father, fountain
66/78	LDUWTB	Lord, dismiss us with thy blessing
78	CYSPAN	Come, ye sinners, poor and needy

Additional references:

1. G. Pullen Jackson, *White Spirituals in Southern Uplands*, no. 80a
2. J. Moffatt and M. Patrick, eds., *Handbook to the Church Hymnary*, rev. ed., no. 661
3. Wasson, *HI*, no. 10818
4. Temperley, *HTI*, no. 16564

GREENVILLE (ABSENCE)   HWT: 1878

1. 3321122321
2. 5543321231
3. 3321122321
4. 5543321231
5. 3345566543
6. 33455665
7. 3321122321
8. 5543321231   Meter: 87.87D

1808	X						
1822	X						
1833	3321122315	BANGNMH	ABSENCE	OTGHGA		F	2/3
1837	3321122321	LANEG-H	ABSENCE	OTGHGA		G	3/4
1848	X						
1849	X						
1853	3321122321	WOODILZ	GREENVILLE	HTODJH	Rousseau	F	1/4
1856	3321122321	WOODINLZ	GREENVILLE	HTODJH	Rousseau	F	1/4
1857	3321122321	=====HU	GREENVILLE	GTTAFF		F	2/4
1866	3321122321	PHILPNHT	GREENVILLE	LDUWTB	Rousseau	F	1/4
1878	3321122321	NELSHWT	GREENVILLE	CYSPAN	Rousseau	F	1/4

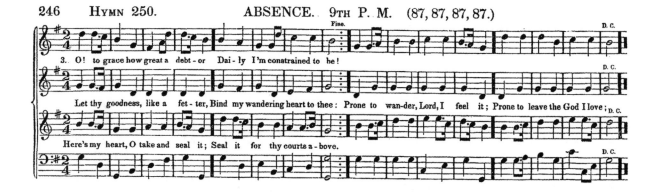

246   HYMN 250.   ABSENCE. 9TH P. M.   (87, 87, 87, 87.)

28. **KENTUCKY** arr. Lucius Chapin (1760–1842)

a. First published in *David's Harp*, Baltimore, 1813.[40]

b. KENTUCKY is a triple-time tune in the major mode that accompanies Short Meter texts. Folklike in quality, it is pentatonic.

c. Three sections of the tune use the isorhythm ♩♩ ♪ ♪ ♪ ♪ ♩ with iambic influence. The tune spans an octave (between dominants) and relies on primary harmonic structures.

d. The 1833 source uses ¢ as its time signature and uses "graces" consistently to fill in the steps where the tune rises a fourth. The texture is three part. In 1837, however, four-part harmony is used, and the "graces" have disappeared. The tune remains unaltered from this time.

   After 1853, the tune is displayed in all sources as being in 3/4 time, using calm harmonic lines more attuned to vocal use. In the 1853 source, the tune is located in part III: "Revival Hymns and Music."

e. Texts used:

22/33/57/66	ACTKIH	A charge to keep I have
37	OTICRW	O that I could repent with all
53/56	CYTLTL	Come ye that love the Lord
78	WLOHTT	We lift our hearts to thee

Additional references:
1. Temperley, *HTI*, no. 14405
2. Wasson, *HI*, no. 24361

KENTUCKY   HWT: 1878

1. *51612165*
2. *51612321*
3. *53216132165*
4. *51612321*   Meter: SM

1808 X						
1822 *516216551*	BANGNMH	KENTUCKY	ACTKIH		C	2/3
1833 *516216551*	BANGNMH	KENTUCKY	ACTKIH		C	2/3
1837 *5161216551*	LANEG-H	KENTUCKY	OTICRW		B♭	3/4
1848 X						
1849 X						
1853 *5161216551*	WOODILZ	KENTUCKY	CWTLTL	Western	B♭	3/4
1856 *5161216551*	WOODINLZ	KENTUCKY	CYTLTL	Western	B♭	1/4
1857 *5161216551*	=====HU	KENTUCKY	ACTKIH	Western	B♭	2/4
1866 *5161216551*	PHILPNHT	KENTUCKY	ACTKIH	ChapinA	B♭	1/4
1878 *5161216551*	NELSHWT	KENTUCKY	WLOHTT	Ingalls	A♭	1/4

142   Hymn 54.   KENTUCKY. S. M.

1. O that I could re-pent, With all my i-dols part; And to thy gra-cious eye pre-sent An hum-ble, con-trite heart:

2. A heart with grief op-prest For hav-ing grieved my God; A troubled heart that can-not rest, Till sprinkled with thy blood.

29. **LENOX** by Lewis Edson (1748–1820)

a. First published in [Simeon Jocelin], *The Chorister's Companion, or Church Music Revised*, New Haven, 1782. It had previously been sung to Watts' Psalm 148, "Ye tribes of Adam, join with heaven."[41]

b. LENOX is a major mode tune in Particular Meter which appeared more than any other fuging tune of its day. In this study it is set with three texts; the textless tune is also presented proximate to three additional texts.

c. The fugue begins at line 5 of the text and spreads over twenty-six quarter-note beats. The opening phrases begin and end with consonances, though within the phrase unexpected progressions can occur (e.g., 1857: measure 11, submediant chord instead of expected tonic; open fifths in measure 12; probable misspelling in measure 12, final beat).

d. Most settings open with a half-note chord; 1837, 1853, and 1856 open with a quarter note, being a unison dominant anacrusis in the latter two cases. The 1849 source introduces passing tones in measures 3, 4, 7, 8, 10, 11, and 14. It also omits the imitative section, and using the original melody (second from bottom) proceeds in homophonic style to the end. All other presentations omit any passing tones and retain the fugue, though with slight variations in the imitation and harmony. The 1878 source presents a homophonic setting, indicating the trend towards standard 4 part (two staff) writing. The final cadence is a simple V–I progression except in 1849, where a 4/3 suspension commences the cadence; 1853; 1856; and 1878, where a dominant seventh is given as the penultimate chord.

e. Texts used:

08/22/33/37/49/78	AMSASO	Arise, my soul, arise, shake off
53/56	YTRRTS	Yes, the Redeemer rose; the Savior
57/66/78	BYTTBT	Blow ye the trumpet, blow

Additional references:
1. Crawford, *Core Repertory*, no. 43
2. Temperley and Manns, *Fuging Tunes*, no. 337
3. Temperley, *HTI*, no. 4280
4. Wasson, *HI*, no. 17139

LENOX   HWT: 1878

1. 111*565*
2. *5*12321
3. 135312
4. 231271
5. *5*1115*666*
6. 12223111
   56661271   Meter: 66.66.88

1808	1115655123		LENOX	AMSASO	Erbin's	C	3/4
1822	1115655123	BANGNMH	LENOX	AMSASO			
1833	1115655123	BANGNMH	LENOX	AMSASO		C	3/4
1837	1115655123	LANEG-H	LENOX	AMSASO	Edson	C	3/4
1848	X						
1849	1115655123	DINGCDH	LENOX	AMSASO	Edson	C	3/4
1853	5115655123	WOODILZ	LENOX	YTRRTS	Edson	C	3/4
1856	5115655123	WOODINLZ	LENOX	YTRRTS	Edson	C	3/4
1857	1115655123	=====HU	LENOX	BYTTBT	Edson	C	2/4
1866	1115655123	=====NHT	LENOX	BYTTBT	EdsonJ	B♭	1/4
1878	1115655123	NELSHWT	LENOX	AMSASO BYTTBT	EdsonL	B♭	1/4

30. **LISBON** by Daniel Read (1757–1836)

a. First published in Daniel Read, *The American Singing Book*, New Haven, 1785. It was formerly sung to Watts' "Welcome, sweet day of rest" from *Hymns and Spiritual Songs, Book 2*, no. 14.[42]

b. LISBON is a major mode fuging tune in Short Meter. Until 1810 it was most often linked with the text "Welcome, sweet day of rest." It is the shortest fuging tune in this study. In the author's *New Haven Collection*, 1818, he "corrected" LISBON, together with several of his other tunes. This tune and WINDHAM made the Read name famous.

c. As long as it remains a fuging tune, the tune opens with two short phrases having a mixture of long and short notes. The voices proclaim the third line of text with sequential entries in bass, soprano, alto, and tenor, as opposed to the usual fuging order of bass, soprano, tenor, alto. The tune spans an octave between dominant pitches. In the final source, 1878, the tune becomes homophonic throughout, in triple time.

d. LISBON appears as a fuging tune in six of the seven sources in this study. The 1833 setting uses a time signature of ¢ and commences with a whole (gathering) note. The voices enter imitatively on line 3 of text.

    The 1837 source uses a time signature of 4/4 rather than 2/2 and is identical in harmony to 1833. Both versions use shape notes for the pitches. The 1853 and 1856 versions use a 3/2 time signature; after the second phrase, the bass and tenor enter duetlike for one phrase. They are rejoined by alto and soprano for phrase 4. Phrase 5 echoes phrase 3, but in soprano-alto duet, also repeating the text of phrase 3. Phrase 6 closes the piece in SATB harmony.

    The 1857 and 1866 sources revert to the older fuging tune style, with two opening phrases of homophony followed by an imitative section; the time signature reverts to duple time (2/2). A further change is seen in the third measure of the soprano entry, where the original eighth-note ascending scale is altered rhythmically to a dotted eighth-sixteenth pattern. The 1878 source presents the tune in a new key (A) and in the alternate time signature of 3/4. The fuging entries and textual repeats are gone.

e. Texts used:

08	ACIYDM	And can I yet delay my little
33/37	CYTLTL	Come, ye that love the Lord

| 53/56/57/78 | WSDORT | Welcome, sweet day of rest |
| 66 | AMNFAD | Away, my needless fears and doubts |

Additional references:
1. Crawford, *Core Repertory*, no. 44
2. Temperley, *HTI*, no. 4609a, b
3. Wasson, *HI*, no. 17561

LISBON   HWT: 1878

1. 165123
2. 321432
3. 51112333
4. 554321   Meter: SM

1808 1651233214		LISBON	ACIYDM	Read	B♭	3/4
1822 X						
1833 1651233214	BANGNMH	LISBON	CYTLTL	Read	B♭	3/4
1837 1651233214	LANEG-H	LISBON	CYTLTL	ReadJ	B♭	3/4
1848 X						
1849 X						
1853 1651233214	WOODILZ	LISBON	WSDORT	Read	B♭	1/4
1856 1651233214	WOODINLZ	LISBON	WSDORT	Read	B♭	1/4
1857 1651233214	=====HU	LISBON	WSDORT	Read	B♭	2/4
1866 1651233214	PHILPNHT	LISBON	AMNFAD	Read	B♭	1/4
1878 1651233214	NELSHWT	LISBON	WSDORT	Read	A	1/4

31. LITCHFIELD (ADISHAM)

a. First published in Andrew Law, *The Musical Primer*, Cheshire, 1793.[43]

b. This tune is a Long Meter tune in the major mode in duple time. Although basically a "plain tune," its appearances in 1833 and 1837 include one antiphonal section.

c. The tune spans a ninth (lower dominant to higher sixth degree) and includes fifteen slurs or melismas. The four phrases are symmetrical.

d. The 1833 and 1837 settings use diatonic chords supporting the stately melody. The third slur of these presentations includes three notes, whereas all later slurs consist of pairs of notes.

    All settings include the raised fourth to suggest the dominant key at the halfway cadence. From 1853 onwards, however, the second half begins with use of the dominant chord of the supertonic, enriching the harmonic content.

e. Texts used:

22/33/37	JSRWTS	Jesus shall reign where'er the sun
53/56	RMSETR	Return my soul, enjoy thy rest
57	EPWHAB	Eternal Power, whose high abode
66	OGTAMG	O God, thou art my God alone

Additional references:
1. Temperley, *HTI*, no. 6387
2. Wasson, *HI*, no. 17612

LITCHFIELD (ADISHAM)   NHT: 1866

1. 112345431271
2. 51212343121765
3. 5534423311232
4. 512345654321   Meter: LM

1808 X

1822	1123454312	BANGNMH	ADISHAM/LITCHFIELD	JSRWTS		B♭	3/4
1833	1123454312	BANGNMH	ADISHAM/LITCHFIELD	JSRWTS		B♭	3/4
1837	1123454312	LANEG-H	LITCHFIELD	JSRWTS		B♭	3/4
1848 X							
1849 X							
1853	1123454312	WOODILZ	LITCHFIELD	RMSETR		A	3/4
1856	1123454312	WOODINLZ	LITCHFIELD	RMSETR		A	3/4
1857	1123454312	=====HU	LITCHFIELD	EPWHAB		A	2/4
1866	1123454312	PHILPNHT	LITCHFIELD	OGTAMG	Law	A	1/4
1878 X							

90   Hymn 479   LITCHFIELD. L. M.

1. Je - sus shall reign where - 'er the sun Does his suc - ces - sive jour - neys run; His king - dom

spread from shore to shore, Till moons shall wax and wane no more.

32. LITTLE MARLBOROUGH

a. First published in Aaron Williams, *The Universal Psalmodist*, London, 1763, and associated with the text, "Welcome, sweet day of rest" (see above, no. 30). First printed in the United States in [Daniel Bayley], *A New and Compleat Introduction to the Grounds and Rules of Musick*, Newbury, 1764.[44]

b. This minor mode tune in triple time was a popular Short Meter tune, linked with many differing texts, chief among which was Watts' Psalm 90, "Lord what a feeble piece."

c. The tune's first and last phrases are remarkably alike, giving a structure of *abca*[1]. The tenor line (staff 2) is almost a tune in itself, closely shadowing the melody.

d. In 1833, the melody ends with the rhythmic pattern ♩ ♩ ♩ ♩ ♩; in 1837 the rhythm of the parallel measure is ♩ ♩ ♩ ♩ ♩. Both editions use the pitches 1 3421; examples in 1853, 1856, 1857, and 1866 show the use of 1 3217 1, using a rhythmic pattern of ♩ ♩ ♩♩ ♩ ♩.

The bass line skips to provide harmonic support, and in 1833 and 1837 uses the naturalized seventh for a relative major dominant and root chord in measures 5 and 7. In later versions, these are altered to be regular dominant triads.

e. Texts used:

22/33/37	ACIYDM	And can I yet delay my little
53/56	TGIWIT	To God in whom I trust
57	MFHAFM	My former hopes are fled
66	HCASKH	Here can a sinner know his sins

Additional references:
1. Crawford, *Core Repertory*, no. 45
2. Temperley, *HTI*, no. 2934
3. Wasson, *HI*, no. 17649

LITTLE MARLBOROUGH (minor)   NHT: 1866

1. 5132171
2. 235432
3. 25313215
4. 5132171   Meter: SM

1808 X						
1822	5132171235	BANGNMH	LITTLE MARL	ACIYDM	a	3/4
1833	5132171235	BANGNMH	LITTLE MARL	ACIYDM	a	3/4
1837	5132171235	LANEG-H	LITTLE MARL	ACIYDM	a	3/4
1848 X						
1849 X						
1853	5132171235	WOODILZ	LITTLE MARL	TGIWIT	a	1/4
1856	5132171235	WOODINLZ	LITTLE MARL	TGIWIT	a	1/4
1857	5132171235	=====HU	LITTLE MARL	MFHAFM	a	2/4
1866	5132171235	PHILPNHT	LITTLE MARL	HCASKH Williams Coll	a	1/4
1878 X						

HYMN 67, 2D PART — LITTLE MARLBOROUGH. S. M. — 141

1. And can I yet de - lay, My lit - tle all to give! To tear my soul from earth a - way, For Je - sus to re - ceive!

2. Nay, but I yield, I yield! I can hold out no more: I sink, by dy - ing love compelled, And own thee con-quer - or!

33. **LUTHER'S HYMN** (JUDGMENT, MONMOUTH)

a. Its first publication was probably Klug's *Geistliche Lieder*, Wittenberg, 1529, since it is found in the 1533 source, the earliest extant edition of this hymnal. Though missing from *Lyra Davidica*, it does occur in Jacobi's *Psalmodia Germanica*, 1722. The first North American publication was in David Pool and Josiah Holbrook, *The American and European Harmony, or Abington Collection of Sacred Musick*, Providence, 1813.[45]

b. LUTHER'S HYMN is a duple-time tune-with-extension which is variously classed as Long Meter (six eight-syllable lines) or Peculiar Meter (87.87.887). It is in the major mode.

c. The tune uses the first five notes of the key in steady half and quarter notes, with the addition of the sixth above only once, and three pitches below the keynote.

d. The melody appears identically in all settings, though the anticipation note of measures 9 and 23 is shown as a grace. To 1837, the settings use simple chordal support for the melody; 1848 changes the style and content of the harmony for all subsequent versions by introducing passing notes and greater interest in interior lines.

e. Texts used:

22/33/37/48	WJHTSD	Would Jesus have the sinner die?
49/53/56/66/78	GGWDIS	Great God! What do I see and hear!
53	IROJLH	In robes of Judgment lo! he comes
57	OJFOTA	O Jesus, full of truth and grace

Additional references:
1. Crawford, *Core Repertory*, no. 39
2. Temperley, *HTI*, no. 994c
3. Wasson, *HI*, no. 18442

LUTHER'S HYMN (JUDGMENT, MONMOUTH)   HWT: 1878

1. 11321223
2. 134543321
3. 11321223
4. 134543321
5. 34321712
6. 31715123   Meter: 88.88.88
   134543321   *or* 87.87.887

1808 X

1822	1132122313	BANGNMH	LUTHER'S	WJHTSD	Luther	A	3/4
1833	1132122313	BANGNMH	LUTHER'S	WJHTSD	Luther	A	3/4
1837	1132122313	LANEG-H	LUTHER'S	WJHTSD	Luther	A	3/4

1848	1132122313	JACKSSH	LUTHER'S	WJHTSD	Luther	A	3/4
1849	1132122313	DINGCDH	JUDGMENT	GGWDIS	Luther	A	3/4
1853	1132122313	WOODILZ	MONMOUTH	IROJLH/ GGWDIS	Luther	G	1/4
1856	1132122313	WOODINLZ	MONMOUTH	GGWDIS	Luther	G	2/4
1857	1132122313	=====HU	MONMOUTH	OJFOTA	Luther	G	2/4
1866	1132122313	PHILPNHT	MONMOUTH	GGWDIS	Luther	G	1/4
1878	1132122313	NELSHWT	JUDGMENT	GGWDIS	J.Klug Gesangbuch	A	1/4

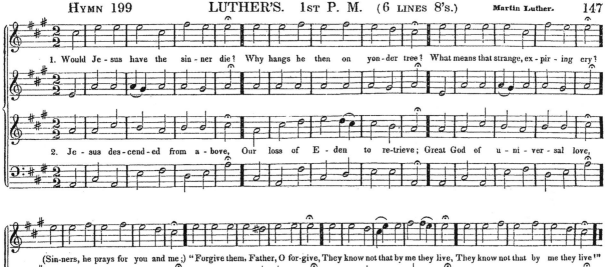

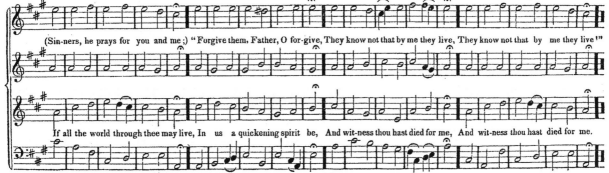

34. LUTON by Rev. George Burder (1752–1832)

a. First published in *The Gospel Magazine, or Treasury of Divine Knowledge*, Vol. 4, London, 1777. It first appears in the United States in Samuel Holyoke, *The Columbian Repository of Sacred Harmony*, Exeter, [1803].[46]

b. LUTON is a Long Meter "plain tune" in triple time in the major mode.

c. Comprised of four four-measure phrases, the tune covers a whole octave. At the halfway point, the melody ends on the dominant, permitting a brief suggestion of the dominant key. In 1833, the fourth section of the tune shows a "grace" of two notes on the upbeat.

d. Nearly all settings rely upon simple harmonic structure, with the use of a raised fourth to suggest the flavor of the dominant key. In 1848, the inner harmonies include four chromatic progressions, as well as use of the dominant seventh chord in noncadential situations.

e. Texts used:

22/33	TMFDTS	The morning flowers display their sweets
37/48	GGAWSS	Great God, attend while Sion sings
49	GGAWZS	Great God, attend while Zion sings
53/56	WAMPOH	With all my powers of heart

57	JTEKAT	Jesus, thou everlasting King, accept
66	FOMBTE	Father of mercies, bow thine ear
78	COMSIS	Come, o my soul, in sacred lays

Additional references:
1. Temperley, *HTI*, no. 3929
2. Wasson, *HI*, no. 18449

LUTON   HWT: 1878

1. 55654321
2. 887654343215
3. 55566778
4. 85434564321   Meter: LM

1808 X

1822 5565432188	BANGNMH	LUTON	TMFDTS	Burder	E♭	3/4
1833 5565432188	BANGNMH	LUTON	TMFDTS	Burder	E♭	3/4
1837 5565432188	LANEG-H	LUTON	GGAWSS	Burder	E♭	3/4
1848 5565432188	JACKSSH	LUTON	GGAWSS	Burder	E♭	3/6
1849 5565432188	DINGCDH	LUTON	GGAWZS	Burder	E♭	3/4
1853 5565432188	WOODILZ	LUTON	WAMPOH	Burder	E♭	1/4
1856 5565432188	WOODINLZ	LUTON	WANMPO	Burder	E♭	1/4
1857 5565432188	=====HU	LUTON	JTEKAT	Burder	E♭	2/4
1866 5565432188	PHILPNHT	LUTON	FOMBTE	BurderG	E♭	1/4
1878 5565432188	NELSHWT	LUTON	COMSIS	BurderG	E♭	1/4

35. **LYONS** arr. from Johann Michael Haydn (1737–1806)

a. First appeared in Gardiner's *Sacred Melodies from Haydn, Mozart and Beethoven and other composers, adapted to the best of English Poets and appropriated for the use of the British Church*, Vol. 2, London, 1815,[47] where it was set for voices and orchestra to "O praise ye the Lord." First appearance in the United States in Rev. John Tufts, *An Introduction to the Singing of Psalm-Tunes*, Boston, 1726.[48]

b. LYONS is a major mode "plain tune" in 10.10.11.11 meter in triple time.

c. The tune falls into four symmetrical phrases, the second and fourth being identical except in one rhythmic subdivision.

d. The tune never varies throughout the period under study. The harmonization of the earliest and the latest settings includes a descending chromatic line in the alto at phrase 3; the harmonizations of 1853, 1856, 1857, and 1866 use the same bass "pedal point" but use only diatonic chords in sequence.

e. Texts used:

33/37	REWAAI	Rejoice evermore with angels above
48	AHKLDF	O heavenly King, look down from above
49/66	TTAADA	Though troubles assail, and dangers
53/56/57	ABTWMI	Appointed by thee, we meet in thy
78	OWTKAG	O worship the King, all glorious

Additional references:
1. Temperley, *HTI*, no. 15176
2. Wasson, *HI*, no. 18500

LYONS

HWT: 1878

1. 5112314432
2. 51123454321
3. 55567712234
4. 511233454321

Meter: 10.10.11.11
or 10.11.10.11

1808 X
1822 X

1833	5112314432	BANGNMH	LYONS	REWAAI	Haydn	B♭	3/4
1837	5112314432	LANEG-H	LYONS	REWAAI	Haydn	B♭	3/4
1848	5112314432	JACKSSH	LYONS	OHKLDF	Haydn	B♭	3/6
1849	5112314432	DINGCDH	LYONS	TTAADA	Haydn	B♭	3/4
1853	5112314432	WOODILZ	LYONS	ABTWMI	Haydn	B♭	3/4
1856	5112314432	WOODINLZ	LYONS	ABTWMI	Haydn	B♭	3/4
1857	5112314432	=====HU	LYONS	ABTWMI		B♭	2/4
1866	5123414432	PHILPNHT	LYONS	TTAADA	HaydnM	B♭	1/4
1878	5112314432	NELSHWT	LYONS	OWTKAG	HaydnF	A	1/4

HYMN 277   LYONS. 13TH P. M.   (10 10, 11 11.)   Haydn. 289

1. Re-joice ev - er-more, with an-gels a bove, In Je - sus - 's power, in Je - sus - 's love: With glad ex - ult - a - tion your

2. Thou, Lord, our re - lief in trou-ble hast been; Hast saved us from grief, hast saved us from sin; The power of thy Spi - rit hath

tri-umph pro - claim, As - crib - ing sal - va - tion to God and the Lamb.

set our hearts free, And now we in - her - it all ful - ness in thee.

19

36. MAJESTY by William Billings (1746–1800)

a. First published in William Billings, *The Singing Master's Assistant*, Boston, 1778.[49] Early appearances are coupled with Thomas Sternhold's text, "The Lord descended from above," with corresponding word painting in the shape of the tune (descending, above).

b. This is a major mode tune written to accompany two stanzas of Common Meter text (CM doubled) in duple time. It was formerly matched with Psalm 147 of Watts.

c. The first half of the tune contains characteristics of "old Methodist" style, with two or more notes per syllable; it spans a full octave after only two measures. The second half becomes syllabic and commences with a solo line, which is not followed by either imitative entries or fuging.

d. In all but 1849, the voicing is reduced to two parts in measures 7–9; in 1857 the melody becomes a unison soprano with (small note) instrumental harmony supporting, and the underlay is phrased three-plus-one in contrast to all other texts, which are underlaid with one syllable for each pair of melody notes.

e. Texts used:

22/33	OTTWTH	O that thou wouldst the heavens rent
37/49	OFATTT	O for a thousand tongues to sing
53/56/78	TLDFAA	The Lord descended from above
57	STTGJP	Sing to the great Jehovah's praise
66	BBOELO	Blest be our everlasting Lord

Additional references:
1. Crawford, *Core Repertory*, no. 47
2. Temperley, *HTI*, no. 4014
3. Wasson, *HI*, no.18678

MAJESTY   HWT: 1878

1. 587865314318
2. 76545678
3. 56426531543215
4. 4313587654321
5. 13124311587678
6. 58885666
7. 568765
8. 78564587654321   Meter: CM D

1808 X						
1822	5878653143 BANGNMH	MAJESTY	OTTWTH		F	3/4
1833	5878653143 BANGNMH	MAJESTY	OTTWTH		F	3/4
1837	5828653143 LANEG-H	MAJESTY	OFATTT	Billings	F	3/4
1848 X						
1849	5878653143 DINGCDH	MAJESTY	OFATTT	Billings	D	3/4
1853	5878653143 WOODILZ	MAJESTY	TLDFAA	Billings	F	3/4
1856	5878653143 WOODINLZ	MAJESTY	TLDFAA	Billings	F	3/4
1857	5878653143 =====HU	MAJESTY	STTGJP		F	2/4
1866	5878653143 PHILPNHT	MAJESTY	BBOELO	Billings	F	1/4
1878	5878653143 NELSHWT	MAJESTY	TLDFAA	Billings	F	1/4

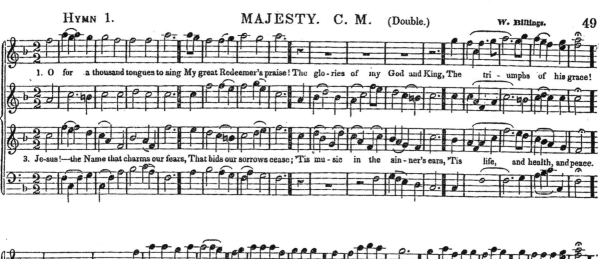

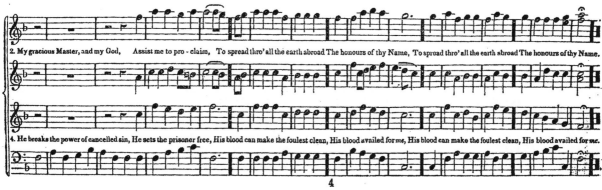

37. **MARTYRDOM** (DRUMCLOG, FENWICK, AVON) by Hugh Wilson (1764–1824)

a. First published in Scotland in R. A. Smith, *Sacred Music Sung in St. George's Church Edinburgh*, 1825. *Hymns Ancient and Modern*, 1861, gives the tune in 4/4 time, but in the appendix of 1868, no. 310, triple time is used.[50] George Pullen Jackson notes that McCutchan records that it may have been in use twenty-five years before its printed appearance.[51] It likely appeared in the United States for the first time in *Sacred Music*, as above.[52]

b. MARTYRDOM is a Common Meter "plain tune" in the major mode.

c. Written as a psalm tune for class use, it originally appeared in 4/4 time,[53] being later changed to triple time, in which form it appears in the tunebook studied. It retains a predictable long-short ♩. rhythmic pattern in each measure as it traces the range of an octave.

d. The melody remains unchanged in the period under study. In the 1848 and 1849 sources it is called MARTYRDOM; 1849 includes the following footnote:

> This tune is called "Fenwick" and "Drumclog," in Europe: and "Avon" in this country. It is erroneously attributed in most publications to "Gamble."

In 1853 and 1856 the title reads MARTYRDOM or AVON. In subsequent sources it is called AVON. The 1853 source is the only one to include a figured bass under the bass line.

e. Texts used:

48	OTICML	O that I could my Lord receive
49	HSOSBN	How sad our state by nature is
53/56	OTWTMH	O Thou, whose tender mercy hears
57	OTIWAH	O that I were as heretofore

| 66 | MGMGTT | My God, my God to thee I cry |
| 78 | FHMRSB | Forever here my rest shall be |

Additional references:
1. Jackson, *Down-East Spirituals*, no. 151
2. McCutchan, *Our Hymnody*, no. 70
3. Wasson, *HI*, no. 19000

MARTYRDOM (FENWICK, AVON, DRUMCLOG)   HWT: 1878

1. 516512321
2. 3532132
3. 53213432
4. 35612321   Meter: CM

1808	X
1822	X
1833	X
1837	X
1848	5165123213	JACKSSH	MARTYRDOM	OTICML	Gamble	B♭	3/4
1849	5165123213	DINGCDH	MARTYRDOM	HSOSBN	Wilson	B♭	3/4
1853	5165123213	WOODILZ	MARTYRDOM	OTWTMH	Scottish	B♭	3/4
1856	5165123213	WOODINLZ	MARTYRDOM	OTWTMH	Scottish	B♭	3/4
1857	5165123213	=====HU	AVON	OTIWAH	Wilson	B♭	2/4
1866	5165123213	PHILPNHT	AVON	MGMGTT	WilsonH	B♭	1/4
1878	5165123213	NELSHWT	AVON	FHMRSB	WilsonH	A♭	1/4

MARTYRDOM.* C. M.

H. WILSON, of Fenwick, Scotland.

MODERATO.

1. How sad our state by na-ture is; Our sin, how deep it stains; And Sa-tan binds our cap-tive souls Fast in his sla-vish chains.

2. But there's a voice of sov-'reign grace Sounds from the sa-cred word:—Ho! ye de-spair-ing sin-ners, come, And trust a faith-ful Lord.

* This tune is also called "Fenwick" and "Drumclog," in Europe ; and "Avon," in this country. It is erroneously attributed in most publications to "Gamble."

38. MEAR (NEW MEAR)

a. Crawford locates the first publication in *A Set of Tunes in 3 Parts*, [London], ca. 1720. Temperley, however, lists Charles Woodmason, *A Collection of Psalm Tunes*, London, [1734–1737], as the original publication, and *The Tunes of the Psalms*, Boston, 1737, as the first American appearance.[54] It was printed 121 times prior to 1810. The original text, which remained popular for a century, was from Watts, Ps. 96, CM, "Sing to the Lord, ye distant lands."[55]

b. MEAR is a tune in the major mode using triple time in Common Meter. It accommodated many differing texts.

c. The tune is remarkable for containing almost no decoration. Its very even harmonic progression relies on the I, V, and VI chords except for a surprising subdominant harmony at the climax in measure 8. Crawford notes that MEAR was collected ca. 1980 from the oral tradition of Primitive Baptists in the Blue Ridge region of Virginia and North Carolina.

d. MEAR appears in all tunebooks in this study, although the research of Baldridge had missed its occurrence in *David's Companion*, 1808.[56] Some versions add passing notes to the tune in two places (in measure 3: 123 replaces 13; in measure 13: 4321 replaces 421). The final version of 1878 reverts to the earliest shape. The 1853 source presents a tenor line flourish in the closing cadence.

e. Texts used:

22/33/37	OFACWW	O for a closer walk with God
48	OWDIMSL	O why did I my Savior leave?
49	IWBTOT	I would be thine; O take
53/56	OTAJST	O 'twas a joyful sound to hear
57	LAIAIK	Lord, all I am is known to thee
66	GMIAMW	God moves in a mysterious way
78	VMTFPF	Vain man, thy fond pursuits
	OGOHIA	O God, our help in ages past

Additional references:
1. Crawford, *Core Repertory*, no. 49
2. Jackson, *Another Sheaf of White Spirituals*, no. 55
3. McCutchan, *Our Hymnody*, no. 617
4. Temperley, *HTI*, no. 909b
5. Wasson, *HI*, no. 19170

MEAR (NEW MEAR)   HWT: 1878

1. 15533132
2. 231545
3. 56551432
4. 153421   Meter: CM

1808	1553313223		MEAR	OFACWW		G	3/4
1822	1553313223	BANGNMH	MEAR	OFACWW		G	3/4
1833	1553313223	BANGNMH	MEAR	OFACWW		G	3/4
1837	15533132231	LANEG-H	MEAR	OFACWW		G	3/4
1848	15533132231	JACKSSH	MEAR	OWDIMSL		G	3/4
1849	15533123223	DINGCDH	MEAR	IWBTOT		G	3/4
1853	15533132231	WOODILZ	MEAR	OTAJST		F	1/4
1856	15533132231	WOODINLZ	MEAR	OTAJST		F	1/4
1857	15533132231	=====HU	MEAR	LAIAIK	Luther	F	2/4
1866	15533123223	PHILPNHT	MEAR	GMIAMW	WilliamsC	G	1/4
1878	15533132231	NELSHWT	MEAR	VMTFPF	Williams Welsh Air	F	1/4

HYMN 89.   MEAR.   C. M.

1. O for a clo-ser walk with God, A calm and heavenly frame; A light to shine up-on the road That leads me to the Lamb.

2. Where is the-bless-ed-ness I knew, When first I saw the Lord? Where is the soul-re-fresh-ing view Of Je-sus and his word.

39. **NEW SABBATH** by Isaac Smith (1734–1805)

a. First published in Stephen Addington, *A Collection of Psalm tunes*, 8th ed., London, 1788. The first U.S. publication was in Amos Pilsbury, *The United States' Sacred Harmony*, Boston, 1799.[57]

b. NEW SABBATH is a Long Meter "plain tune" in triple (3/4) time in the major mode.

c. This plain tune of four phrases incorporates an antiphonal phrase in the sources from 1822, 1833, and 1837. The range of melody is a ninth, and rhythmic emphasis is secured by having a slurred melisma or a half-note value to commence each measure.

d. The tune of the final phrase shows some variation over this period:

1808/22/33	1 *543*513 321 2342 17 1
1837	1 *543*512 321 2342 17 1
1853/56/57	1 *543*512 321 217 1

The harmonies are conservative, with introduction of a secondary dominant (measure 11) in all sources after 1853.

e. Texts used:

08	WEHSWB	What equal honors shall we bring
22/33	JMSBFO	Jesus my saviour, brother, friend
37	GHBTWD	Go, Holy Book, thou word divine
53/56	FTAJST	Forgiveness! 'tis a joyful sound to
57	JIWTGR	Jesus, in whom the Godhead's rays

Additional references:
1. Diehl, *Hymns and Tunes*, p. 759
2. Temperley, *HTI*, no. 4946a
3. Wasson, *HI*, no. 20657

NEW SABBATH   HU: 1857

1. 856554345862878
2. *327532758654332*
3. 5678562887
4. 85435*823*282878   Meter: LM

1808	8565533458	EVANJDC	NEW SABBATH	WEHSWB		D	1/2
1822	8565543458	BANGNMH	NEW SABBATH	JMSBFO		D	3/4
1833	8565543458	BANGNMH	NEW SABBATH	JMSBFO		D	3/4
1837	8565543458	LANEG-H	NEW SABBATH	GHBTWD	Smith	D	3/4
1848	X					
1849	X					
1853	8565543458	WOODILZ	NEW SABBATH	FTAJST	Smith	C	1/4
1856	8565543458	WOODINLZ	NEW SABBATH	FTAJST	Smith	C	1/4
1857	8565543458	=====HU	NEW SABBATH	JIWTGR	Smith	C	2/4
1866	X					
1878	X					

92 HYMN 642. NEW SABBATH. L. M. Isaac Smith.

1. Go, Ho - ly Book, thou word di - vine, Of Him who spake as man ne'er spake; Go, for Om - ni - po-

tence is thine, And to thy truths the na - tions wake.

40. NUREMBURG by Johann Rudolphe Ahle (1625–1673)

a. First published in John Christian Jacobi, *A Collection of Divine Hymns, translated from the High Dutch*, London, 1720. First U.S. publication in Jacob Eckhard, *Choral-Book*, Boston, 1816.[58]

b. This is a duple time "plain tune" in the major mode which uses meter of 4 Sevens, except as noted in part d below.

c. The chief characteristic of the tune is that phrases 2, 3, and 4 commence with four repeated pitches. The opening phrase simply traces the tonic and dominant chord. In some sources, the first half is repeated in order to accommodate six lines of poetry instead of four.

d. The tune remains constant throughout except in 1853, when it is turned into a Long Meter tune with the following annotation:

> NUREMBURG. L.M: Or 7's by omitting the first note to each line

In each case, the phrase begins with an upbeat eighth-note pitch then repeated immediately; this produces the necessary additional melody note to accommodate the Long Meter text. The keys used are B-flat (1837, 1848, 1856, and 1866), and G (1853 and 1866), and A (1878). As mentioned above, six lines of text (instead of four) are accommodated by repetition of the first two phrases in 1856, 1857, and 1866.

e. Texts used:

37/48	LWWASO	Lord, whom winds and seas obey
53	LEGCTH	Let everlasting glories crown thy head
56	OTGWHP	O thou God who hearest prayer
57	SPOIRS	Savior, Prince of Israel's race, save me
66	WSTWWF	Weary souls that wander wide from
78	GBTGAG	Glory be to God above, God from

Additional reference:
Temperley, *HTI*, no. 923a, d

NUREMBURG   HWT: 1878

1. 3125312
2. 11112321
3. 5555627
4. 11112321

Meter: 77.77 *or*
88.88 *or* 77.77.77

1808 X							
1822 X							
1833 X							
1837	3125312111	LANEG-H	NUREMBURG	LWWASO	German	B♭	3/4
1848	3125312111	JACKSSH	NUREMBURG	LWWASO	German	B♭	3/4
1849 X							
1853	3312253121	WOODILZ	NUREMBURG	LEGCTH	German	G	1/4
1856	3125312111	WOODINLZ	NUREMBURG	OTGWHP	German	B♭	1/4
1857	3125312111	=====HU	NUREMBURG	SPOIRS	German	B♭	2/4
1866	3125312111	PHILPNHT	NUREMBURG	WSTWWF	AhleJ	G	1/4
1878	3125312111	NELSHWT	NUREMBURG	GBTGAG	AhleJ	A	1/4

HYMN 686.   NUREMBURG.   5TH P. M.   (77, 77.)   German.

1. Lord, whom winds and seas o-bey, Guide us through the wa-tery way; In the hol-low of thy hand, Hide, and bring us safe to land.

2. Je-sus, let our faith-ful mind, Rest on thee a-lone re-clined; Ev-ery anxious thought repress, Keep our souls in per-fect peace.

* From "The Choir,"—by permission.

41. **OLD HUNDRED** (OLD HUNDREDTH)

a. First published in *Psalms of David*, 4th ed., Geneva, [1561]. First published in the United States in *The Tunes of the Psalms*, Boston, 1698. Printed 226 times before 1810.[59]

b. This plain, major mode, Long Meter tune enjoys use more than any other tune. It is often presented without a text.

c. The phrases are carefully balanced in structure: five stepwise notes precede a leap for each of the first three phrases; the final phrase begins with two leaps, closing with stepwise motion.

d. Except for the 1848 source, where many passing notes are introduced for inner parts, this tune remains constant and the settings very similar through the period. The key used is A major, except for the final source (1878), which uses G major.

e. Texts used:

08/22/33/37/48/49/57/66	BJATYN	Before Jehovah's awful throne
53/56/78	FATDBT	From all that dwells below

Additional references:
1. Crawford, *Core Repertory*, no. 68
2. Frost, *English and Scottish Psalm Tunes*, 114
3. Temperley, *HTI*, no. 143a, c
4. Wasson, *HI*, no. 22276

OLD HUNDRED (OLD HUNDREDTH)   HWT: 1878

1. 11765123
2. 33321432
3. 12321671
4. 53124321   Meter: LM

Year	Tune	Source	Name	Setting	Composer	Key	Time
1808 1176512333		OLD HUNDRED	BJATYN	Luther	A	3/4
1822 1176512333		OLD HUNDRED	BJATYN		A	3/4
1833 1176512333	BANGNMH	OLD HUNDRED	BJATYN		A	3/4
1837 1176512333	LANEG-H	OLD HUNDRED	BJATYN	Luther	A	3/4
1848 1176512333	JACKSSH	OLD HUNDRED	BJATYN	Luther	A	3/4
1849 1176512333	DINGCDH	OLD HUNDRED	BJATYN	Luther	A	3/4
1853 1176512333	WOODILZ	OLD HUNDRED	FATDBT	Luther	A	1/4
1856 1176512333	WOODINLZ	OLD HUNDRED	FATDBT	Luther	A	1/4
1857 1176512333	=====HU	OLD HUNDRED	BJATYN		A	2/4
1866 1176512333	PHILPNHT	OLD HUNDRED	BJATYN	FrancG	A	1/4
1878 1176512333	NELSHWT	OLD HUNDRED	FATDBT	FrancG	G	1/4

HYMN 266..   OLD HUNDRED. L. M.   Martin Luther.

1. Be-fore Je-ho-vah's aw-ful throne, Ye na-tions, bow with sacred joy; Know that the Lord is God a-lone, He can cre-ate, and he de-stroy.

2. His sovereign power, without our aid, Made us of clay, and formed us men: And when like wandering sheep we strayed, He brought us to his fold a-gain.

42. PARK STREET by Frederic M. A. Venua (1786–1872)

a. This tune was included by Gardiner in *Sacred Melodies*, Vol. 2, London, 1815, with the text "Thee will I love, O Lord," arranged for strings, harp, organ, and voices. In the United States it appeared in the *Handel and Haydn Society Collection of Church Music*, Lowell Mason, ed., 1822, set to "Hark! how the choral song of heaven."[60]

b. This tune-with-extension (in four early sources including antiphonal sections) appears in the major mode using triple time for Long Meter text.

c. A characteristic of the tune is the repeated pitch of the first measure of phrases 1, 2, and 5. In each instance, the supporting parts (e.g., bass line) move by leap for interest. Phrase 4 has an internal echo or imitation when proclaiming the fourth line of poetry. That line is repeated but to a differing tune in phrase 5 (the extension).

d. The tune does not change in the period 1808–1878, and the settings show little change.

e. Texts used:

33	TLOGTP	Thou Lamb of God, thou Prince
48	LHSABA	Lord, how secure and blest are they
37/49	OATETS	On all the earth thy Spirit shower
53/56	HHTCSO	Hark! how the choral song of heaven
57	TSTTIF	This stone to thee in faith, we lay
66	AWSTHF	Abraham, when severely tried, his faith
78	LRTTAG	Lo! round the throne a glorious band

Additional references:
1. Wasson, *HI*, no. 23022
2. Temperley, *HTI*, no. 15192

PARK STREET   HWT: 1878

1. 1111232171
2. 3333527165
3. 52233443
4. 536444253
   1111712171   Meter: LM

1808 X
1822 X

1833	11112321713	BANGNMH	PARK-STREET	TLOGTP		B♭	3/4
1837	11112321713	LANEG-H	PARK STREET	OAETSS	Venua	B♭	3/4
1848	11112321713	JACKSSH	PARK-STREET	LHSABA	Venua	B♭	3/6
1849	11112321713	DINGCDH	PARK STREET	OATETS	Venua	B♭	3/4
1853	11112321713	WOODILZ	PARK-STREET	HHTCSO	Venua	A	1/4
1856	11112321713	WOODINLZ	PARK-STREET	HHTCSO	Venua	A	1/4
1857	11112321713	=====HU	PARK STREET	TSTTIF	Venua	A	2/4
1866	11112321713	PHILPNHT	PARK STREET	AWSTHF	Venua	A	1/4
1878	11112321713	NELSHWT	PARK STREET	LRTTAG	Venua	G	1/4

HYMN 458   PARK STREET L. M.   Venua.   97

1. On all the earth thy Spir-it shower, The earth in right-eous-ness re-new: Thy king-dom come, and hell's o'er-power,

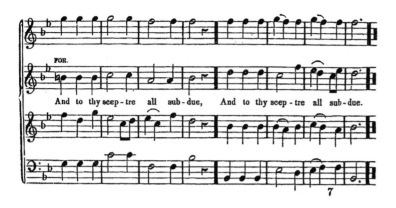

And to thy scep-tre all sub-due,   And to thy scep-tre all sub-due.

43. PECKHAM (RIPPON) by Isaac Smith (1734–1805)

a. First published in Isaac Smith, *A Collection of Psalm Tunes*, London, ca. 1779–1780. First U.S. publication in Samuel Holyoke, *The Columbian Repository of Sacred Harmony*, Exeter, 1803.[61]

b. PECKHAM is a Short Meter "plain tune" in the major mode in triple time.

c. The tune uses the wide range of a tenth, and every measure (except cadence measures) contains at least one slurred group of notes, usually for beats 1 and 2. The 1808 source includes a repeat of phrase 3, which gives the tune an extension in this instance only.

d. The harmonic structure of the melody does not change, but the tune contents evolve interestingly over the period.

1808	8 54358*	432 18 765 678654 58 *328* 543 456782 87
1822/33	8 54358*	432 18 765 678654 58 *328* 53 456782 87
1837	8 54358*	432 18 765 678654 58 *328* 7653 456782 87
1848	8 54358*	432 18 765 678654 58 *328* 53 4562 87
1853	8 5435	432 18 765 678654 55 *328* 7653 4562 87
1857	8 5435	432 18 765 678654 55 *328* 7653 4562 87

* triplet figure

The harmonies are similar throughout, with an occasional printer's error (see 1837, p. 119, measure 2, where G is given instead of A).

e. Texts used:

08/22/33	TJOQAD	Thou judge of quick and dead
37	STCOTL	Sinners the call obey! The latest
48	OTICRW	O that I could repent with all
53	MSWJAW	My soul with joy attend while Jesus
57	LGTHGI	Lord God, the Holy Ghost! in this

Additional reference:
Temperley, *HTI*, no. 4158a

PECKHAM (RIPPON)   HU: 1857

1. 854354321
2. 87656786545
3. 3*3*287653456287
4. 5878*3*2878   Meter: SM

1808 8543584321	EVANJDC	RIPPON	TJOQAD	Miller	D	1/2
1822 8543584321		RIPPON/PECKHAM	TJOQAD	Smith	D	2/3
1833 8543584321	BANGNMH	RIPPON/PECKHAM	TJOQAD	Smith	D	2/3
1837 8543584321	LANEG-H	PECKHAM	STCOTL	Smith	D	3/4
1848 8543584321	JACKSSH	PECKHAM	OTICRW	Smith	D	3/4
1849 X						
1853 8543543218	WOODILZ	PECKHAM	MSWJAW	Smith	C	1/4
1856 X						
1857 8543543218	=====HU	PECKHAM	LGTHGI	SmithI	C	2/4
1866 X						
1878 X						

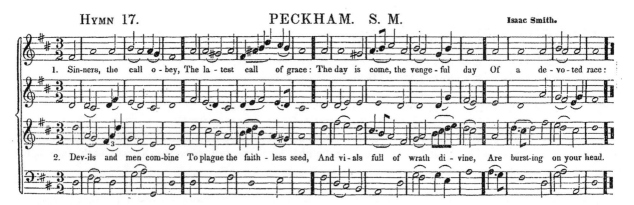

44. PENITENCE by William A. Oakley (1809–1881)

a. The first documented appearance seems to be in the tunebook of 1837 (see below).[62]

b. PENITENCE is a "plain tune" in the major mode for the meter 76.76.78.76. Its triple time is noted as 3/8 throughout the period.

c. In lilting fashion the tune adopts a long-short pattern with one harmony for each measure. Only I, IV, and V harmonies are used. The tune is identical for phrases 3 and 4, as well as 7 and 8, and in 1857, 1866, and 1878 the *dal Segno* is indicated for use with new text.

d. Both tune and settings are consistent throughout the period.

e. Text used:
All sources: JLTPEC   Jesus, let thy pitying eye call back

Additional reference:
Wasson, *HI*, no. 23265

PENITENCE   HWT: 1878

1. 85*3*288765
2. 566578
3. *3283*288765
4. 588*328*
5. 534556785
6. 5687658*382*
7. *3283*288765
8. 588*328*

Meter: 76.76.78.76

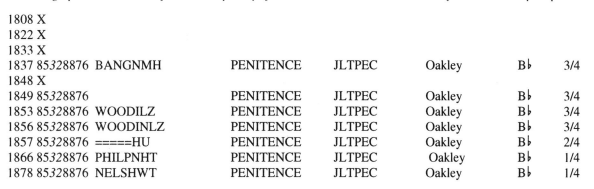

1808 X							
1822 X							
1833 X							
1837	85328876	BANGNMH	PENITENCE	JLTPEC	Oakley	B♭	3/4
1848 X							
1849	85328876		PENITENCE	JLTPEC	Oakley	B♭	3/4
1853	85328876	WOODILZ	PENITENCE	JLTPEC	Oakley	B♭	3/4
1856	85328876	WOODINLZ	PENITENCE	JLTPEC	Oakley	B♭	3/4
1857	85328876	=====HU	PENITENCE	JLTPEC	Oakley	B♭	2/4
1866	85328876	PHILPNHT	PENITENCE	JLTPEC	Oakley	B♭	1/4
1878	85328876	NELSHWT	PENITENCE	JLTPEC	Oakley	B♭	1/4

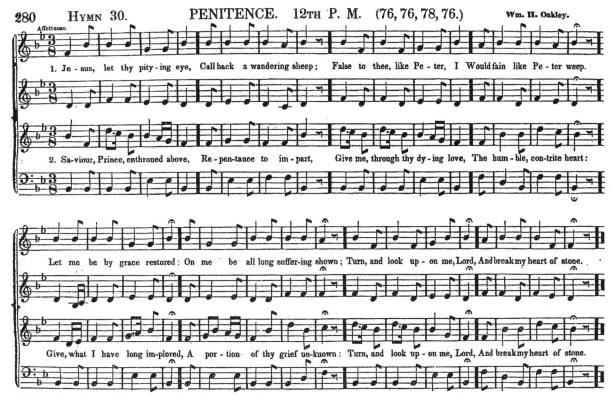

45. **PETERBOROUGH** by Ralph Harrison (1748–1810)

a. Harrison composed the tune in 1786.[63] It was first published in Lewis and Thaddeus Seymour, *The Musical Instructor*, New York, 1803.[64]

b. PETERBOROUGH (Peterboro') is a "plain tune" in the major mode which uses Common Meter in duple time.

c. The tune has a narrow range of five notes, and is supported by conventional harmonies. Its progress is usually step-wise, and the underlay syllabic with only two short slurred passages near the final cadence.

d. The tune never varies in pitch sequence throughout the period, and the harmonies change but little. There are changes in the rhythmic layout within the frame of duple time, signified by signatures of 2/2, ₵, or 4/4. For example, the 1837 source uses a half rest in measure 7 to prepare the upbeat, the 1878 source indicates no delay or preparation, and all other sources use a fermata on the final note of the preceding phrase.

e. Texts used:

| 22/33/37 | LAIAIK | Lord, all I am is known |

| 53/56/78 | OMMSTR | Once more, my soul, the rising day |
| 57 | HFWCCU | Hail Father, whose creating call unnumbered |

Additional references:
1. Temperley, *HTI*, no. 10186
2. Wasson, *HI*, no. 23361

PETERBOROUGH   HWT: 1878

1. 13344321
2. 355432
3. 32231432
4. 232354321   Meter: CM

1808 X						
1822	1334432135	BANGNMH	PETERBOROUGH	LAIAIK		A	3/4
1833	1334432135	BANGNMH	PETERBOROUGH	LAIAIK		A	3/4
1837	1334432135	LANEG-H	PETERBOROUGH	LAIAIK		A	3/4
1848 X						
1849 X						
1853	1334432135	WOODILZ	PETERBOROUGH	OMMSTR		G	1/4
1856	1334432135	WOODINLZ	PETERBOROUGH	OMMSTR		G	1/4
1857	1334432135	=====HU	PETERBOROUGH	HFWCCU	Harrison	G	2/4
1866 X						
1878	1334432135	NELSHWT	PETERBOROUGH	OMMSTR	Harrison	G	1/4

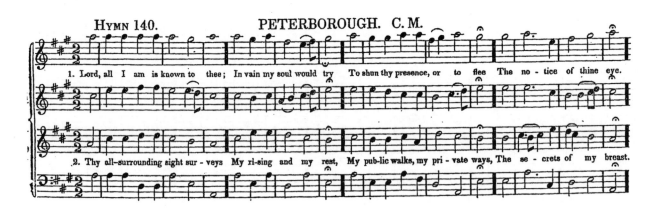

46. **PIETY** by Thomas Clark (1775–1859)

a. First published in Andrew Law, *Supplement to the Musical Primer*, Philadelphia, 1811.[65]

b. This is a Common Meter tune in duple time using the major mode. In some sources it has antiphonal sections, and in others has both extension phrases and antiphonal sections.

c. The author is noted variously as Clark, Clarke, and Carle. The tune changes in one respect only. Until 1837 the tune of phrase 5 reads 5 646 535 424 3, in contrast with the later 5 64 53 42 3. In the 1853 source, directions are given for "soli" and "chorus" singing of the final two phrases, enhancing the antiphonal character.

d. The 1833, 1837, 1853, and 1866 sources contain settings that are both antiphonal and extended.
The scheme is as follows:

| Phrase 1 | 4-part | | first line of text |
| Phrase 2 | tune/alto | (antiphonal) | second line of text |

Phrase 3	4-part	(extended)	repeat text of phrase 2
Phrase 4	4-part		third line of text
Phrase 5	tune/bass	(antiphonal/extended)	repeat text of phrase 4
Phrase 6	4-part		fourth line of text

The 1849, 1856, and 1857 sources use the same tune and harmonic support, but utilize a six-line text. These are plain antiphonal tunes.

e. Texts used:

33/37	JHDTIM	Jesus hath died that I might live
49	LAOETV	Let all on earth their voices raise
53	HIHWFT	Happy is he who fears the Lord
56	OCISTM	O could I speak the matchless worth
57	TGOPTG	Thou God of power, thou God of love
66	OFAOFT	O for an overcoming faith to cheer

Additional reference:
Temperley, *HTI*, no. 13830

PIETY   HU: 1866

1. 8878832878
2. 5678786543
   532878
3. 5882232865
   56453423
4. 58232878   Meter: CM (with ext.) *or* 886 D

1808 X
1822 X

1833	8878832878	BANGNMH	PIETY	JHDTIM	Clark	D	3/4
1837	8878832878	LANEG-H	PIETY	JHDTIM	Clark	D	3/4
1848	X						
1849	8878832878	DINCDH	PIETY	LAOETV	Clark	D	3/4
1853	8878832878	WOODILZ	PIETY	HIHWFT	Carle	C	3/4
1856	8878832878	WOODINLZ	PIETY	OCISTM	Carle	C	1/4
1857	8878832878	=====HU	PIETY	TGOPTG	Clarke	C	2/4
1866	8878832878	PHILPNHT	PIETY	OFAOFT		C	1/4
1878	X						

56 HYMN 325.   PIETY. C. M.   Thos. Clark.

PIA. Treblet.   FOR.

1. Je-sus hath died that I might live, Might live to God a - lone, Might live to God a-lone; In him e - ter - nal life re - ceive,

In him e - ter - nal life re - ceive, And be in spir - it one.

47. PLEYEL'S HYMN (CONDOLENCE, GERMAN HYMN) by Ignace Pleyel (1757–1831)

a. This tune is derived from the Andante movement of a string quartet in G major published in 1788. First appearance as a Long Meter hymn was in *Arnold and Callcott's Psalms*, 1791,[66] with the text by J. Addison, "The spacious firmament on high." It was first published in 77.77 meter in *Select Hymns for the Voice and Harpsichord*, London, [1790]. The first appearances in the United States were in [Benjamin Carr?], *Sacred Harmony*, Philadelphia, [1803–1804]; or in S. and J. Cole of Baltimore, *Sacred Music, published for the Use of the Cecilian Society*, Baltimore, 1803.[67]

b. This is a "plain tune" in the major mode using duple time. Usually it is meant for use with 4 Sevens, though use with Long Meter is mentioned in the 1853 and 1856 sources.

c. The phrases of this tune are isorhythmic. Spread over an octave, the second and fourth phrases are identical in content, and the third has the same rhythm and descending character of phrases 2 and 4. In the two sources (see above) where Long Meter is suggested, the second note of each phrase is subdivided in order to accommodate the extra syllable. A discussion of the tune's relatedness to the Pleyel original is available in Hill's dissertation.[68]

d. The tune and settings are consistent throughout the period under study.

e. Texts used:

22/33/37	HAVDTS	Hark! a voice divides the sky
48	EROLIK	Earth, rejoice! Our Lord is King
49	LJGLIT	Loving Jesus, gentle Lamb, in thy
53/56	TTPFAL	To thy pastures fair and large
	KATTGB	Kingdoms and thrones to God belong
57/78	DOMCTB	Depth of mercy, can there be
66	HSTBWS	Hasten sinner, to be wise! Stay
78	HFSLBT	Heavenly Father, sovereign Lord, be

Additional references:
1. Jackson, *Down East-Spirituals*, no. 65
2. Temperley, *HTI*, no. 5356a, g
3. Wasson, *HI*, no. 23535

PLEYEL'S HYMN (CONDOLENCE, GERMAN HYMN)   HWT: 1878

1. 3523423
2. 3523421
3. 2312765
4. 3523421   Meter: 77.77

1808 X
1822 3523423352 BANGNMH   CONDOLENCE   HAVDTS   Pleyel   B♭   3/4

1833	3523423352	BANGNMH	CONDOLENCE	HAVDTS	Rippon	B♭	3/4
1837	3523423352	LANEG-H	CONDOLENCE	HAVDTS	Pleyel	B♭	3/4
1848	3523423352	JACKSSH	PLEYEL'S HY	EROLIK	Pleyel	G	3/4
1849	3523423352	DINGCDH	GERMAN HY	LJGLIT	Pleyel	A	3/4
1853	3552342335	WOODILZ	PLEYEL'S HY	TTPFAL/KATTGB	Pleyel	G	1/4
1856	3523423352	WOODINLZ	PLEYEL'S HY	TTPFAL/KATTGB	Pleyel	G	1/4
1857	3523423352	=====HU	PLEYEL'S HY	DOMCTB	Pleyel	A	2/4
1866	3523423352	PHILPNHT	PLEYEL'S HY	HSTBWS	Pleyel	G	1/4
1878	3523423352	NELSHWT	PLEYEL'S HY	DOMCTB	Pleyel	G	1/4

48. **PLYMOUTH DOCK** by Andrew Law (1749–1821)

a. First published in William Edward Miller, *David's Harp*, London, ca. 1803. In the United States it first appeared in James Evans, *David's Companion*, New York, 1808.[69]

b. This "plain tune" in the major mode is set for 6 Eights and proceeds in duple time (¢, 4/4, 2/2) or, in 1857, in a mixture (2/2, 3/2).

c. This tune recalls the "old Methodist" style with a rudimentary harmonic setting, and many melismas or slurs. Stepwise motion is interrupted occasionally by leaps of four or six steps. It remains unchanged throughout the period.

d. There are basically three settings of this tune: the 1808 version in two parts, which includes a repeat of the final two phrases; the 1822, 1833, and 1837 setting, which uses basic harmonies and fermatas or rests to separate phrases; and the 1848, 1857, and 1866 setting, which uses many passing notes, accidentals suggesting related keys, and some chromatics.

e. Texts used:

08	COTTUW	Come O thou traveller unknown
22/33/37/57	LGIHLU	Lo! God is here; let us adore
48	CFSAHG	Come, Father, Son and Holy Ghost
66	POHBSB	Prisoners of hope, be strong, be bold

Additional references:
1. Temperley, *HTI*, no. 10053
2. Wasson, *HI*, no. 23551

PLYMOUTH DOCK   NHT: 1866

1. 1543234512345
2. 565678354321
3. 543216543212
4. 13587665

5. 5854365432
6. 5834654321   Meter: 88.88.88

1808	1543234512		PLYMOUTH DOCK	COTTUW	G	1/2
1822	1543234512	BANGNMH	PLYMOUTH DOCK	LGIHLU	G	2/3
1833	1543234512	BANGNMH	PLYMOUTH DOCK	LGIHLU	G	2/3
1837	1543234512	LANEG-H	PLYMOUTH DOCK	LGIHLU	E♭	3/4
1848	1543234512	JACKSSH	PLYMOUTH DOCK	CFSAHG	F	3/6
1849	X
1853	X
1856	X
1857	1543234512	=====HU	PLYMOUTH DOCK	LGIHLU	F	2/4
1866	1543234512	PHILPNHT	PLYMOUTH DOCK	POHBSB LawA	F	1/4
1878	X

148   Hymn 285   PLYMOUTH DOCK.   1st P. M.   (6 lines 8's.)

1. Lo! God is here! let us a-dore, And own how dreadful is this place! Let all with-in us feel his power, And silent, bow before his face!

2. Lo! God is here! him day and night Th'u-ni-ted choirs of angels, sing: To him, enthroned above all height, Heaven's host their noblest praises bring:

Who know his power, his grace who prove, Serve him with fear, with reverence, love.

Dis-dain not, Lord, our mean - er song, Who praise thee with a stammering tongue.

49. **PORTUGAL** by Thomas Thorley

a. Temperley states in the *Hymn Tune Index* that this was first published in *The Gospel Magazine, or Treasury of Divine Knowledge*, Vol. 5, London, 1778. First published in the United States by Samuel Holyoke, Oliver Holden, and Hans Gram, *The Massachusetts Compiler*, Boston, 1795.[70] Printed fifty-four times prior to 1810.[71] It often carried the text written by Anne Steel, "How lovely, how divinely sweet."[72]

b. In the major mode, this "plain tune" sets one stanza of Long Meter text in duple time and was seen frequently with "How loudly, how divinely sweet" up to 1810.

c. The tune contains alternating half notes and slurred quarters. Phrase 4 copies the opening phrase exactly. The 1853, 1856, 1857, and 1866 sources omit the tenor voice in phrase 3, creating an "antiphonal" effect.

d. Phrases are separated from each other by a half note and/or a rest in a manner of "gathering note." The shape of the first part of the tune varies markedly in phrase 2 in early sources. Pitch differences, placed between brackets, are as follows:

1808	3 {21212 57217}	6 5
1822/33	3 {21 212572 1}	6 5
1837	3 {21 752 17}	6 5
1853, etc.	3 {21 7231 7}	6 5

The triplets of 1822 and 1833 gradually become smoothed out in the version of 1853 and subsequent sources.

e. Texts used:

08/22/33/37	HTMTFT	Happy the man that finds the grace
53/56/57	SITWMG	Sweet is the work, my God, my King
66	HATARL	Holy and true and righteous Lord

Additional references:
1. Crawford, *Core Repertory*, no. 63
2. Temperley, *HTI*, no. 3965a, b
3. Wasson, HI, no. 23621

PORTUGAL   NHT: 1866

1. 51231354321
2. 3217231765
3. 553564235315332
4. 51231354321   Meter: LM

1808	5123135432		PORTUGAL	HTMTFT		A	1/2
1822	5123135432	BANGNMH	PORTUGAL	HTMTFT	Thorley		
1833	5123135432	BANGNMH	PORTUGAL	HTMTFT	Thorley	G	3/4
1837	5123135432	LANEG-H	PORTUGAL	HTMTFT	Thorley	G	3/4
1848 X							
1849 X							
1853	5123135432	WOODILZ	PORTUGAL	SITWMG	Thorley	G	1/4
1856	5123135432	WOODINLZ	PORTUGAL	SITWMG	Thorley	G	1/4
1857	5123135432	=====HU	PORTUGAL	SITWMG	Thorley	G	2/4
1866	5123135432	PHILPNHT	PORTUGAL	HATARL	Thorley	G	1/4
1878 X							

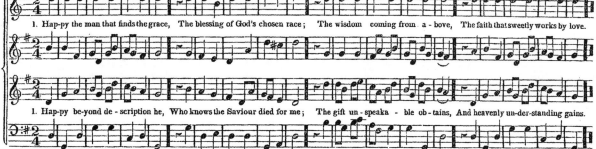

50. **ROCHESTER**

a. First published in Israel Holdroyd, *The Spiritual-Man's Companion*, London, ca. 1722. First published in the United States in James Lyon, *Urania*, Philadelphia, 1761.[73] Printed eighty-three times prior to 1810.[74] Its earliest text was from Watts, Ps. 73, "God my supporter and my hope."

b. This major mode Common Meter "plain tune" in duple time was paired with many different texts.

c. ROCHESTER is strongly characterized by dactyls: ♪ ♪ ♪ ♩ ♩. Its regular mixture of long and short values recalls Genevan tune style. The tune rises by a sixth in the first half of the tune, and descends to the lower dominant close to the end.

d. The tune appears in 1822, 1833, and 1837 in duple time, whereas later sources use triple (3/2) meter. Beginning in 1837, phrase 2 includes a raised subdominant as penultimate pitch in the tune.

e. Texts used:

22/33/37	GGTMTS	Great God! to me the sigh
53/56	MSCMTD	My soul, come mediate the day
57	TDNBHD	That doleful night before his death
66	TLHBMG	Thou, Lord hast blessed my going

Additional references:
1. Crawford, *Core Repertory*, no. 75
2. Temperley, *HTI*, no. 967a
3. Wasson, *HI*, no. 25534

ROCHESTER   NHT: 1866

1. 11231271
2. 345645
3. 54365432
4. 3154321   Meter: CM

1808 X							
1822	1123127134	BANGNMH	ROCHESTER	GGTMTS		A	3/4
1833	1123127134	BANGNMH	ROCHESTER	GGTMTS		A	3/4
1837	11231271345	LANEG-H	ROCHESTER	GGTMTS		A	3/4
1848 X							
1849 X							
1853	1123127134	WOODILZ	ROCHESTER	MSCMTD	English	G	1/4
1856	1123127134	WOODINLZ	ROCHESTER	MSCMTD	English	G	1/4
1857	1123127134	=====HU	ROCHESTER	TDNBHD	Williams	G	2/4
1866	1123127134	PHILPNHT	ROCHESTER	TLHBMG	Holdroyd	G	1/4
1878 X							

18   HYMN 180   ROCHESTER. C. M.

1. Great God! to me the sight af-ford, To him of old al-low'd; And let my faith be-hold its Lord, De-scending in a cloud.

3. Je-ho-vah, Christ, I thee a-dore, Who gav'st my soul to be! Foun-tain of be-ing, and of power, And great in ma-jes-ty.

51. **ST. ANN'S** by William Croft (1678–1727)

a. First published in Brady and Tate, *A Supplement to the New Version*, 6th ed., London, 1708. First published in the United States in William Dawson, *The Youths Entertaining Amusement*, Philadelphia, 1754.[75] Printed eighty-eight times before 1810.[76] Originally, it carried Watts' text from *Hymns and Spiritual Songs, Book 2*, "My God, my portion and my love."

b. This major mode Common Meter tune in duple time, often printed textless, was very popular in New England.

c. A very angular tune spanning a rising minor seventh, it is constructed in a pattern of ascent, with a dip to the dominant at the midpoint. It remains constant throughout the period in its tune shape, except for 1857, where the close of phrase 3 reads 865 instead of the usual 867. Passing note and secondary harmonies are used with variety.

d. In 1822 and 1833, the first and third phrases are marked with a fermata on the last pitch, and a rest separates the second and third phrases. In 1837, only two fermatas are at the midpoint and end. Subsequent sources omit all "holds," indicating that the steady half-note values are to be sung in time. Only in 1878, in an attempt to recover some original intent, does the score once again include two fermatas, those at midpoint and end.

The 1866 source curiously specifies 3/2 time, but is actually 2/4 plus 3/2 in this pattern for each phrase: ♩♩♩♩♩♩♩.

e. Texts used:

22/33/37	MGMPAM	My God, my portion and my love
48	LUYHTT	Lift up your hearts to things above
53/56	HSTYST	How shall the young secure their hearts
57	OGWPTA	O God we praise thee and confess
66	JTLTTT	Jesus the Life, the Truth, the Way
78	OWAKAE	O where are kings and empires now

Additional references:
1. Crawford, *Core Repertory*, no. 77
2. Temperley, *HTI*, no. 664a
3. Wasson, *HI*, no. 25918

ST. ANN'S   HWT: 1878

1. 53658878
2. 585645
3. 78627867
4. 5678278   Meter: CM

1808 X							
1822	5365887858	BANGNMH	ST. ANN'S	MGMPAM	Croft	C	3/4
1833	5365887858	BANGNMH	ST. ANN'S	MGMPAM	Croft	C	3/4
1837	5365887858	LANEG-H	ST. ANN'S	MGMPAM	Croft	C	3/4
1848	5365887858	JACKSSH	ST. ANN'S	LUYHTT	Croft	D	3/6
1849 X							
1853	5365687858	WOODILZ	ST. ANN'S	HSTYST	Croft	D	1/4
1856	5365687858	WOODINLZ	ST. ANN'S	HSTYST	Croft	D	1/4
1857	5365887858	=====HU	ST. ANN'S	OGWPTA	Croft	D	2/4
1866	5365887858	PHILPNHT	ST. ANN'S	JTLTTT	CroftW	C	1/4
1878	5365887858	NELSHWT	ST. ANN'S	OWAKAE	CroftW	C	1/4

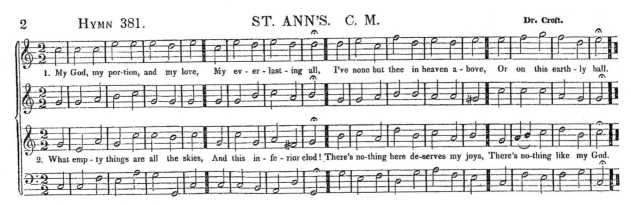

2 HYMN 381.   ST. ANN'S. C. M.   Dr. Croft.

1. My God, my por-tion, and my love, My ev-er-last-ing all, I've none but thee in heaven a-bove, Or on this earth-ly ball.

2. What emp-ty things are all the skies, And this in-fe-rior clod! There's no-thing here de-serves my joys, There's no-thing like my God.

52. ST. MARTIN'S (GAINSBOROUGH) by William Tans'ur (1706–1783)

a. First published in William Tans'ur, *The Royal Psalmodist Compleat*, [n.p.], 1748. First published in the United States in Thomas Walter, *The Grounds and Rules of Musick Explained*, [7th ed.], Boston, ca. 1759. Printed 137 times prior to 1810. It formerly was paired with Watts' "Behold the glories of the Lamb."

b. This major mode Common Meter "plain tune" in triple time appeared with many texts.

c. Main characteristics of this tune are the dotted rhythm patterns within frequent slurs throughout the tune. It contains for the most part stepwise motion, and alternates cadences which end on the dominant (first and third) and the tonic (second and fourth).

d. The tune never varies, and the settings change only in minor details, such as addition or omission of passing notes.

e. Texts used:

22/33/37/57	OGOHIA	O God! our help in ages past
53/56	OTTWAC	O Thou, to whom all creatures bow
66	LWWBBT	Lord! when we bend before thy throne
78	CHSHDW	Come, Holy Spirit, heavenly Dove, with
	CLUUTG	Come, let us use the grace divine

Additional references:
1. Crawford, *Core Repertory*, no. 82
2. Temperley, *HTI*, no. 1929
3. Wasson, *HI*, no. 26247

ST. MARTIN'S (GAINSBOROUGH)   HWT: 1878

1. 112151233454312
2. 354312171
3. 3456543345432
4. 565432171   Meter: CM

1808	1121512334	EVANJDC	GAINSBOROUGH	GHFAW		A	3/4
1822	1121512334	BANGMH	GAINSBOROUGH	OGOHIA	Smith	A	3/4
1833	1121512334	BANGNMH	GAINSBOROUGH	OGOHIA	Smith	A	3/4
1837	1121512334	LANEG-H	GAINSBOROUGH	OGOHIA	Tansur	A	3/4
1848	X						
1849	X						
1853	1121512334	WOODILZ	ST. MARTIN'S	OTTWAC	Tansur	G	1/4
1856	1121512334	WOODINLZ	ST. MARTIN'S	OTTWAC	Tansur	G	1/4
1857	1121512334	=====HU	ST. MARTIN'S	OGOHIA	Tansur	G	2/4

| 1866 1121512334 | PHILPNHT | ST. MARTIN'S | LWWBBT | Tansur | G | 1/4 |
| 1878 1121512334 | NELSHWT | ST. MARTIN'S | CHSHDW | Tansur | G | 1/4 |

53. ST. MICHAEL'S (HANOVER)

a. In all sources it is attributed to Rippon or Handel. Frost claims it is first found in the Tate and Brady *Supplement to the New Version of Psalms*, 1708, without a name.[77] Temperley in the *Hymn Tune Index* locates the name HANOVER first in William Lawrence, *A Collection of Tunes*, London, 1722.[78] Wesley used the name BROMSWICK in *The Foundery Collection*, 1742, and renamed it TALLY'S for *Sacred Melody*, 1765. It is usually attributed to Dr. Croft, who edited the 1708 book two years before Handel arrived in England. First published in the United States in John Tufts, *An Introduction to the Singing of the Psalm-Tunes*, 5th ed., Boston, 1726.

b. This tune is a "plain tune" in triple meter in the major mode. Its meter is 10.10.11.11.

c. The tune is marked by an arch shape to each half of the tune, and a solid half-note rhythm, which moves in steps much of the time. The end of the tune is marked by an unusual number of leaps. Except for the 1848 source, all versions use home-key harmonies with the addition of the raised fourth for the dominant cadence that ends phrase 2.

d. The tune evolves in its profile in the following ways:

1808,				
1822/33,				
1848:	5112351271 232171217655	712316	43215	56712536271
1853/56:	5112551271 2321712165	512316	43215	56712536271
1866:	5112351271 23217121765	512316	43215	56712536271

It is the 1848 source that introduces frequent use of secondary dominants, and florid passing notes, but the 1866 version reverts to the simplicity of earlier versions.

e. Texts used:

08/22/33	OATPBT	O all that pass by to Jesus
48	ATTTLW	All thanks to the Lamb, who gives
53/56	TTAADA	Though troubles assail, and dangers affright
66	APTTLA	All praise to the Lamb! accepted I am

Additional references:
1. Crawford, *Core Repertory*, no. 72
2. Temperley, *HTI*, no. 657a
3. Wasson, *HI*, no. 11283

ST. MICHAEL'S (HANOVER)   NHT: 1866

1. *5112351271*
2. *23217121765*
3. *51231643215*
4. *56712536271*   Meter: 10.10.11.11

1808 *5112351271*	EVANJDC	HANOVER	OATPBT	Rippon	B♭	1/2
1822 *5112351271*	BANGNMH	HANOVER	OATPBT	Handel	B♭	3/4
1833 *5112351271*	BANGNMH	HANOVER	OATPBT	Handel	B♭	3/4
1837 X						
1848 *5112351271*	JACKSSH	HANOVER	ATTTLW	Handel	A♭	3/4
1849 X						
1853 *5112551271*	WOODILZ	ST. MICHAEL'S	TTAADA	Handel	A	1/4
1857 X						
1856 *5112351271*	WOODINLZ	ST. MICHAEL'S	TTAADA	Handel	A	1/4
1866 *5112351271*	PHILPNHT	ST. MICHAEL'S	APTTLA		B♭	1/4
1878 X						

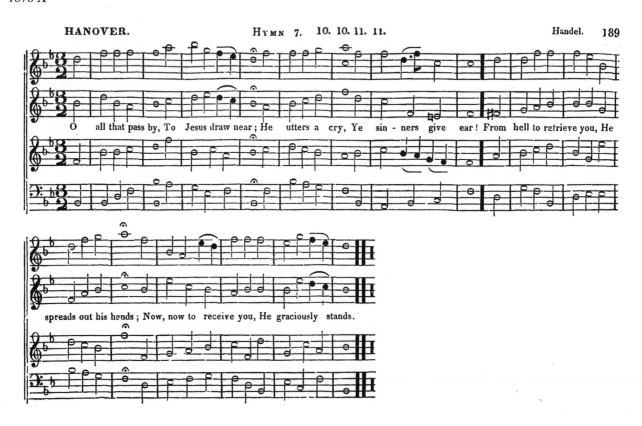

54. ST. THOMAS by Aaron Williams (1731–1776)

a. First published in Thomas Knibb, *The Psalm Singer's Help*, London, ca. 1769.[79] First published in the United States in Andrew Law, *Select Harmony*, Cheshire, CT, 1778, and printed fifty-one times prior to 1810.[80] Its early appearances accompanied Watts' Psalm 148, "Let every creature join to praise."

b. This major mode Short Meter tune in duple time was printed with many differing texts. It is a "plain tune" except for 1853, 1856, and 1857, where the tenor voice is given in small notes only; ST. THOMAS may be termed a plain antiphonal tune for these versions.

c. Phrases 1 and 3 of this tune contain leaps within the octave, whereas phrases 2 and 4 proceed entirely by step motion. There is an attempt to embellish the tune in 1848, but the tune profile is the same at the beginning and the end of this nineteenth-century period.

d. Most sources indicate that the final note of each phrase is to be elongated through use of a fermata, or a related rest. The 1848 source drops all such indications. The tune's profile also changes in 1848 through use of passing notes, especially in phrase 3: 1837—5 31 *25* 13 55 6; 1848—5 31 *217* 134 55 6.

The influence of "correct" music is felt in subsequent versions. The 1849 source reclaims use of fermatas, and is cautious in use of passing tones. In sources from 1853, 1856, and 1857, there is antiphonal writing as noted above, but the overall content compares with 1849. The next notable change is the 1878 source, where rhythms are "smoothed out" (e.g., the beginning of phrase 2 becomes ♩. ♩ ♩ instead of ♩. ♪ ♩).

e. Texts used:

22/33	JMLATF	Jesus, my Lord, attend thy feeble
37	OMTPWI	O may the powerful word inspire
48	BBTTTB	Blest be the tie that binds
49	TBTCRI	To bless thy chosen race in mercy
53/56	MSRHPW	My soul, repeat his praise
57/66	AASTSO	Awake and sing the song of Moses
78	OCADIM	O come and dwell in me

Additional references:
1. Crawford, *Core Repertory*, no. 83
2. Temperley, *Music of the English Parish Church*, 1: 176
3. Temperley, *HTI*, no. 2933b
4. Wasson, *HI*, no. 26374

ST. THOMAS

HWT: 1878

1. 5113212
2. 34543432
3. 53125135
4. 5654321

Meter: SM

1808 X							
1822	5113212345	BANGNMH	ST. THOMAS	JMLATF	Handel	A	3/4
1833	5113212345	BANGNMH	ST. THOMAS	JMLATF	Handel	A	3/4
1837	5113212345	LANEG-H	ST. THOMAS	OMTPWI	Williams	A	3/4
1848	5112321234	JACKSSH	ST. THOMAS	BBTTTB	Williams	A	3/6
1849	5113212345	DINGCDH	ST. THOMAS	TBTCRI	Williams	A	3/4
1853	5113212345	WOODILZ	ST. THOMAS	MSRHPW	Williams	G	1/4
1856	5113212345	WOODINLZ	ST. THOMAS	MSRHPW	Williams	G	1/4
1857	5113212345	=====HU	ST. THOMAS	AASTSO	Williams	G	2/4
1866	5113212345	PHILPNHT	ST. THOMAS	AASTSO	Williams Co	G	1/4
1878	5113212345	NELSHWT	ST. THOMAS	OCADIM	Handel	G	1/4

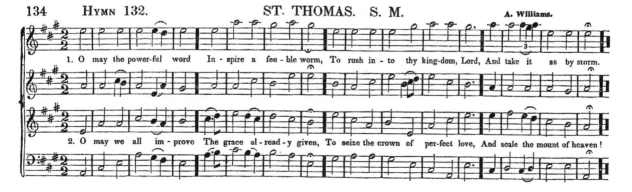

134   Hymn 132.   ST. THOMAS.   S. M.   A. Williams.

1. O may the power-ful word In-spire a fee-ble worm, To rush in-to thy king-dom, Lord, And take it as by storm.

2. O may we all im-prove The grace al-read-y given, To seize the crown of per-fect love, And scale the mount of heaven!

55. SCOTLAND by John Clarke-Whitfield (1770–1836)

a. First published appearance is unknown.

b. This example is a "set piece" in triple time which is extended by a repeat of the second half. It accompanies text with the meter 12.12.12.12.

c. A feature of the tune is melodic use of primary chords. The 1853 and 1856 sources show a "corrected" version of the tune, but 1857, 1866, and 1878 reclaim the original melodic profile.

d. The profile of phrase 3 undergoes change in 1853 and 1856:

```
    1837    2 235432 353 212342 355 54321 166 51332
    1853    2 242 353 242 355 531 166 513 32
```

The harmonic setting remains simple based on primary chords in all tunebooks examined.

e. Text used:

1833/37/53/56/57/66/78   TVOFGC   The voice of free grace cries

Additional reference:
Wasson, *HI*, no. 26813

SCOTLAND   HWT: 1878

```
1. 5565513321235
2. 5531161651332
3. 2235432353211234235
4. 554321161651332
x  235335121231
    (or 12121)
```
                                                                                Meter: 12.12.12.12

1808 X						
1822 X						
1833 5565513321	BANGNMH	VOICE OF	TVOFGC	Clark	B♭	3/4
1837 5565513321	LANEG-H	VOICE OF	TVOFGC	Clark	B♭	3/4
1848 X						
1849 X						
1853 3456551332	WOODILZ	SCOTLAND	TAGTTG	Clarke	A	3/4
1856 3456551332	WOODINLZ	SCOTLAND	TVOFGC/TAGTTG		A	3/4
1857 5565513321	=====HU	VOICE OF FREE	TVOFGC	Clarke	B♭	2/4
1866 5565513321	PHILPNHT	SCOTLAND	TVOFGC	ClarkeJ	B♭	1/4
1878 5565513321	NELSHWT	SCOTLAND	TVOFGC	ClarkeJ	A	1/4
(345655133)						

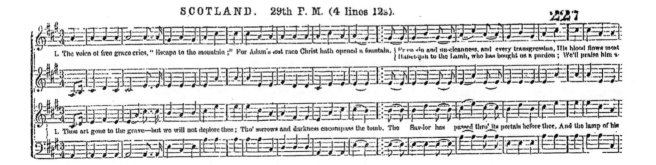

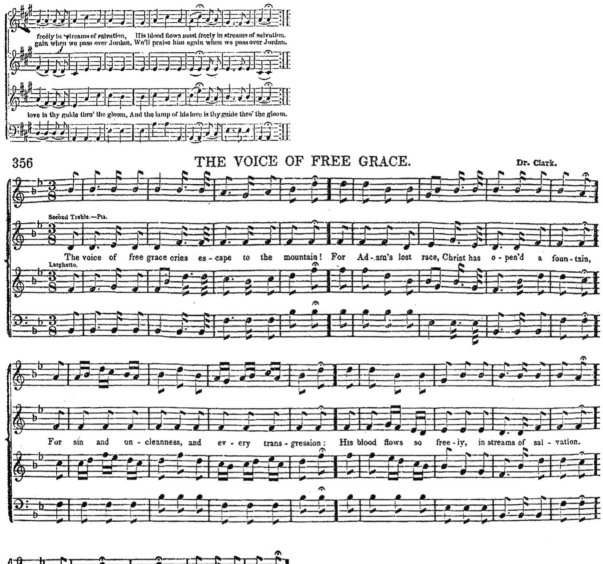

56. **SHIRLAND** by Samuel Stanley (1767–1822)

a. First published in Samuel Stanley's *Twenty-Four Tunes in Four Parts, composed chiefly to Dr. Watts' Psalms and Hymns*, Birmingham, [1802]. First publication in the United States in Joel Harmon, *Musical Primer*, Harrisburg, ca. 1814, and in Isaac Cole, *The Philadelphia Third Presbyterian Church Collection*, Philadelphia, 1815.[81]

b. SHIRLAND is a plain antiphonal tune in duple time in the major mode. It accompanies Short Meter texts.

c. There are many slurred passages. The third and longest phrase is frequently set in three parts (antiphonal) as seen in many compositions of the period.

d. The tune does not change throughout the period. Variations in the settings are seen with particular reference to phrase 3, where three-part writing prevails until the 1849 source, in which two parts are in bold, and two parts are in small notation. The 1857 and 1866 sources revert to the simpler three-part style, but 1878 provides four parts for the whole piece, with rapidly shifting harmonies supporting the active tune.

e. Texts used:

22/33/37/49	MGMLML	My God, my life, my love
48	JMTMWM	Jesus, my truth, my way, my sure
53/56	BTMSBH	Behold! the morning sun begins his
57	JWLTTT	Jesus, we look to thee, thy promise
66	HTTSDT	Hail to the Sabbath day! The day
78	HICFRI	Here I can firmly rest; I dare

Additional references:
1. Temperley, *HTI*, no. 7866b
2. Wasson, *HI*, no. 27318

SHIRLAND   HWT: 1878

1. 12342571
2. 172536545
3. 1332244335544332
4. 23456321   Meter: SM

1808 X

1822	1234257117	BANGNMH	SHIRLAND	MGMLML		A	3/4
1833	1234257117	BANGNMH	SHIRLAND	MGMLML		A	3/4
1837	1234257117	LANEG-H	SHIRLAND	MGMLML	Stanley	A	3/4
1848	1234257117	JACKSSH	SHIRLAND	JMTMWM	Stanley	A	3/4
1849	1234257117	DINGCDH	SHIRLAND	MGMLML	Stanley	A	3/4
1853	1234257117	WOODILZ	SHIRLAND	BTMSBH	Stanley	G	1/4
1856	1234257117	WOODINLZ	SHIRLAND	BTMSBH	Stanley	G	1/4
1857	1234257117	=====HU	SHIRLAND	JWLTTT	Stanley	G	2/4
1866	1234257117	PHILPNHT	SHIRLAND	HTTSDT	Stanley	G	1/4
1878	1234257117	NELSHWT	SHIRLAND	HICFRI	Stanley	G	1/4

57. **SICILIAN HYMN** (DISMISSAL)

a. The melody, which may have been carried from Italy by poet J. G. von Herder to Germany (ca. 1789), appeared in the *European Magazine* 22, 1792. It first appeared in England in *Improved Psalmody*, W. D. Tattersall, ed., ca. 1793.[82] Temperley locates the first U.S. appearance in John Aitkin, *Aitkin's Collection of Divine Music*, Philadelphia, 1806.[83] It may have appeared in earlier to the text "Lord, dismiss us," gaining its alternate name, DISMISSAL, or in many sources such as Joel Harmon, *Musical Primer*, Harrisburg, ca. 1814, DISMISSION.

b. This is a plain antiphonal tune in the major mode. It uses duple time and accompanies text with 4 Sevens or 87.87 meter. In the 1849 source it is attributed to Mozart.

c. When paired with 4 Sevens text, the first and third phrases end with a slurred group; when the meter is 87.87, there is a new syllable for each beat. An interesting feature is the mixture of note values: quarters, eighth-note pairs, dotted eighth, sixteenth, and half-note patterns.

d. The 1822 and 1833 and 1848 sources are the only ones to contain no antiphonal section. The shape of the tune never changes, although a repeat of the second half (to accommodate extra text) is introduced with the 1848 source and imitated in 1853, 1856, 1857, and 1866.

e. Texts used:

22/33/37	LWCBTN	Lord, we come before thee now
48	OTGOMS	O thou God of my salvation
49	CMSTSP	Come, my soul, thy suit prepare
53/56/66	LDUWTB	Lord, dismiss us with thy blessing
57	GMOTGJ	Guide me, O thou great Jehovah

Additional references:
1. W. Baeumker, *Katholische deutsche Kirchenlied*, 1962
2. Johann von der Heydt, *Geschichte der Evangelischen Kirchenmusik*, 1926
3. Temperley, *HTI*, no. 6141b, g
4. Wasson, *HI*, 27385

SICILIAN HYMN (DISMISSAL)   NHT: 1866

1. 56543456543
2. 55678765
3. 232344343455   Meter: 77.77
4. 87658654321   *or* 87.87.47 *or* 87.87.87

1808 X

1822	5654345654	BANGNMH	SICILIAN HY	LWCBTN	F	2/3
1833	5654345654	BANGNMH	SICILIAN HY	LWCBTN	F	2/3
1837	5654345654	LANEG-H	SICILIAN HY	LWCBTN	F	3/4
1848	5654345654	JACKSSH	SICILIAN HY	OTGOMS	F	3/4
1837	5654345654	LANEG-H	SICILIAN HY	LWCBTN	F	3/4
1849	5654345654	DINGCDH	SICILIAN HY	CMSTSP Mozart	F	3/4
1853	5654345654	WOODILZ	SICILIAN HY	LDUWTB Mason	F	3/4
1856	5654345654	WOODINLZ	SICILIAN HY	LDUWTB	F	3/4
1857	5654345654	=====HU	SICILIAN HY	GMOTGJ	F	2/4
1866	5654345654	PHILPNHT	SICILIAN HY	LDUWTB Mozart	F	1/4

1878 X

58. SILVER STREET (FALCON STREET, NEWTON) by Isaac Smith (1734–1805)

a. First published in Isaac Smith, *A Collection of Psalm Tunes in Three Parts*, London, [1779–1780]. First published in the United States in [Simeon Jocelin], *The Chorister's Companion*, 2nd ed., New Haven, 1788.[84] Printed sixty-one times prior to 1810. It was seen often with Watts' Psalm 95.

b. This tune in Short Meter in the major mode uses duple time. Baldridge names it a "revival tune" up to 1837, due to the inclusion of a refrainlike "Hallelujah" ending.[85] Thereafter, sources contain a thirteen-measure "plain tune" without the refrain section. It is attributed variously to Miller, to J. Smith, and to Isaac Smith in the tunebooks of this survey.

c. SILVER STREET is an angular tune punctuated by rests occurring between phrases.

d. The 1808 source is remarkable in the use of secondary dominant material in the cadences of both phrases 2 and 3. The "Hallelujah" ending in this and the 1822, 1833, and 1837 sources is in antiphonal style, with a solo voice inviting the response. The 1848 is the first to drop the refrain, and many chromatic and secondary dominant additions are employed. The 1878 source is the only one to smooth out the opening rhythm, in which ♩. ♪ ♩ ♩ 𝄾 becomes ♩ ♩ ♩ ♩.

e. Texts used:

22/33/37/48	CYTLTL	Come, ye that love the Lord
53/56/57/78	CSHPAA	Come, sound his praise abroad, and hymns
66	WSDORT	Welcome, sweet day of rest that saw

Additional references:
1. Crawford, *Core Repertory*, no. 57
2. Temperley, *HTI*, no. 4091a
3. Wasson, *HI*, no. 27443

SILVER STREET (FALCON STREET, NEWTON)   HWT: 1878

1. 855358
2. *32*586545
3. 58*3*85656787
4. 567823*28*   Meter: SM

1808	8553583258	EVANJDC	FALCON ST	CYTLTL	Miller	C	3/4
1822	8553583258	BANGNMH	FALCON ST	CYTLTL	Smith	C	3/4
1833	8553583258	BANGNMH	FALCON ST	CYTLTL	Smith	C	3/4
1837	8553583258	LANEG-H	FALCON ST	CYTLTL	Smith	C	3/4
1848	8553583258	JACKSSH	FALCON ST	CYTLTL	Smith	C	3/6
1849	X						
1853	X						

1856	8553583258	WOODINLZ	SILVER STR	CSHPAA	Smith	C	1/4
1857	8553583258	=====HU	SILVER STR	CSHPAA	Smith	C	2/4
1866	8553583258	PHILPNHT	SILVER STR	WSDORT	Smith	C	1/4
1878	8553583258	NELSHWT	SILVER STR	CSHPAA	Smith	C	1/4
				GTACSH			

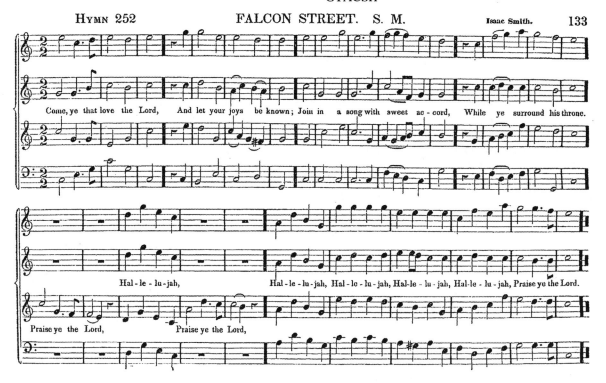

HYMN 252   FALCON STREET. S. M.   Isaac Smith.   133

Come, ye that love the Lord, And let your joys be known; Join in a song with sweet ac - cord, While ye surround his throne.

Hal - le - lu - jah, Hal - le - lu - jah, Hal - le - lu - jah, Hal-le - lu - jah, Hal-le - lu - jah, Praise ye the Lord.

Praise ye the Lord, Praise ye the Lord,

59. STEPHEN'S

a. First published at the end of Rev. William Jones, *Ten Church Pieces for the Organ*, [1789], where it is set to Psalm 23 and called St. Stephen's Tune.[86] The first appearance in the United States is Samuel Dyer, *A New Selection of Sacred Music, comprising . . . psalms and hymn tunes*, Baltimore, 1817.[87]

b. This Common Meter "plain tune" is set in the major mode in duple time.

c. Slurred pairs are often encountered on the weak beats of 2 and 4 of the measure. The tune employs mostly stepwise motion. The use of a secondary dominant should be noted in all sources to commence the final phrase, rather than support a cadence.

d. The rhythm of the passing notes in measures 1 and 4 changes to a dotted pattern in 1849, 1856, 1857, and 1866. The 1878 source reverts to the 1833 and 1837 pattern of passing quarter notes.

e. Texts used:

33/37/49/56/57	FHMRSB	Forever here my rest shall be
66	JMLICT	Jesus my Lord, I cry to thee
78	FHWTGS	Father, how wide thy glory shines

Additional references:
1. Temperley, *HTI*, no. 5168
2. Wasson, *HI*, no. 26358

STEPHEN'S   HWT: 1878

1. 1532121712
2. 34512321
3. 342345217
4. 6512321   Meter: CM

1808	X						
1822	X						
1833	1532121712	BANGNMH	STEPHENS	FHMRSB	Jones	B♭	3/4
1837	1532121712	LANEG-H	STEPHENS	FHMRSB	Jones	B♭	3/4
1848	1531217123	JACKSSH	ST. STEPHEN'S	MSMAFW	Jones	A	3/4
1849	1532121712	DINGCDH	STEPHENS	FHMRSB	Jones	A	3/4
1853	X						
1856	1532121712	WOODINLZ	STEPHENS	FHMRSB	Jones	A	2/4
1857	1532121712	=====HU	STEPHEN'S	FHMRSB	Jones	A	2/4
1866	1532121712	PHILPNHT	ST. STEPHEN'S	JMLICT	Jones	A	1/4
1878	1532121712	NELSHWT	STEPHENS	FHWTGS	Jones	G	1/4

50   HYMN 305.   STEPHENS.   C. M.   John Jones.

1. For ev - er here my rest shall be, Close to thy bleed-ing side; This all my hope, and all my plea, For me the Sa-viour died.

2. My dy-ing Sa-viour, and my God, Foun-tain for guilt and sin, Sprin-kle me ev - er with thy blood, And cleanse and keep me clean.

60. **STONEFIELD** (DOVERSDALE) by Samuel Stanley (1767–1822)

a. First published in Edward Miller, *Dr. Watts's Psalms and Hymns, Set to Music*, London, [1800]. The first U.S. appearance is Samuel Dyer, *A New Selection of Sacred Music*, Baltimore, 1817.[88]

b. This is a plain antiphonal tune in the major mode which accompanies Long Meter text in triple (3/2) time.

c. STONEFIELD rises and falls by step motion most of the time, and uses secondary dominants in orthodox fashion. The third phrase is charming in its sequential structure.

d. The tune remains unchanged except in two instances in these tunebooks. The opening motive reads 1 3432 1, except in 1848, where the profile is 1 5432 1. The harmonies are identical for each. In the same source, a passing note is inserted in measure 6 to fill in the leap of a third.

   The antiphonal section is typically the third phrase, where the tenor is always omitted, although in 1849, 1853, and 1856 the bass is provided in small-note notation only.

e. Texts used:

33/37	FOAWPV	Father of all, whose powerful voice
48	TLIKAE	The Lord is King, and earth
49	FATDBT	From all that dwells below the skies
53/56	HSFTGS	How sweetly flowed the gospel sound
57	HEOTTD	Ho! every one that thirsts draw

Additional references:
1. Temperley, *HTI*, no. 8256
2. Wasson, *HI*, no. 28711

STONEFIELD (DOVERSDALE)   HU: 1857

1. 13432155678
2. 888756545
3. 55654344454323
4. 55678554321   Meter: LM

1808 X							
1822 X							
1833	1343215567	BANGNMH	STONEFIELD	FOAWPV	Stanley	E	3/4
1837	1343215567	LANEG-H	STONEFIELD	FOAWPV	Stanley	E	3/4
1848	1543215567	JACKSSH	STONEFIELD	TLIKAE	Stanley	E	3/4
1849	1343215567	DINGCDH	STONEFIELD	FATDBT	Stanley	E	3/4
1853	1343215567	WOODILZ	STONEFIELD	HSFTGS	Stanley	E♭	1/4
1856	1343215567	WOODINLZ	STONEFILED	HSFTGS		E♭	1/4
1857	1343215567	=====HU	STONEFIELD	HEOTTD		E♭	2/4
1866 X							
1878 X							

61. **SWANWICK** by James Lucas (b. ca. 1762)

a. First published (variant form) in William Dixon, *Psalmodia Christiana*, Guildford, 1789. First appearance in the United States is likely *The Beauties of Psalmody . . . adapted to Dr. Watts's Psalms and Hymns*, Baltimore, 1804.[89]

b. This is an antiphonal tune-with-extension in the major mode using triple time (3/4). The musical extension requires the repeat of the fourth line of the Common Meter text.

c. The tune is in five phrases with no repeats; the third phrase is printed in two, three, or four parts and may include an ornament (measure 9) of eighth note plus two sixteenths, or a triplet figure. The figure is dropped altogether after 1857. Secondary dominants are orthodox; phrase 5 uses descending chromatics in all but 1822 and 1833.

d. The melody changes in only one respect in this period. The opening of phrase 4 changes from *5567* 1 to *557* 1. Whereas most sources place the third and/or fourth phrases over a pedal point, the 1848 source places the dominant pedal in the alto line, with the bass exploring chromatics.

e. Texts used:

22/33/37/49/57	IKTMRL	I know that my Redeemer lives
48	EWTWPT	Eternal Wisdom! thee we praise; thee
53/56	AYPAAE	Arise, ye people and adore; exulting
66	WGGTSP	What glory gilds the sacred page

Additional references:
1. Temperley, *HTI*, no. 5104
2. Wasson, *HI*, no. 29015

SWANWICK

NHT: 1866

1. 51123132171
2. 34321765
3. 332117554332
4. 5567123443212171

Meter: CM

1808 X

1822	5113313217	BANGNMH	SWANWICK	IKTMRL	Lucas	B♭	3/4
1833	5113313217	BANGNMH	SWANWICK	IKTMRL	Lucas	B♭	3/4
1837	5112313217	LANEG-H	SWANWICK	IKTMRL	Lucas	B♭	3/4
1848	5112313217	JACKSSH	SWANWICK	EWTWPT	Lucas	B♭	3/4
1849	5112313217	DINGCDH	SWANWICK	IKTMRL	Lucas	B♭	3/4
1853	5112313217	WOODILZ	SWANWICK	AYPAAE	Lucas	A	1/4
1856	5112313217	WOODINLZ	SWANWICK	AYPAAE	Lucas	A	1/4
1857	5112313217	=====HU	SWANWICK	IKTMRL	Lucas	A	2/4
1866	5112313217	PHILPNHT	SWANWICK	WGGTSP	LucasJ	A	1/4

1878 X

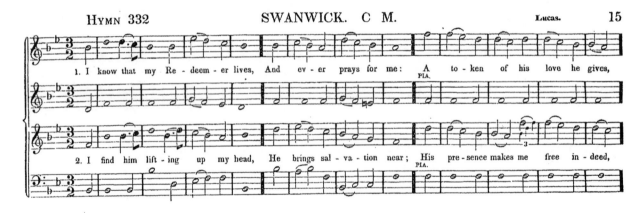

62. THATCHER (DAVID, GERMANY, HALLAM, HANDEL, THACHER) by G. F. Handel (1685–1759)

a. The original tune first appeared in Handel's opera *Sosarme* (1732).[90] The first appearance of the tune as examined is in [Henry Ranlet?], *The Village Harmony*, 7th ed., Exeter, 1806.[91]

b. This "plain tune" in the major mode accompanies Short Meter; it uses triple time.

c. It is attributed to Handel in most sources. There is no apparent reason for the name changes.

d. There is one rhythmic variant in the tune in the 1822 and 1833 sources, namely in measure 5. In these sources, the melodic rhythm is short-long, whereas in subsequent sources it is long-short. In pitch the tune is consistent throughout the period, except in 1848 in the version called DAVID, which bears the footnote (174):

This melody is the same subject as the tune HANDEL.

In this source the meter becomes 4 Sixes and 2 Eights rather than Short Meter.

e. Texts used:

22/33/37	GTGOHO	Glory to God on high; our peace
48	MGLLTT	My gracious, loving Lord, to thee
	TGOTAL	Thou God of truth and love
49	OBTLMS	O bless the Lord, my soul
53/56	TGIWIT	To God in whom I trust
57	IOAQST	If on a quiet sea, toward heaven
66	GWMHTH	Glad was my heart to hear
78	GWMHTH	Glad was my heart to hear
	TGITGW	This God is the God we adore

Additional references:
1. Temperley, *HTI*, no. 5698d
2. Wasson, *HI*, no. 29588

THATCHER (DAVID, HALLAM, HANDEL, GERMANY, THACHER)   HWT: 1878

1. 13215432
2. *5123671*
3. 15433211712
4. 3456321   Meter: SM

1808 X

1822 1321543251	BANGNMH	THACHER	GTGOHO	Handel	A	3/4
1833 1321543251	BANGNMH	THACHER	GTGOHO	Handel	G	3/4
1837 1321543251	LANEG-H	THACHER	GTGOHO	Handel	A	3/4
1848 1321543251	JACKSSH	HANDEL	MGLLTT	Handel	A	3/4
1321543251	JACKSSH	DAVID	TGOTAL	Handel	B♭	3/4
1849 1321543251	DINGCDH	THATCHER	OBTLMS	Handel	A	3/4
1853 1321543251	WOODILZ	THATCHER	TGIWIT	Handel	G	3/4
1856 1321543251	WOODINLZ	THATCHER	TGIWIT	Handel	G	3/4
1857 1321543251	=====HU	THATCHER	IOAQST	Handel	G	2/4
1866 1321543251	PHILPNHT	THATCHER	GWMHTH	Handel	G	1/4
1878 1321543251	NELSHWT	THATCHER	GWMHTH	Handel	G	1/4

63. TRINITY (ITALIAN HYMN) by Felice de Giardini (1716–1796)

a. This tune first appeared in *A Collection of Psalm and Hymn Tunes*, edited by Martin Madan, London, [1760–1763]. The first U.S. source is Andrew Law, *A Collection of Hymn Tunes*, Cheshire, [1783].[92]

b. This "plain tune" in the major mode accompanies text in the meter 664.6664. It uses triple time (3/4).

c. The tune's hallmark is the triadic opening motif, which is echoed in measure 7. It is given an antiphonal-tune treatment in 1866 when in phrases 4 and 5 the tenor is omitted, and the bass is sketched. It is underlaid with only this text in this period, although it appears opposite other texts in 1857 and 1866.

d. The tune evolves in small ways over the period. The opening rhythm in sources 1822 and 1833 is . . . . . ♩ ♩ , whereas source 1837 reads . . . ♩ ♩. The tune profile in these cases is 531 27; and all subsequent sources show . . . ♩‿. . for the profile 531 217.

The final two phrases show changes such as the following:

22/33/37	111 565 432 1
48/53/56/57/78	135 565 432 1
66	131 565 432 1

The 1848 source also shows changes in measures 9–12.

e. Text used:

| 22/33/3748/53/56/57/66 | CTAKHU | Come, thou almighty King; help us |

Additional reference:
Temperley, *HTI*, no. 2792

TRINITY (ITALIAN HYMN)   NHT: 1866

1. 5312171
2. 12345432
3. 5315
4. 567654567654
5. 131565
6. 4321   Meter: 664.6664

1808 X

1822	5312711234	BANGNMH	TRINITY	CTAKHU	Giardini	G	3/4
1833	5312711234	BANGNMH	TRINITY	CTAKHU	Giardini	G	3/4
1837	5312711234	LANEG-H	TRINITY	CTAKHU	Giardini	G	3/4
1848	5312171123	JACKSSH	TRINITY	CTAKHU	Giardini	G	3/4

1849 X							
1853	5312171/123	WOODILZ	ITALIAN HY	CTAKHU	Giardini	G	1/4
1856	5312171123	WOODINLZ	ITALIAN HY	CTAKHU	Giardini	G	1/4
1857	5312171123	=====HU	ITALIAN HY	CTAKHU	Giardini	G	2/4
1866	5312171123	PHILPNHT	ITALIAN HY	CTAKHU	Giardini	G	1/4
1878 X							

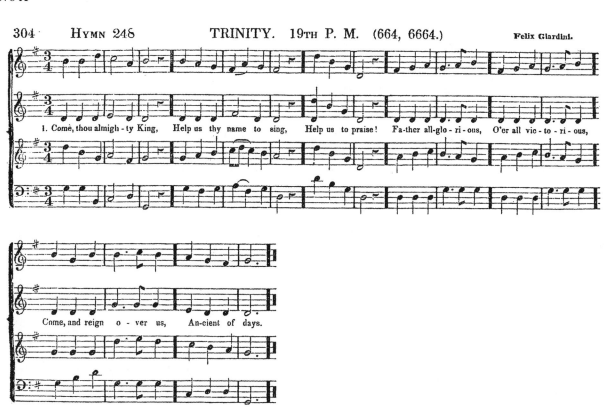

64. **TRIUMPH** by Thomas Clark (1775–1859)

a. The tune first appeared in *David's Harp*, Baltimore, 1813.[93]

b. The meter of the tune is 77.87.77.87, and it uses duple time (4/4) in the major mode. Its range is an octave and a fourth; secondary dominants are used in the traditional cadential way. Although an extension occurs in some sources, this tune is a usually a "plain antiphonal tune."

c. In 1833, the second half is repeated; hence it is an antiphonal tune-with-extension. In 1848 all four parts continue throughout, hence it is a "plain tune." All other examples are "plain antiphonal tune" settings, due to the brief thinning of the texture in phrase 3 followed immediately by full voices in phrase 4.

d. The tune remains consistent throughout, and harmonic support varies only as detailed in c (above).

e. Texts used:

22/33/37/57/66	HOTCTW	Head of the church triumphant
48	JTATGT	Jesus, take all the glory; thy
56	WATABA	Worship and thanks and blessing

Additional reference:
Temperley, *HTI*, no. 14409

TRIUMPH   NHT: 1866

1. 53432112354332
2. 5112234587576545
3. 5313586275765455
4. 58875665431321711   Meter: 77.87.77.87

1808 X

1822	5343211235	BANGNMH	TRIUMPH	HOTCTW	F	2/3
1833	5343211235	BANGNMH	TRIUMPH	HOTCTW	F	2/3
1837	5343211235	LANEG-H	TRIUMPH	HOTCTW	F	3/4
1848	5343211235	JACKSSH	TRIUMPH	JTATGT Clark	F	3/4
1849 X						
1853 X						
1856	5343211235	WOODINLZ	TRIUMPH	WATABA	F	2/4
1857	5343211235	=====HU	TRIUMPH	HOTCTW	F	2/4
1866	5343211235	PHILPNHT	TRIUMPH	HOTCTW ClarkT	F	1/4
1878 X						

320   Hymn 275.   TRIUMPH.   25th P. M.   (77, 87, 77, 87.)

1. Head of the Church triumph-ant, We joy-ful-ly a-dore thee; Till thou ap-pear, thy mem-bers here Shall sing like those in glo-ry.

2. While in af-flic-tion's fur-nace, And passing through the fire, Thy love we praise which knows no days, And ev-er brings us nigh-er.

We lift our hearts and voi-ces With blest an-ti-ci-pa-tion, And cry a-loud, and give to God The praise of our sal-va-tion.

We clap our hands ex-ult-ing In thine al-migh-ty fa-vour: The love divine which makes us thine, Can keep us thine for-ev-er

65. **TRURO** by Dr. Charles Burney (1726–1814)

a. This tune first appeared in *Musica Sacra*, Bath, ca. 1778. First U.S. appearance in Hans Gram, Samuel Holyoke, and Oliver Holden, *The Massachusetts Compiler of Theoretical and Practical Elements of Sacred Vocal Music,* Boston, 1795.[94]

b. This "plain tune" in the major mode accompanies Long Meter in duple time.

c. The tune is characterized by leaps to begin each phrase, followed by stepwise motion. The third phrase is entirely in the dominant key, through early use of the secondary dominant chord.

d. The 1808, 1822, and 1833 versions share in common the trill ornament on the penultimate note of the tune, as well as a small-note decoration three measures from the end. The decoration is gradually absorbed into the tune, and reads: 8 7654 32 1. Its effect on the tune may be seen in the following comparison:

1808/22/33 (measure 14)	5 58 234 32 1
1848	5 58 24 32 1
1837/57/66/78	5 58 2654 32 1

e. Texts used:

22/33/37/57/66	PYTLTG	Praise ye the Lord! 'tis good
48	HTMTFT	Happy the man that finds the grace
53/56	NTTLAN	Now to the Lord a noble song
78	JTEKAT	Jesus, thou everlasting King accept

Additional references:
1. Temperley, *HTI*, no. 3991a
2. Wasson, *HI*, no. 30432

TRURO   HWT: 1878

1. 13455678
2. 5854321432
3. 2567228765
4. 5582654321   Meter: LM

1808 1345567858		TRURO	PYTLTG		F	2/3
1822 1345567858	BANGNMH	TRURO	PYTLTG		F	2/3
1833 1345567858	BANGNMH	TRURO	PYTLTG		F	2/3
1837 1345567858	LANEG-H	TRURO	PYTLTG	Burney	D	3/4
1848 1345567858	JACKSSH	TRURO	HTMTFT	Burney	E♭	3/4
1849 X						
1853 1345567858	WOODILZ	TRURO	NTTLAN	Burney	D	1/4
1856 1345567858	WOODINL	TRURO	NTTLAN	Burney	D	1/4
1857 1345567858	=====HU	TRURO	PYTLTG	Burney	D	2/4
1866 1345567858	PHILPNHT	TRURO	PYTLTG	BurneyC	D	1/4
1878 1345567858	NELSHWT	TRURO	JTEKAT	BurneyC	D	1/4

66. **UXBRIDGE** by Lowell Mason (1792–1872)

a. It may have first appeared in *The Boston Handel and Haydn Society Collection of Church Music*, 9th ed., 1830, set to the text "At anchor laid, remote from home."[95]

b. This "plain tune" in the major mode accompanies Long Meter text in duple time.

c. The isorhythm ♩ ♪ ♪ ♪ ♪ ♪ ♩ governs each phrase of this tune. This arch-shaped tune ascends from the lower tonic to the upper tonic and back again to close.

d. The tune and its settings remain consistent throughout the period.

e. Texts used:

33/37/49	DNOSOG	Draw near, O Son of God
53/56/78	THDTGL	The heavens declare thy glory Lord
66	HUOLTY	Help us, O Lord thy yoke
78	OHHHLB	O holy, holy, holy Lord, bright

Additional reference:
Wasson, *HI*, no. 30874

UXBRIDGE

HWT: 1878

1. 11232171
2. 35567865
3. 58565432
4. 23554321

Meter: LM

1808	X						
1822	X						
1833	1123217135	BANGNMH	UXBRIDGE	DNOSOG	MasonL	F	3/4
1837	1123217135	LANEG-H	UXBRIDGE	DNOSOG	Mason	F	3/4
1848	X						
1849	1123217135	DINGCDH	UXBRIDGE	DNOSOG	Mason	F	3/4
1853	1123217135	WOODILZ	UXBRIDGE	THDTGL	Mason	E	1/4
1856	1123217135	WOODINLZ	UXBRIDGE	THDTGL	Mason	E	1/4
1857	X						
1866	1123217135	PHILPNHT	UXBRIDGE	HUOLTY	MasonL	E	1/4
1878	1123217135	NELSHWT	UXBRIDGE	OHHHLB	MasonL	E	1/4
				THDTGL			

98   Hymn 461.   UXBRIDGE. L. M.   Lowell Mason.

1. Draw near, O Son of God, draw near, Us with thy flaming eye behold; Still in thy Church vouchsafe t' appear, And let our can-dle-stick be gold.

2. Still hold the stars in thy right hand, And let them in thy lus-tre glow, The lights of a be-night-ed land, The an-gels of thy Church be-low.

67. **WARSAW** (BALTIMORE) by Thomas Clark (1775–1859)

a. First published in Thomas Clark, *A Third Set of Psalm & Hymn Tunes*, London, [1807]. In the United States, it first appeared in Charles Woodward, *Sacred Music in Miniature*, Philadelphia, 1812.[96]

b. The "plain tune" in duple time accompanies the meter 66.66.88.88 (except in 1822, 1833, and 1837) and is in the major mode.

c. The tune ranges over a tenth, and includes many slurred pairs. Its meter in 1822, 1833, and 1837 is 66.66.86.86, but 66.66.88.88 in sources after 1848. Secondary dominants are used conventionally except in 1853 and 1856 where they are avoided altogether.

d. The tune profiles of the closing two phrases differ in the following ways:

1822/33:	5	54	35	86	55	84	32	15	54	35	86	55	87654	32	1
1837:	5	54	35	86	55	84	32	15	54	35	86	55	864	32	1
1848:	5	54	35	876	55	82	*3*854	32	1						
1853/56:	5	54	35	86	55	82	*3*854	32	1						

e. Texts used:

22/33/37	YSSTSF	Ye simple souls that stray far from
48	CLOVJI	Come, let our voices join in one
53/56/57	JATGNO	Join all the glorious names of wisdom

Additional references:
Temperley, *HTI*, no. 11876
Wasson, *HI*, no. 31723

WARSAW (BALTIMORE)   HWT: 1878

1. 854315
2. 345678287
3. 5876562
4. 34654321
5. 55435865   Meter: 66.66.88.88
6. 582*3*854321   *or* 66.66.86.86

1808 X							
1822	8543153456	BANGNMH	BALTIMORE	YSSTSF	Clark	E	3/4
1833	8543153456	BANGNMH	BALTIMORE	YSSTSF	Clark	E	3/4
1837	8543153456	LANEG-H	BALTIMORE	YSSTSF	Clark	E	3/4
1848	5854315345	JACKSSH	WARSAW	CLOVJI	Clark	E♭	3/4
1849 X							
1853	8543153456	WOODILZ	WARSAW	JATGNO	Clark	D	1/4
1856	8543153456	WOODINLZ	WARSAW	JATGNO	Clark	D	1/4
1857	8543153456	=====HU	WARSAW	JATGNO	Clark	D	2/4
1866 X							
1878	8543153456	NELSHWT	WARSAW	AYSAAH MSAAIP	ClarkT	D	1/4

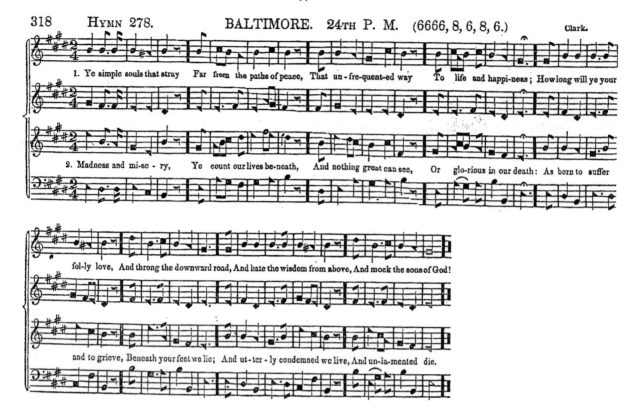

318 HYMN 278.   BALTIMORE. 24TH P. M. (6666, 8, 6, 8, 6.)   Clark.

1. Ye simple souls that stray Far from the paths of peace, That un-fre-quent-ed way To life and happi-ness; How long will ye your

2. Madness and mi-se - ry, Ye count our lives be-neath, And nothing great can see, Or glo-rious in our death: As born to suffer

fol-ly love, And throng the downward road, And hate the wisdom from above, And mock the sons of God!

and to grieve, Beneath your feet we lie; And ut-ter-ly condemned we live, And un-la-mented die.

68. **WARWICK** by Samuel J. Stanley (1767–1822)

a. First published in Edward Miller, *The Psalms of David*, London, [1790]. First U.S. appearance in Andrew Law, *The Art of Singing*, Cambridge, 1805.[97]

b. This "plain tune" in duple time accompanies Common Meter text and is in the major mode.

c. WARWICK is an angular tune, with slurred pairs placed frequently on the first two beats of the measure. Secondary dominant harmony is used in the conventional way.

d. The openings of the 1822, 1833, 1837, 1848, and 1849 sources share the following profile: 1 3586 5456 532 1. The same passage in the 1853, 1856, 1857, and 1866 sources is: 1 3586 56 5321.

　　Another melodic variant is in measure 3, where 3 567 87654 5 (1857 and 1866) gives way in the 1878 source to 3 56 87654 5.

　　The rhythm of 1822 and 1833 shows a holding note preceding a rest between phrases. That is discontinued in 1837 and subsequent versions, where the beat is uninterrupted. In 1878, however, the midpoint is marked by a whole note tied to a half note for the effect of a fermata or hold.

e. Texts used:

| 22/33/37/48/49/57 | CLUUTG | Come, let us use the grace divine |
| 53/56/66/78 | LITMTS | Lord, in the morning thou shalt |

Additional references:
1. Temperley, *HTI*, no. 8267
2. Wasson, *HI*, no. 31735

WARWICK   HWT: 1878

1. 13586565321
2. 356876545
3. 564865342543
4. 56782878   Meter: CM

1808 X
1822 X

1833	1358654565	BANGNMH	WARWICK	CLUUTG	Stanley	E♭	3/4
1837	1358654565	LANEG-H	WARWICK	CLUUTG	Stanley	E♭	3/4
1848	1358654565	JACKSSH	WARWICK	CLUUTG	Stanley	E♭	3/4
1849	1358654565	DINGCDH	WARWICK	CLUUTG	Stanley	E♭	3/4
1853	1358656532	WOODILZ	WARWICK	LITMTS	Stanley	D	1/4
1856	1358656532	WOODINLZ	WARWICK	LITMTS	Stanley	D	1/4
1857	1358656532	=====HU	WARWICK	CLUUTG	Stanley	D	2/4
1866	1358656653	PHILPNHT	WARWICK	LITMTS	Stanley	D	1/4
1878	1358656532	NELSHWT	WARWICK	LITMTS	Stanley	D	1/4

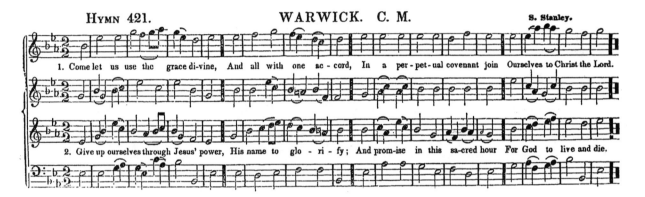

69. **WATCHMAN** by James Leach (1762–1798)

a. First published in James Leach, *A Second Sett of Hymn and Psalm Tunes*, London, [1789–1798]. First U.S. appearance is Amos Pilsbury, *The United States' Sacred Harmony*, Boston, 1799.[98]

b. WATCHMAN is a Short Meter "plain tune" in the major mode in duple time.

c. The tune begins in an angular fashion, but employs stepwise motion in the second half, noticeably in the descent of a ninth, pitch by pitch. The secondary dominant influence is unusual in its use over the whole of phrases 2 and 3.

d. Evolution of the tune is seen in the following instances:
    (i) The 1808, 1822, and 1833 versions include a rest at the midpoint to separate the phrases, whereas other sources allow the tune to continue in strict time.
    (ii) The tune of phrase 2 in early and later sources reads 5 458 76 5, but in 1853, 1856, and 1857 reads 5 456 76 5. This is an example of the "smoothing out" of the melody common in midcentury practice, also seen in the penultimate measure, where the leap of a third is filled in with a passing note.

e. Texts used:

08	AWSIAF	Ah, when shall I awake from sin
22/33/37/49	WSTLCA	When shall thy love constrain and force
48	GOALBW	God of almighty love, by whose
53/56	MGMLML	My God, my love, my life

| 57 | RIJBTU | Rejoice in Jesus' birth; to us |
| 66 | SOSMTG | Saviour of sinful men, thy goodness |

Additional references:
1. Temperley, *HTI*, no. 6812
2. Wasson, *HI*, no. 31800

WATCHMAN   NHT: 1866

1. 135832
2. 5458765
3. 582876543215
4. 5678654321   Meter: SM

1808 1358325458		WATCHMAN	AWSIAF	Leach	E	3/4
1822 1358325458	BANGNMH	WATCHMAN	WSTLCA	Leach	E	2/3
1833 1358325458	BANGNMH	WATCHMAN	WSTLCA	Leach	E	2/3
1837 1358325456	LANEG-H	WATCHMAN	WSTLCA	Leach	E♭	3/4
1848 1358325458	JACKSSH	WATCHMAN	GOALBW	Leach	E	3/4
1849 1358325458	DINGCDH	WATCHMAN	WSTLCA	Leach	E♭	3/4
1853 1358325456	WOODILZ	WATCHMAN	MGMLML	Read	E	1/4
1856 1358325456	WOODINLZ	WATCHMAN	MGMLML	Read	E	1/4
1857 1358325456	=====HU	WATCHMAN	RIJBTU	Read	E	2/4
1866 1358325458	PHILPNHT	WATCHMAN	SOSMTG	LeachJ	E	1/4
1878 X						

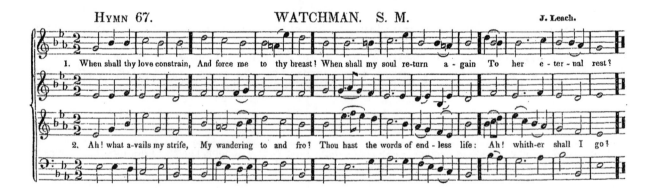

70. **WELLS** probably by Israel Holdroyd (1702–1753)

a. First published in Israel Holdroyd, *The Spiritual-Man's Companion*, London, ca. 1722. The text was from Watts, *Hymns and Spiritual Songs, Book 1*, no. 88: "Life is the time to serve the Lord." Crawford locates the first U.S. publication in James Lyon, *Urania* [see note 8, below], Philadelphia, 1761. Printed 160 times prior to 1810.[99] Temperley, however, cites [untitled collection], Boston, 1755, ca. 1760.[100]

b. This major mode Long Meter tune in duple time was almost as popular as OLD HUNDRED. Early appearances were textless.

c. Each half of WELLS has the same shape, rising to the upper tonic, and ending a phrase later on the lower tonic. The phrases are isorhythmic. The secondary dominant is introduced in a standard way in both the first and third phrases rather than at the midpoint.

d. The tune and its settings are consistent throughout the period.

e. Texts used:

08	OTWATS	O thou, whom all thy saints
22/33/37	GOMLWJ	God of my life, what just return
53/56	LITTTS	Life is the time to serve the Lord
57	SPLOLF	Show pity, Lord, O Lord forgive
66	GSOBAO	Great Source of being and of love
78	WLPIPL	While life prolongs its precious life

Additional references:
1. Crawford, *Core Repertory*, no. 94
2. Temperley, *HTI*, no. 975a
3. Wasson, *HI*, no. 32221

WELLS   HWT: 1878

1. 13587865
2. 55553421
3. 34567865
4. 23453421   Meter: LM

1808	13586555		WELLS	OTWATS		F	1/2
1822	1358786555	BANGNMH	WELLS	GOMLWJ	Holdrayd	F	3/4
1833	1358786555	BANGNMH	WELLS	GOMLWJ	Holdroyd	F	3/4
1837	1358786555	LANEG-H	WELLS	GOMLWJ	Holdrad	F	3/4
1848	X						
1849	X						
1853	1358786555	WOODILZ	WELLS	LITTTS	Holdrad	E♭	1/4
1856	1358786555	WOODINLZ	WELLS	LITTTS	Holdrad	E♭	1/4
1857	1358786555	=====HU	WELLS	SPLOLF	Holdrayd	E♭	2/4
1866	1358786555	PHILPNHT	WELLS	GSOBAO	Holdroyd	E♭	1/4
1878	1358786555	NELSHWT	WELLS	WLPIPL	Holroyd	D	1/4

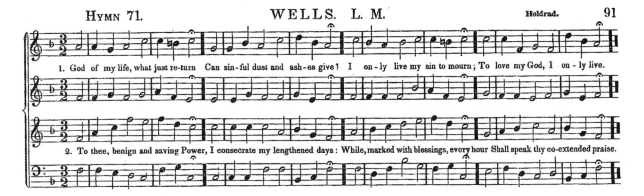

71. **WILLOWBY** (WILLOUGHBY) by Crane (19th c.)

a. First published in [Simeon Jocelin], *The Chorister's Companion*, 2nd ed., New Haven, 1788.[101]

b. This "plain tune" in the major mode and duple time accompanies texts of 886 (doubled) meter.

c. Motifs in the tune are used sequentially to create a sense of unity and folk character. The third and sixth phrases are identical. Secondary dominant influences are absent.

d. In later versions, there are accretions to the tune such as passing notes meant to fill in the leaps, or the pickup to the fourth phrase in sources after 1849. The tune also shows some changes in note values of eighth-note pairs, which sometimes adopt a dotted eighth–sixteenth pattern.

e. Texts used:

08/22/33	BIMOWH	Be it my only wisdom here to serve
37/49/53/56	JTSOAO	Jesus, thou soul of all our joys
57/66	COMPID	Come on, my partners in distress

Additional references:
1. Temperley, *HTI*, no. 4911
2. Wasson, *HI*, no. 32937

WILLOWBY (WILLOUGHBY)   NHT: 1866

1. 511131222
2. 3444323332
3. 13215671
4. 345565434454
5. 32333452232
6. 13215671   Meter: 886 D

1808 5111312223		WILLOWBY	BIMOWH		A	1/2
1822 5111312223	BANGNMH	WILLOWBY	BIMOWH		A	1/2
1833 5111312223	BANGNMH	WILLOWBY	BIMOWH		A	1/2
1837 5111312223	LANEG-H	WILLOWBY	JTSOAO		A	3/4
1848 X						
1849 5111312223	DINGCDH	WILLOUGHBY	JTSOAO		A	3/4
1853 5111312223	WOODILZ	WILLOUGHBY	JTSOAO		A	3/4
1856 5111312223	WOODINLZ	WILLOUGHBY	JTSOAO		A	3/4
1857 5111312223	=====HU	WILLOUGHBY	COMPID		A	2/4
1866 5111312223	PHILPNHT	WILLOUGHBY	COMPID	Crane	A	1/4
1878 X						

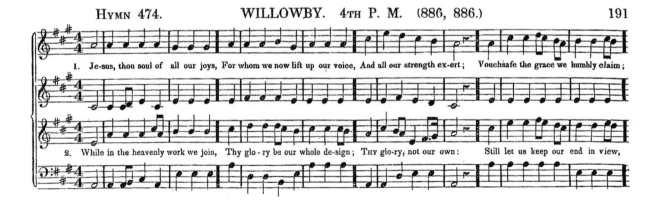

Hymn 474.   WILLOWBY.   4th P. M.   (886, 886.)   191

Com-pose in - to a thank-ful frame, And tune thy peo - ple's heart.

And still the plea-sing task pur - sue, To please our God a - lone.

72. **WILMOT** arr. from Carl Maria von Weber (1786–1826)

a. First published by Lowell Mason in 1832.[102]

b. This major mode tune for 77.77 or 87.87 meter is a "plain tune" in duple time.

c. The tune is angular in profile, and is supported by harmonies that are basic to the key, with no use of secondary dominants.

d. The tune changes only when the meter changes to accommodate an eighth syllable in the first or third lines. In those instances, a note is added, by which 13215 1321 becomes 13215 13215.

e. Texts used:

33/57	LWCBTN	Lord, we come before thee now
49	BAJITM	Bright and joyful is the morn
53/56	LTLJLH	Lo! The Lord Jehovah liveth; He
66	COTHKA	Children of the heavenly King, as we
78	HWMTHV	Hark! what mean those holy voices

Additional reference:
Wasson, *HI*, no. 32952

WILMOT   HWT: 1878

1. 1321513215
2. *615332171*
3. *4651321715*   Meter: 87.87
4. *6153271*   *or* 77.77

1808 X
1822 X
1833 X

1837	1321513215	LANEG-H	WILMOT	LWCBTN	Weber	C	3/4
1848	X						
1849	1321513216	DINGCDH	WILMOT	BAJITM	Weber	C	3/4
1853	1321513215	WOODILZ	WILMOT	LTLJLH	Von Weber	C	1/4
1856	1321513215	WOODINLZ	WILMOT	LTLJLH	Von Weber	C	1/4
1857	1321513216	=====HU	WILMOT	LWCBTN	Von Weber	C	2/4
1866	1321513216	PHILPNHT	WILMOT	COTHKA		C	1/4
1878	1321513215	NELSHWT	WILMOT	HWMTHV	Von Weber	B♭	1/4

Appendix A

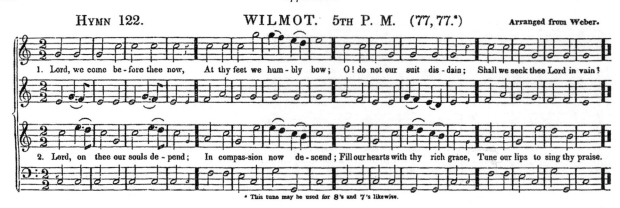

Hᴍɴ 122.   WILMOT. 5ᴛʜ P. M. ('77, 77.*)   Arranged from Weber.

* This tune may be used for 8's and 7's likewise.

73. **WINDHAM** by Daniel Read (1757–1836)

a. First published in Daniel Read, *The American Singing Book*, New Haven, 1785.[103] Printed sixty-five times prior to 1810, often with the text from Watts, *Hymns and Spiritual Songs, Book 2*, no. 158, "Broad is the road that leads to death."

b. This minor mode Long Meter "plain tune" in triple time was closely identified with the text above, but in various printings, with no particular text.

c. The rhythms of this melody copy those of WELLS exactly as far as the final phrase, where it turns to use of successive quarter notes. Crawford points out that it may have been composed as early as 1775 but not published till 1785. The tune elicited unique praise from musicians of the day.[104]

d. The tune remains consistent throughout the period. All versions maintain the rhythm ♩ ♩ ♩ ♩ ♩ ♩ ♩ ♩ for phrases 1 to 3. The final phrase changes the rhythmic structure to ♩ ♩ ♩ ♩ ♩ ♩ ♩ ♩, which in the 1853, 1857, and 1866 sources is marked by altering the time to 2/2 from 3/2.

e. Texts used:

33/37/57/78	STISST	Stay, thou insulted spirit, stay though
49/53	SPLOLF	Show pity Lord, O Lord, forgive
56	BITRTL	Broad is the road that leads
66	HDTFOS	He dies! the friend of sinners

Additional references:
1. Crawford, *Core Repertory*, no. 97
2. Jackson, *Down-East Spirituals*, no. 103
3. Wasson, *HI*, no. 32995
4. Temperley, *HTI*, no. 4628

WINDHAM (minor)   HWT: 1878

1. 13455321
2. 13235432
3. 234588878
4. 55654321   Meter: LM

1808 X						
1822 X						
1833	1345532113	BANGNMH	WINDHAM	STISST	Read	e	3/4
1837	1345532113	LANEG-H	WINDHAM	STISST	Read	e	3/4
1848 X						

1849	1345532113	DINGCDH	WINDHAM	SPLOLF		e	3/4
1853	1345532113	WOODILZ	WINDHAM	SPLOLF	Read	e	1/4
1856	1345532113	WOODINLZ	WINDHAM	BITRTL	Read	d	1/4
1857	1345532113	=====HU	WINDHAM	STISST	Read	d	2/4
1866	1345532113	PHILPNHT	WINDHAM	HDTFOS	ReadD	d	1/4
1878	1345532113	NELSHWT	WINDHAM	STISST	ReadD	d	1/4

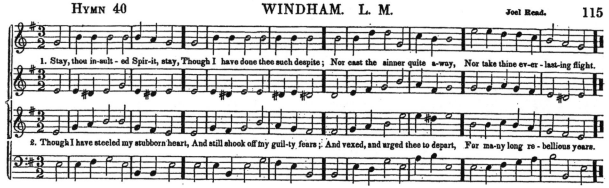

74. **WINDSOR** (OLD WINDSOR)

a. First published in William Damon, *The former Booke of the Musicke of M. William Damon*, [London], 1591. First published in the United States in *The Tunes of the Psalms*, Boston, 1698, bound with *The Psalms, Hymns, and Spiritual Songs*, 9th ed.[105] An early text was from Watts, *Hymns and Spiritual Songs, Book 2*, no. 107, "That awful day will surely come."

b. This minor mode Common Meter tune in duple time (early sources) or triple time (after 1837) is a common tune and was paired with many different texts. It was sung in America before being available in print there.

c. This tune and COLESHILL bear a close relationship, discovered by Erik Routley and noted by Temperley. He proposes that COLESHILL began its existence as an "improvised descant" to WINDSOR.[106]

d. The tune remains the same throughout the period. The 1837 source is the only one in this period to use the time signature ¢. The rhythm only varies in the matter of phrase separation; some versions end the phrase on a note of double value followed by a rest, which may be an approximation of the fermata used in German chorales. Most others employ the fermata sign. The 1866 source is the only one to offer the "gathering note" format, with double-value notes to begin and end each phrase: ♩ ♪ ♪ ♪ ♪ ♪ ♩.

e. Texts used:

08	GIITAE	God is in this and every place
22/33/37	HFTTAD	Hark! from the tombs a doleful
48	TWAENA	Thee we adore, eternal Name! And
53	OGOHIA	O God our help in ages
66	BTSOMN	Behold the Saviour of mankind
78	TADWSC	That awful day will surely come

Additional references:
1. Crawford, *Core Repertory*, no. 98
2. Temperley, *HTI*, no. 271a
3. Wasson, *HI*, no. 33003

WINDSOR (OLD WINDSOR) (minor)   HWT: 1878

1. 11232127
2. 354323

3. 35432117
4. 321171   Meter: CM

1808	1123211735		OLD WINDSOR	GIITAE	Kirby	a	3/4
1822	1123211735	BANGNMH	OLD WINDSOR	HFTTAD	Kirby	a	3/4
1833	1123211735	BANGNMH	OLD WINDSOR	HFTTAD	Kirby	a	3/4
1837	1123211735	LANEG-H	WINDSOR	HFTTAD	Kirby	a	3/4
1848	1123211735	JACKSSH	WINDSOR	TWAENA	Kirby	a	3/4
1849	X						
1853	1123211735	WOODILZ	WINDSOR/DUNDEE	OGOHIA	ScotPs	g	1/4
1856	X						
1857	X						
1866	1123211735	PHILPNHT	WINDSOR	BTSOMN	Ravens	g	1/4
1878	1123212735	NELSHWT	WINDSOR	TADWSC	Kirbye	g	1/4

75. WOODLAND by Nathaniel D. Gould (1781–1864)

a. The source is dated 1832, but first appeared in *National Church Harmony*, Boston, Lincoln, Edmands, 1835, copyright 1833, N. Gould, ed. The composer also provided a version in the minor mode.[107]

b. This major mode tune uses triple time. It accompanies texts of either 86.86 (Common Meter) or 86.886 meter. Its structure is antiphonal tune-with-extension except for 1878, which is fully voiced throughout.

c. The main rhythmic pattern ♩ | ♩. ♪ ♩ ♩. is the uniting characteristic of the tune. Neither secondary dominants nor accidentals are used.

d. The fourth phrase omits the tenor and bass lines for two measures in most sources, although 1853, 1856, and 1857 sources provide a bass line or sketch of one. In other versions, the fourth phrase may be for tune and bass.[108] The 1866 source simply pairs tune and alto in this phrase.

e. Texts used:

37	WJWMTG	With joy we meditate the grace
49/57/66	TIAHOP	There is an hour of peaceful rest
53/56	LOPMTG	Lovers of pleasure more than God
78	FOLTAB	Fountain of life, to all below

Additional reference:
Wasson, *HI*, no. 33360

WOODLAND   HWT: 1878

1. 13353232
2. 355123
3. 32234555
   35431432   Meter: CM
4. 654321   *or* 86.886

1808 X							
1822 X							
1833 X							
1837	1335323235	LANEG-H	WOODLAND	WJWMTG	Gould	G	3/4
1848 X							
1849	1335323235	DINGCDH	WOODLAND	TIAHOP	Gould	G	3/4
1853	1335323235	WOODILZ	WOODLAND	LOPMTG	Nat. Ch. Har.	G	3/4
1856	1335323235	WOODINLZ	WOODLAND	LOPMTG	Nat. Ch. Har.	G	3/4
1857	1335323235	=====HU	WOODLAND	TIAHOP	Gould	G	2/4
1866	1335323235	PHILPNHT	WOODLAND	TIAHOP	Gould	G	1/4
1878	1335323235	NELSHWT	WOODLAND	FOLTAB	Gould	G	1/4

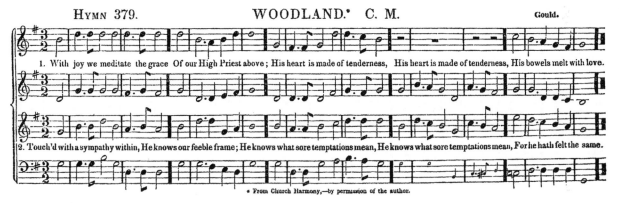

76. **ZION** (SION) by Thomas Hastings (1784–1872)

a. First published in 1831–1832 in Thomas Hastings, *Spiritual Songs for Social Worship*, Utica, New York.[109]

b. This major mode tune in triple time accompanies texts of 87.87.47 meter. In some sources it is an antiphonal tune with extension, in its last format a tune with extension in 87.87.47 meter. In the 1853, 1856, 1857, and 1866 sources, ZION may be considered a gospel tune.

c. The tune has rhythmic and harmonic patterns typical of its genre. The antiphonal phrase (if included) is the fourth one.

d. The 1866 source prints out the whole tune, indicating section 3 to be "Verse" and section 4 the "Chorus." In each case the text is identical, beginning with "Hallelujah." There are several gospel tune characteristics such as one-beat-long dotted rhythms (as upbeat in most measures, as downbeat in the precadential measure of each phrase), the limitations of chords I, IV, and V (there is also one supertonic sixth chord), and the repetition of text to accommodate tune shape.

e. Texts used:

37/57/66	LHCWCD	Lo! he comes with clouds descending
49	ZSWHSZ	Zion, stand with hills surrounded, Zion
53/56/78	GMOTGJ	Guide me, O thou great Jehovah
	OTMTAL	On the mountain tops appearing, lo

Additional reference:
Wasson, *HI*, no. 27684

ZION (SION)   HWT: 1878

1. 55538565
2. 8822878
3. 55538565
4. 8822878
5. 313322171
6. 55535544323   Meter: 87.87.887

1808 X							
1822 X							
1833 X							
1837	5553856588	LANEG-H	ZION	LHCWCD		E	3/4
1848 X							
1849	5553856588	DINGCDH	ZION	ZSWHSZ	Hastings	E♭	3/4
1853	5553856588	WOODILZ	ZION	OTMTAL	Hastings	D	1/4
1856	5553856588	WOODINLZ	ZION	OTMTAL	Hastings	D	1/4
1857	5553856588	=====HU	ZION	LHCWCD	Hastings	D	2/4
1866	5553856588	PHILPNHT	ZION	LHCWCD	Hastings	D	1/4
1878	5553856588	NELSHWT	ZION	GMOTGJ	Hastings	D	1/4
				OTMTAL			

Notes

1. This term is borrowed from Richard Crawford, ed., *The Core Repertory of Early American Psalmody* (Madison, WI: A-R Editions, 1984).

2. If the date of first printing remains unidentified, section a will use the designation "first appearance unknown." It remains possible that a tune may be identified by another name. Due to the general practice of not identifying tune sources in the nineteenth century, the first appearance is often not known.

3. See Nicholas Temperley, *Hymn Tune Index* (Oxford: Clarendon Press, 1998), hereafter designated as *HTI*, IV/658, and D. DeWitt Wasson, compiler, *Hymntune Index and Related Hymn Materials*, Vol. 2 (Lanham, MD, and London, Scarecrow Press, 1998), hereafter designated as *HI*.

4. John Julian, *A Dictionary of Hymnology* (New York: Charles Scribner's Sons, 1892), 1036; and Temperley, *HTI*, III/375.

5. Temperley, *HTI*, III/776.

6. Temperley, *HTI*, III/722.

7. Robert G. McCutchan, *Our Hymnody* (New York: Abingdon-Cokesbury, 1937), 308.

8. Temperley, *HTI*, III/261f. Crawford, *Core Repertory*, xxv, states publication was in John Chetham, *A Book of Psalmody* (London, 1718), with subsequent publication in the United States in James Lyon, *Urania, or a Choice Collection of Psalm-tunes, Anthems, and Hymns* (Philadelphia, 1761).

9. Terry L. Baldridge, "Evolving Tastes in Hymntunes of the Methodist Episcopal Church in the Nineteenth Century" (Ph.D. dissertation, University of Kansas, 1982), 215.

10. Temperley, *HTI*, IV/95.

11. Baldridge, "Evolving Tastes," 282.

12. Temperley, *HTI*, IV/751.

13. Temperley, *HTI*, IV/281.

14. Temperley, *HTI*, III/705.

15. Baldridge, "Evolving Tastes," 294.

16. Temperley, *HTI*, IV/426.

17. Temperley, *HTI*, III/750.

18. Temperley, *HTI*, IV/297. Hezekiah Butterworth, *The Story of the Tunes*, American Tract Society (New York, 1890), 36, cites publication in *Federal Harmony*, 1785. The tune may also have appeared in Swan's first publication, *The Songster's Assistant* (ca. 1800).

19. Hughes, *American Hymns*, 278.

20. Temperley, *HTI*, IV/63. Crawford, *Core Repertory*, xxxi, cites Martin Madan, *A Collection of Psalms and Hymn Tunes* (London, 1769).

21. Temperley, *HTI*, III/341. See also Crawford, *Core Repertory*, xxxi.

22. Carlton R. Young, *Companion to the United Methodist Hymnal* (Nashville: Abingdon Press, 1993), 304.

23. Temperley, *HTI*, IV/426.

24. Fred D. Gealy, with A. Lovelace, C. Young, and E. S. Bucke, eds., *Companion to the Hymnal: A Handbook to the 1964 Methodist Hymnal* (New York: Abingdon Press, 1970), 400. See also Temperley, *HTI*, IV/474, especially no. 11690b.

25. Temperley, *HTI*, IV/474.

26. Temperley, *HTI*, IV/91f.

27. Temperley, *HTI*, V/111.

28. McCutchan, *Our Hymnody*, 99.

29. Temperley, *HTI*, III/149.

30. This is a variant of Playford, *The Whole Book of Psalmes in 3 parts* (London, 1677).

31. Temperley, *HTI*, IV/323.

32. Temperley, *HTI*, IV/630.

33. Hughes, *American Hymns*, 255.

34. Temperley, *HTI*, IV/307, version 8879a.

35. Temperley, *HTI*, IV/205. A later date is posited by Thomas F. Bickley in *David's Harp (1813), a Methodist Tunebook from Baltimore: An Analysis and Facsimile* (MA thesis, American University, Washington, D.C., 1983), 25.

36. Temperley, *HTI*, IV/278.

37. McCutchan, *Our Hymnody*, 235.

38. Hill, "A Study of Tastes," 311.

39. See G. Pullen Jackson, *White Spirituals in Southern Uplands* (Chapel Hill: University of North Carolina Press, 1933), 149, 173f.

40. Temperley, *HTI*, IV/630.

41. Temperley, *HTI*, III/707.

42. Crawford, *Core Repertory*, xli. See also Temperley, *HTI*, III/741.

43. Temperley, *HTI*, IV/130.

44. Crawford, *Core Repertory*, lxii. See also Temperley, *HTI*, III/54f.

45. Temperley, *HTI*, III/291.

46. Temperley, *HTI*, III/659.

47. Hill, "A Study of Tastes," 273, citing Leslie Stephen and Sidney Lee, eds., *The Dictionary of National Biography* (London: Oxford University Press, 1885–1901), Vol. 7, 868.

48. Temperley, *HTI*, III/217.

49. Temperléy, *HTI*, III/668.

50. Frost, ed., *Historical Companion*, 305.

51. George Pullen Jackson, *Down-East Spirituals*, 101.

52. Wasson, *HI*, III/1764.

53. McCutchan, *Our Hymnody*, 101.

54. Temperley, *HTI*, III/272.

55. Crawford, *Core Repertory*, lxii.

56. Baldridge, "Evolving Tastes," 235 and 379.

57. Temperley, *HTI*, III/778.

58. Temperley, *HTI*, III/277.

59. Crawford, *Core Repertory*, li. See also Temperley, *HTI*, III/55f.

60. Temperley, *HTI*, IV/676.

61. Temperley, *HTI*, III/690.

62. Oakley must have published this privately before its appearance in *The Harmonist*, but that source remains undiscovered.

63. Brown and H. Butterworth, *The Story of the Hymns and Tunes* (New York: G. H. Doran, 1906), 48.

64. Temperley, *HTI*, IV/386.

65. Temperley, *HTI*, V/596.

66. Lightwood, *The Music of the Methodist Hymnbook*, 334. See also Temperley, *HTI*, IV/34f.

67. Temperley, *HTI*, IV/34.

68. Hill, "A Study in Tastes," 258.

69. Temperley, *HTI*, IV/378.

70. Temperley, *HTI*, III/661.

71. Crawford, *Core Repertory*, 112.

72. Julian, *A Dictionary of Hymnology*, 1089.

73. Temperley, *HTI*, III/285.

74. Crawford, *Core Repertory*, lv.

75. Temperley, *HTI*, III/22.

76. Crawford, *Core Repertory*, lvi.

77. Temperley, *HTI*, III/414.

78. McCutchan, *Our Hymnody*, 217.

79. Temperley, *HTI*, III/217.

80. Temperley, *HTI*, III/540.

81. Crawford, *Core Repertory*, lxiii.

82. Temperley, *HTI*, IV/236.

83. Fred D. Gealy et al., eds., *Companion to the Hymnal*, 273.

84. Temperley, *HTI*, IV/109f.

85. Temperley, *HTI*, III/676.

86. Baldridge, "Evolving Tastes," 432.

87. Frost, ed., *Historical Companion*, 157, and Temperley, *HTI*, IV/13.

88. Temperley, *HTI*, IV/13.

89. Temperley, *HTI*, IV/266.

90. Temperléy, *HTI*, IV/8.

91. Hill, "A Study in Tastes," 293.

92. Temperley, *HTI*, IV/70.

93. Temperley, *HTI*, III/522.

94. Temperley, *HTI*, IV/631.

95. Temperley, *HTI*, II/664.

96. McCutchan, *Our Hymnody*, 233.

97. Temperley, *HTI*, IV/486.

98. Temperley, *HTI*, IV/266.

99. Temperley, *HTI*, IV/162.
100. Crawford, *Core Repertory*, lxii.
101. Temperley, *HTI*, III/287.
102. Temperley, *HTI*, III/774.
103. Wasson, *HI*, III/2563.
104. Temperley, *HTI*, III/744.
105. Crawford, lxiv.
106. Temperley, *HTI*, III/129.
107. Nicholas Temperley, quoted in Crawford, *Core Repertory*, xxxii.
108. Hughes, *American Hymns*, 45.
109. Hill, "A Study of Tastes," 277.
110. Stanley Sadie, ed., *New Grove Dictionary of Music and Musicians*, Vol. 11.

Appendix B
Annotated Bibliography of Tunebooks Used in the Survey

1808

David's Companion, being a choice selection of hymn and psalm tunes adapted to the words and measures of the Methodist Pocket Hymnbook, containing a variety of tunes to all the metres that are now in use in the different churches; with many new tunes, principally from Dr. Miller, Leach and other composers. New York: J. Evans, 1808. 80 pages.

Semiofficial. Book recommended for use by congregations. Evans also published the 1811 edition, *David's Companion, or The Methodist Standard,* which was intended to be used in conjunction with Wesley's "Large Hymnbook" (1780) of which the eighteenth London edition was used as the basis for the Baltimore reprint of 1814. Having been recommended by the General Conference, these books mark the entry of vernacular American melodies into official church use. Bickley contends that rural lay dissatisfaction with denominational leadership caused suspicion of any book recommended by the leadership.[1] The problem may have been exacerbated in the new country by the fact that tune sources were from (old) England and New England. The 108 tunes follow a "Plain and Easy Introduction to the Science of Music for the Use of Evans's Singing School." The collection is organized so that tunes appear in groups according to meter. At the end of the tunebook, the supplement is advertised.

One stanza of text is interlined in a score presented in two or three staves, with the melody always being the staff above the bass line.

Meters included:

Long Meter	17
Common Meter	20
Short Meter	10
6 Eights	7
4, 6, 8 Sevens	13
Other meters	41

The copy at the Methodist Archives, Drew University, contains a supplement that provides these in addition: BURNHAM, PENITENT, ST. MARTIN'S, GAINSBORO, SICILIAN. This tunebook was re-edited in 1811 and 1817, and finally appeared as *Wesleyan Selection* in an 1820 edition.

1822

The Methodist Harmonist, containing a great variety of tunes collected from the Best Authors, adapted to all the various metres in the Methodist Hymn-Book and Designed for the Use of the Methodist Episcopal Church in the United States. To which is added a choice selection of Anthems and Pieces. New York: Published by N. Bangs and T. Mason for the Methodist Episcopal Church, 1822. xi, 247 pages.

Compiled by a committee appointed by Nathan Bangs and Thomas Mason, publishing agents of the Methodist Episcopal Church, composed of the following persons: John M. Smith, Daniel Ayres, John D. Myers, and G. P. Disoway. Reprinted in 1823, 1825, 1827, and 1831.

In the 1831 edition examined at the New York Public Library, Music Division, the preface of 1821, signed by Smith, Ayres, Myers, and Disoway was retained. The first eight pages present "A Brief Introduction to the Science of Music." The tunes are arranged by meter: Common, Long, Short, 6 Eights, as well as other metrical divisions.

Beside each tune name appears the number of the hymn to be found in the words-only hymnbook (e.g., ARLINGTON Hymn 546. CM). The text of one verse only is interlined in the score. Principal tunes are grouped as:

Long Meter	45
Common Meter	65
Short Meter	30
6 Eights	12
886 D	13
4, 6, 8 Sevens	18
Other meters	25
Anthems	12
Total	220

Indexes

1833

The Methodist Harmonist, containing A Collection of Tunes from the Best Authors, Embracing Every Variety of Metre, and adapted to the Worship of the Methodist Episcopal Church, to which is added A Selection of Anthems, Pieces, and Sentences for Particular Occasions. New Edition, Revised and Greatly Enlarged. New York: B. Waugh and T. Mason for the Methodist Episcopal Church at the Conference Office, 1833. xiii, 362 pages.

The General Conference of 1832 requested preparation and publication of a revised and improved tunebook "with a view . . . to suit the different habits and tastes of the lovers of sacred music . . . at the same time recommended that the edition be issued with patent or angular notes."[2] A committee consisting of George Coles and others revised it. Tunes numbering 292 follow the section called "A Brief Introduction To The Science Of Music" consisting of five pages of music theory, concluding with two pages of exercises and a "Dictionary of Musical Terms."

In response to the request from the General Conference, the edition is printed with "patent or angular" (shape) notes. The music is set out on three or four staves, the melody next to the bass line. Tunes are categorized by meter; tune name and meter are clearly indicated, though authors and sources are not always apparent. At the top of every tune appears a hymn number as a reference to the current hymnbook (words only). One stanza of text is interlined, and one to four additional verses may appear below the musical notation.

Long Meter	45
Common Meter	65
Short Meter	30
6 Eights	13
4, 6, 8 Sevens	18
Other meters	109
Anthems	12
Total	292

Appendix: Alphabetical Tunes; Metrical Tunes; Anthems and Pieces.

1837

The Harmonist: being a Collection of Tunes from the Most Approved Authors; Adapted to Every Variety of Metre in the Methodist Hymn-Book. And, for particular occasions, a Selection of Anthems, Pieces, and Sentences. New Edition in Patent Notes—Revised and Greatly Enlarged. New York: Published by G. Lane and P. P. Sandford (James Collord, Printer), [2nd ed.], 1842. xiv, 384 pages.

The music theory section of the book is double the size of that in the preceding tunebook, comprising ten pages. The preface mentions the source as being similar material in *The Boston Handel and Haydn Society Collection of Church Music* (Boston: Boston Handel and Haydn Society, 1822) reprinted with consent of the proprietor.

The layout of the tunes has been altered in this collection to occupy less space, in facilitating the insertion of hymn texts. It was thought that practice would be gained in "applying different hymns to the tune, which is very desirable."[3]

Regarding fuging tunes, "a few have been retained . . . as, in every section of the country, there are some persons who are very partial to them."[4] This decision was taken despite admonishments to avoid fuging tunes (*Discipline*) and "modern taste proscrib[ing] their use."

Tunes are printed on four staves, with the "Air" nearest the bass line. One to four stanzas are interlined, and tunes are categorized according to meter. With each tune appears the number related to the text located in the current hymnbook.

The collection closes with thirty-three "Anthems, Sentences, &c." Included are two settings of "Glory be to the Father," and one of "Holy Lord God of Sabaoth," a practice begun at this time and retained in subsequent hymn- and tunebooks. Tunes appear in groups as follows:

Long Meter	73
Common Meter	115
Short Meter	45
6 Eights	29
4 Sevens	16
6 Sevens	10
8 Sevens	15
Other meters	127
Total	430

1848

Sacred Harmony: A Collection of Music, adapted to the Greatest Variety of Metres Now in Use: And, for Special Occasions, A Choice Selection of Sentences, Anthems, Motets, and Chants harmonized, and Arranged with an Accompaniment for the Organ or Piano Forte, by Samuel Jackson, *With An Improved System of Elementary Instruction.* New York: Lane and Tippett, 1848. xxxix, 396 pages.

As the title page indicates, the collection begins with a section of elementary instruction divided into seventeen lessons. The tunes, grouped by meter, precede Sentences, Anthems, Motets, Sanctus settings, and Doxologies and Chants.

Long Meter	64
Common Meter	73
Short Meter	43
6 Eights	24
4, 6, 8 Sevens	31
Other meters	102
Sentences, Anthems, Motets	29
Doxologies, chants	30
Total	396

Tunes are printed on four staves; located on the staff above the bass line, the tune appears as part of a four-part keyboard/choral setting. While it may appear that six parts have been printed, the alto and tenor parts (on the top two staves) have been replicated in the keyboard score.

One stanza of text is interlined with each tune. Many new sources are evident in this collection: "From the Missal Book"; "Beethoven"; "V. Novello," indicating a leaning towards classical European tune repertoire. On the other hand, a folk tune like Switzerland (no. 188) is brought into hymnic use. Use of chromaticism is apparent in almost every harmony; great attention has been given to the interest within every vocal line.

There are three appendixes: Alphabetical Tune; Metrical; Sentences, Anthems, Motets and Chants. The latter category seems especially large, and includes the following:

Venite	Chants by Boyce, Mornington
Gloria Patri	Chants by Croft, Travers, Tallis, Purcell
Te Deum	Chant by Mather
Benedicite	Chant by Hodges
Jubilate Deo	Chants by Fitzherbert, Battishill
Benedictus	Chants by Russell, Soaper
Responses (to the Commandments)	Chants by Farrant, Porter
Glorias (Gloria tibi)	Anon.
Gloria in Excelsis	Anon., Coolidge
Cantate Domino	Chants by Mornington, Jackson
Bonum est confiteri	Chants by Hodges, Norris
Deus Misereatur	Chants by Coolidge, Anon.
Benedic anima mea	Chants by Nares, Anon.
Laudate Dominum	Chant by Taylor
Chant for Thanksgiving Day	by Cook
Chant for Ash Wednesday	by Cambridge
Chant for Good Friday	by Attwood
Burial of the Dead	by V. Novello

1849

The Devotional Harmonist: a Collection of Sacred Music, comprising a large variety of New and Original Tunes, Sentences, Anthems, etc., in addition to many of the most Popular Tunes in common use. Presenting a Greater Number of Metres than Any Book Heretofore Published, to which is prefixed A Progressive System of Elementary Instruction for Schools and Private Tuition. Charles Dingley, ed. New York: George Lane and Levi Scott, 1849. 424 pages.

The preface presents an apology for the process and result in the *Devotional Harmonist*: the compilers drew upon all available resources; they relied especially on *The Harmonist* (1837); in dealing with new compositions they acted without knowing the location or person of origin.

The editor commends the opening section of instruction, which is "strictly inductive and practical," and provides "Elements of Vocal Music" borrowing freely from Pfeiffer and Naegeli, under the direction of Pestalozzi. Rudiments of musical form and notation as well as vocalises and a listing of principal musical terms are presented.

The tunes are shown in open score (four staves), with one to four stanzas interlined. Tunes are metrically grouped.

Long Meter	88
Common Meter	127
Short Meter	52
6 Eights	18
4, 6, 8 Sevens	38
Other meters	156
Anthems, Sentences	32
Total	511

Following the tunes with meter 87.87.887 additional tunes appear arranged again in groupings by meter. This section is mentioned in the preface as containing pieces "not suitable as hymn tunes nor proper to come under the head of set pieces"; this may bear reference to the inclusion of fuging tunes as well as anthem texts and "Sentences." Wesley's favorite, "Vital Spark of heavenly flame" (The Dying Christian), finds its place here. It should be noted that "Silent Night," which first appeared in 1833, appears in this American collection!

The appendix includes alphabetical tune and metrical indexes, as well as an index of first lines (hymn texts).

1853

The Lute of Zion: A Collection of Sacred Music designed for the Use of The Methodist Episcopal Church: consisting of a choice collection of new tunes from the best foreign and American composers, with most of the old tunes in common use; together with a concise elementary course, simplified and adapted to the capacities of beginners, &c, &c. By I. B. Woodbury, ed. New York: F. J. Huntington and Mason Brothers, 1853. 352 pages.

As noted on the title page, an instructional section entitled "Elements of music made easy" is included at the front of the volume. All rudiments of music notation are covered, as well as classification of voices, "explosive tone and staccato" singing, as well as directions for performing ornaments. In keeping with use in a singing school, Rounds and Melodies for Class Practice are provided. The section ends with "Instructions for Playing the Organ, Piano-Forte, Melodeon and Seraphine by Figures."

Tunes are presented in four-part harmony in two configurations: close score (two staves) with the melody in the soprano on top, or open score (four staves) with the melody next above the bass line. Figures for the bass are included as necessary for keyboard realization.

Text interlining is usually provided. Close score contains one stanza as a rule (though up to three stanzas may be found) whereas open score contains three stanzas in a plain tune. One stanza is set with a fuging tune, as seen at INVITATION (p. 26). Direction for altering meters can be found beside some tunes. For example, NUREMBURG is listed as LM with the text "Let everlasting glories crown" along with the following notation: "NUREMBURG. L.M: Or 7's by omitting the first note to each line" (p. 36).

Headed by a performance direction (e.g., "Gentle," "Firmly," "Spirited"), tunes are grouped by meter as follows:

Long Meter	166
Common Meter	157
Short Meter	67
6 Eights	15
4, 6, 8 Sevens	29
Other meters	115
Total	549

Part Second of the volume provides "Anthems and Select Pieces," some of which clearly acknowledge instrumental accompaniment (thirty selections).

Part Third gives "Revival Hymns and Music" in two, three, or four parts with a variety of scorings (thirty-three selections).

Part Fourth presents "Sabbath School Hymns and Music" in two or three parts with choruses often in four parts (twenty-four selections).

Part Fifth provides "Melodies for the Singing School, Social Circle, and Concert Room" (thirty-nine selections).

Indexes: Alphabetical Tunes; Metrical Index; First Line Index.

1856

THE NEW LUTE OF ZION: A Collection of Sacred Music, designed for the Use of Congregations Generally, but more especially The Methodist Episcopal Church. By I. B. Woodbury. New York: Carlton and Porter, 1856. xxxvii, 368 pages.

The preface notes that this collection is "not designed for the fastidious and scientific musician whose highest delight, and perhaps sole worship, is music as an art, but for those who love to worship God in the simple song of praise."

A section entitled "The Music Teacher" presents ten lessons on musical rudiments, including an extensive lesson on vocalizing. Seventeen songs and glees are printed on two, three, or four staves for practice at singing school sessions. Tunes are presented on two staves (close score) with the tune in the soprano, or on four staves (open score) with the tune on the line next above the bass. Only a few settings use the three-stave style, with the tenor on the topmost line, with tune and alto on the middle staff, bass on the bottom.

Text is always interlined to show one or more stanzas. Tunes are grouped by meter in the following order:

Long Meter	165
Common Meter	177
Short Meter	77
6 Eights	16
4, 6, 8 Sevens	42
Other meters	210
Total	687

Part Second provides "Anthems and Select Pieces" mostly in open score with text interlined (forty-seven selections). Fourteen "Chants" are provided for both psalms and pointed prose of a devotional nature.

Part Third provides "Pieces for prayer and Social Meetings, Revivals, and Music for the Old Folks." A note under the title declares: "A few of the old tunes in this department are very imperfect in their structure, but as any effort towards appropriate correction would nearly destroy their identity, they have been inserted without the slightest revision" (316). There are both plain tunes and fuging tunes with texts interlined (ninety-two selections).

1857

Hymns for the Use of The Methodist Episcopal Church with Tunes for Congregational Worship. New York: Published by Carlton and Porter, 1857. 368 pages.

This is the first collection in this study to have a new shape and layout. Whereas tunebooks to 1856 were oblong in shape, opening on the short side, the 1857 collection opens on the long side, with the pages taller than heretofore.

The preface states the object of the book to be "in the most quiet and satisfactory way, to promote congregational singing." Only the hymns of the standard hymnbook were used; old tunes were used as suitable, new tunes were drawn chiefly from *The New Lute of Zion (NLZ)*. Those tunes found in *NLZ* could be found by referring to the bracketed number at the top of the page. Some alterations to new tunes were made to "adapt them to congregational use."

The publishers chose two "experienced and popular choristers" (S. Main and W. C. Brown) to edit the collection. It was decided to use "several tunes in the minor key. The reason for this is that no compositions are better adapted for devotional purposes. They need not be confined to grace subjects, but may be used with the best effect to express sentiments of thanksgiving and praise" (4).

The tunes are presented in four-part harmony, on three staves. The uppermost contains the tenor alone; the middle staff contains the tune and alto; the lowest staff shows the bass line. The text for the first stanza of a hymn is interlined. The author or source of the tune is shown beside the tune name; authors of texts are missing. All hymns are designated by the number in the official hymnbook; between three and eight hymn texts occupy space below the tune and/or on the opposite page.

The subject index headings are as found in 1866 *New Hymn and Tunebook*. Tunes are no longer presented in groupings according to meter, but are presented in random order laid out so that matching meters are on opposing pages.

Long Meter	47
Common Meter	79
Short Meter	42
6 Eights	26
4, 6, 8 Sevens	21
Other meters	81

Chants   2

Total   298

1866

NEW HYMN AND TUNEBOOK: *An Offering of Praise for the Methodist Episcopal Church*. Edited by Philip Phillips. New York: Published by Carlton and Porter, 1866. iv, 432, 63 pages.

The preface stresses the need for each one in a congregation to sing, and to have a hymn and tunebook in every pew. The editor commends the selection of three tunes on each page opposite six hymn texts; one of the tunes is to be a "good old familiar one." In order to advance the cause of heartfelt singing, it is recommended that singing meetings be held weekly to learn new tunes and improve the music.

The tunes are given in four-part harmony (melody in the soprano) on two staves, and the first stanza of a hymn is interlined. Tunes are grouped according to meter: CM, followed by LM, etc. No composers or sources are printed near the music; this information is contained in the "Alphabetical Index of Tunes."

Following 410 pages of hymns, nineteen doxologies are listed. The tunes are grouped as follows:

Long Meter	117
Common Meter	168
Short Meter	78
6 Eights	27
4, 6, 8 Sevens	38
Other meters	103
Appendix (choral)	51
Total	582

Indexes for the hymns, the tunes, the metrical listing, the subject listing, biblical texts, and number/page listing are provided. Under the subject listing are the following:

Introduction to Worship
The Divine Perfections
Jesus Christ (Incarnation and Birth, Sufferings and Death, Resurrection and Ascension, Priesthood and Intercession)
The Holy Spirit
Institutions of the Gospel (The Ministry, The Church, The Sabbath, Baptism, The Lord's Supper)
Provisions and Promises of the Gospel
The Sinner (Depravity, Awakening, Inviting, Penitential)
The Christian Life (Justification by Faith, Adoption and Assurance, Sanctification)
Means of Grace (Prayer and Intercession, Family Devotion, The Closet, Scriptures)
Christian Fellowship (Communion of Saints, Love-Feast)
Duties and Trials (The Warfare, Patience and Resignation, Steadfastness and Growth in Grace)
Humiliation (Unfaithfulness Mourned, Backslidings Lamented)
Rejoicing (Deliverance from Trouble, Communion with God, Prospect of Heaven)
Erection of Churches
Missionary
Sunday Schools
Miscellaneous (Public Fasts, Thanksgivings, Peace, Our Country, Charitable and Benevolent)
Mariners
Time and Eternity (Watch-Night, New-Year, Brevity and Uncertainty of Life)
Death and Resurrection
The Day of Judgment
Close of Worship
Doxologies

An appendix of fifty-one anthems and chants appears in the "Choir Edition," some with annotations such as "For opening or closing Public Worship," or "Temperance Anthem."

1878

Hymnal of the Methodist Episcopal Church With Tunes. New York: Nelson and Phillips, 1878. viii, 504 pages.

The tunes are given in four-part harmony (melody in the soprano) on two staves, with acknowledgment of the tune name and tune composer. Below the tune or opposite, two or more texts are given (author designated as well), for a total of 1117. Nineteen doxologies are listed; the "Occasional Pieces and Chants" are not numbered.

Following the title page and the preface, the table of contents lists the hymns under the following headings:

Worship	The Church
God	Time and Eternity
Christ	Miscellaneous
The Holy Spirit	Doxologies
The Scriptures	Occasional Pieces and Chants
The Sinner	Indexes
The Christian	Ritual

This publication demonstrates a clear break with the tradition of publishing tunes grouped according to meter, and goes much further in supplying congregational hymns for the seasons, for national occasions, and for mariners. In addition, pointed chants for selected psalms and canticles are provided. Of special note is the music for Trisagion and Tersanctus (439ff).

The Index is fulsome, including even a cross reference of all scriptural allusions by hymn number and verse. Also provided are thirty-six columns of subject indexes, and a listing of first lines of verses as well as of hymns' first lines. The Ritual section includes Baptism, Reception of Members, and The Lord's Supper. It was the first Methodist Episcopal Hymnal to include an order of worship. The ritual was authorized by the 1896 General Conference, and included in the front of the 1896 printing of the hymnal.

Metrical groupings are as follows:

Long Meter	77
Common Meter	93
Short Meter	47
6 Eights	14
4, 6, 8 Sevens	41
Other meters	199
Total	471

Of the total of 471, sixty-eight hymns are listed as having alternate tune(s) available. In addition to the nineteen doxologies, thirty-seven occasional pieces and chants are provided.

Notes

1. Thomas F. Bickley, "David's Harp (1813), a Methodist Tunebook from Baltimore: An Analysis and Facsimile" (M.A. dissertation, American University, 1983), 3, 21.
2. "Advertisement to the Revised And Enlarged Edition," *The Methodist Harmonist* (New York, 1833), v.
3. Preface, *The Harmonist* (New York, 1842), iv. The 1837 preface was retained in the 1842 edition.
4. Preface, *The Harmonist*, iv.

Appendix C
Alphabetical List of Tunes

TUNE NAME	COMPOSER/SOURCE	METER
ABSENCE (see **GREENVILLE**)		
ADISHAM (see **LITCHFIELD**)		
1. **ALFRETON**	Beastall, William	LM
ALMA (see **COME, YE DISCONSOLATE**)		
2. **AMSTERDAM**	Nares, James	76.76.77.76
ANTICIPATION (see **BURNHAM**)		
3. **ANTIGUA**	Wells; English Tune	LM
4. **ARLINGTON** (ARNE)	Arne, Thomas	CM
ARNE (see **ARLINGTON**)		
AVON (see **MARTYRDOM**)		
5. **AYLESBURY**	Miller; Green, James; Greene, Dr. M.	SM
BALTIMORE (see **WARSAW**)		
6. **BANISTER** (ROMAINE, DUNKIRK)	Bannister, C. W.	76.76 D
7. **BENEVENTO**	Webbe, Samuel	77.77 D
8. **BRATTLE STREET** (DEVOTION)	Pleyel, Ignace	CM D
9. **BRIDGEWATER**	Edson, Lewis	LM
10. **BRIGHTON**	English	888 D
11. **BURNHAM** (ANTICIPATION)	Clark, Thomas	66.66.88
12. **CAMBRIDGE** (RANDALL)	Randall, John	CM
13. **CHINA**	Swan, Timothy	CM
14. **CHRISTMAS**	Handel, Georg Frideric	CM
15. **COLCHESTER**	Williams, Tans'ur	CM
16. **COME, YE DISCONSOLATE** (ALMA, CONSOLATION, GILFORD, MERCY SEAT)	Webbe, Samuel	11.10 D
CONDOLENCE (see **PLEYEL'S HYMN**)		
CONSOLATION (see **COME, YE DISCONSOLATE**)		
17. **CRANBROOK**	Clark, Thomas	SM
18. **CREATION**	Haydn, Franz Joseph	LM

DAVID (see **THATCHER**)

19.	**DEVIZES**	Tucker, Isaac	CM

DEVOTION (see **BRATTLE STREET**)
DISMISSAL (see **SICILIAN HYMN**)
DOVERSDALE (see **STONEFIELD**)
DRUMCLOG (see **MARTYRDOM**)

20.	**DUKE STREET** (NEWRY)	Hatton, John	LM
21.	**DUNDEE** (FRENCH TUNE)	Scottish; Franc, G.	CM

DUNKIRK (see **BANISTER**)

22.	**EATON**	Wyvill, Zerubbabel	88.88.88

FALCON (see **SILVER STREET**)
FENWICK (see **MARTYRDOM**)

23.	**FOREST**	Chapin, Lucius	LM

FRENCH TUNE (see **DUNDEE**)

GAINSBOROUGH (see **ST. MARTIN'S**)

24.	**GANGES** (GORHAM)	Chandler, S.	886 D
25.	**GENEVA**	Cole, John	CM

GERMAN HYMN (see **PLEYEL'S HYMN**)
GERMANY (see **THATCHER**)
GILFORD (see **COME, YE DISCONSOLATE**)

26.	**GOD OF ABRAHAM**	Beaumont	66.84 D

GORHAM (see **GANGES**)

27.	**GREENVILLE** (ABSENCE)	Rousseau, Jean-Jacques	87.87 D

HALLAM (see **THATCHER**)
HANDEL (see **THATCHER**)
HANOVER (see **ST. MICHAEL'S**)

ITALIAN HYMN (see **TRINITY**)

JUDGMENT (see **LUTHER'S HYMN**)

28.	**KENTUCKY**	Western Air; Chapin, A.; Ingalls, J.	SM
29.	**LENOX**	Edson, Lewis	66.66.88
30.	**LISBON**	Read, Daniel	SM
31.	**LITCHFIELD** (ADISHAM)	Law, Andrew	LM
32.	**LITTLE MARLBOROUGH**	A. Williams' Collection	SM
33.	**LUTHER'S HYMN** (JUDGMENT, MONMOUTH)	Luther, Martin; Klug, J.	LM *or* 87.87.888
34.	**LUTON**	Burder, George	LM
35.	**LYONS**	Haydn, Johann Michael; Haydn, Franz Joseph	10.11.10.11 *or* 10.10.11.11
36.	**MAJESTY**	Billings, William	CM D
37.	**MARTYRDOM** (AVON, DRUMCLOG, FENWICK)	Wilson, Hugh; Scottish; Gamble	CM
38.	**MEAR** (NEW MEAR)	Williams; Welsh Air; Luther	CM

MERCY SEAT (see **COME, YE DISCONSOLATE**)
MONMOUTH (see **LUTHER'S HYMN**)

	NEW MEAR (see **MEAR**)		
	NEWRY (see **DUKE STREET**)		
39.	**NEW SABBATH**	Smith, Isaac	LM
	NEWTON (see **SILVER STREET**)		
40.	**NUREMBURG**	German; Ahle, J.	77.77 *or* 88.88 *or* 77.77.77
41.	**OLD HUNDRED** (OLD HUNDREDTH)	Luther; Franc, G.	LM
	OLD WINDSOR (see **WINDSOR**)		
42.	**PARK STREET**	Venua, Frederic	LM
43.	**PECKHAM** (RIPPON)	Smith, Isaac	SM
44.	**PENITENCE**	Oakley, William A.	76.76.78.76
45.	**PETERBOROUGH**	Harrison, Ralph	CM
46.	**PIETY**	Clark, Thomas; Clarke; Carle	CM (with extension) *or* 886 D
47.	**PLEYEL'S HYMN** (CONDOLENCE, GERMAN HYMN)	Pleyel, Ignace; Rippon	77.77
48.	**PLYMOUTH DOCK**	Law, Andrew	88.88.88
49.	**PORTUGAL**	Thorley, Thomas	LM
	RANDALL (see **CAMBRIDGE**)		
	RIPPON (see **PECKHAM**)		
50.	**ROCHESTER**	Holdroyd, Israel; Williams; English	CM
	ROMAINE (see **BANISTER**)		
51.	**ST. ANN'S**	Croft, William	CM
52.	**ST. MARTIN'S** (GAINSBOROUGH)	Tans'ur, William; Smith	CM
53.	**ST. MICHAEL'S** (HANOVER)	Handel, Georg Frideric	10.10.11.11
54.	**ST. THOMAS**	Williams, Aaron; Handel, G. F.	SM
55.	**SCOTLAND**	Clarke-Whitfield, John	12.12.12.12
56.	**SHIRLAND**	Stanley, Samuel	SM
57.	**SICILIAN HYMN** (DISMISSAL)	Mozart; Mason	77.77 *or* 87.87.47 *or* 87.87.87
58.	**SILVER STREET** (FALCON, NEWTON)	Smith, Isaac; Miller	SM
	SION (see **ZION**)		
59.	**STEPHEN'S**	Jones, William	CM
60.	**STONEFIELD** (DOVERSDALE)	Stanley, Samuel	LM
61.	**SWANWICK**	Lucas, James	CM
62.	**THATCHER** (DAVID, GERMANY, HALLAM, HANDEL, THACHER)	Handel, Georg Frideric	SM
63.	**TRINITY** (ITALIAN HYMN)	Giardini, Felice de	664.6664
64.	**TRIUMPH**	Clark, Thomas	77.87.77.87
65.	**TRURO**	Burney, Charles	LM
66.	**UXBRIDGE**	Mason, Lowell	LM
67.	**WARSAW** (BALTIMORE)	Clark, Thomas	66.66.88.88 *or* 66.66.86.86
68.	**WARWICK**	Stanley, Samuel	CM
69.	**WATCHMAN**	Leach, James; Read	SM
70.	**WELLS**	Holdroyd, Israel (Holroyd, Holdrayd, Holdrad, Holdrayd)	LM
71.	**WILLOWBY** (WILLOUGHBY)	Crane	886 D

72.	**WILMOT**	Weber, Carl Maria von	87.87 *or* 77.77
73.	**WINDHAM**	Read, Daniel	LM
74.	**WINDSOR** (OLD WINDSOR)	Kirbye; Scottish Psalter; Ravenscroft	CM
75.	**WOODLAND**	Gould, Nathaniel; National Church Harmony	CM *or* 86.886
76.	**ZION** (SION)	Hastings, Thomas	87.87.887 *or* 87.87.47

Appendix D
Metrical Index of Tunes

TUNE NAME	NUMBER	TUNE NAME	NUMBER
Long Meter		*Long Meter*	
ALFRETON	1	**WELLS**	70
ANTIGUA	3	**WINDHAM**	73
BRIDGEWATER	9		
CREATION	18	*Common Meter*	
DUKE STREET	20	**ARLINGTON**	4
FOREST	23	**CAMBRIDGE**	12
LITCHFIELD	31	**CHINA**	13
LUTON	34	**CHRISTMAS**	14
NEW SABBATH	39	**COLCHESTER**	15
NUREMBURG	40	**DEVIZES**	19
OLD HUNDRED	41	**DUNDEE**	21
PARK STREET	45	**GENEVA**	25
PORTUGAL	49	**MARTYRDOM**	37
STONEFIELD	60	**MEAR**	38
TRURO	65	**PETERBOROUGH**	45
UXBRIDGE	66	**PIETY**	46

Common Meter

ROCHESTER	50
ST. ANN'S	51
ST. MARTIN'S	52
STEPHEN'S	59
SWANWICK	61
WARWICK	68
WINDSOR	74
WOODLAND	75

CM D

BRATTLE STREET	8
MAJESTY	36

Short Meter

AYLESBURY	5
CRANBROOK	17
KENTUCKY	28
LISBON	30
LITTLE MARLBOROUGH	32
PECKHAM	43
ST. THOMAS	54
SHIRLAND	56
SILVER STREET	58
THATCHER	62
WATCHMAN	69

664.6664

TRINITY	63

66.84 D

GOD OF ABRAHAM	26

66.66.86.86

WARSAW	67

66.66.88

BURNHAM	11
LENOX	29

66.66.88.88

WARSAW	67

76.76 D

BANISTER	6

76.76.77.76

AMSTERDAM	2

76.76.78.76

PENITENCE	44

77.77

NUREMBURG 40

PLEYEL'S HYMN 47

SICILIAN HYMN 57

WILMOT 72

77.77.77

NUREMBURG 40

77.77 D

BENEVENTO 7

77.87.77.87

TRIUMPH 64

86.886

WOODLAND 75

87.87

WILMOT 72

87.87.47

SICILIAN HYMN 57

ZION 76

87.87.87

SICILIAN HYMN 57

87.87 D

GREENVILLE 27

87.87.887

LUTHER'S HYMN 33

ZION 76

886 D

GANGES 24

PIETY 46

WILLOWBY 71

88.88.88

EATON 22

LUTHER'S HYMN 33

PLYMOUTH DOCK 48

888 D

BRIGHTON 10

10.10.11.11

LYONS 35

ST. MICHAEL'S 53

10.11.10.11

LYONS 35

11.10 D   *12.12.12.12*

COME YE DISCONSOLATE   16   **SCOTLAND**   55

Appendix E
Alphabetical List of Composers

COMPOSER	NUMBER	TUNE NAME
Ahle, J.R.	40	**NUREMBURG** (see German)
Arne, T., attrib.	4	**ARLINGTON**
Banister, C.	6	**BANISTER**
Banister, C.	6	DUNKIRK
Banister, C.	6	ROMAINE
Beastall, W.	1	**ALFRETON**
Beaumont	26	**GOD OF ABRAHAM**
Billings, W.	36	**MAJESTY**
Bridgewater	16	**COME YE DISCONSOLATE** (see Webbe, S.)
Burder, G.	34	**LUTON**
Burney, C.	65	**TRURO**
Carle	46	**PIETY**
Chandler, S.	24	**GANGES**
Chapin, A.	23	**FOREST**
Chapin, A.	28	**KENTUCKY** (see Ingalls, Western Air)
Chapin, L.	2	**AMSTERDAM**
Clark, T.	11	**BURNHAM**
Clark, T.	12	**CAMBRIDGE** (see Randall, J.)
Clark, T.	17	**CRANBROOK**
Clark, T.,	46	**PIETY**
Clark, T.	12	RANDALL (see Randall, J.)
Clark, T.	64	**TRIUMPH**
Clark, T.	67	BALTIMORE
Clark, T.	67	**WARSAW**
Clarke, T.	46	**PIETY**
Clarke-Whitfield, J.	55	**SCOTLAND**
Cole, J.	25	**GENEVA**
Crane	71	**WILLOWBY**
Croft, W.	51	**ST. ANN'S**
Cuzens	19	**DEVIZES** (see Rippon, Tucker, I.)

Edson, L./J.	9	**BRIDGEWATER**
Edson, L./J.	29	**LENOX** (see Erbin's)
English	10	**BRIGHTON** (see Mason)
English	50	**ROCHESTER** (see Holdroyd, Williams)
English Tune	3	**ANTIGUA** (see Wells)
Erbin's	29	**LENOX** (see Edson, L./J.)
Franc	41	**OLD HUNDRED** (see Luther)
Franc	41	**OLD HUNDREDTH** (see Luther)
Franc, G.	21	**DUNDEE** (see Scottish)
Franc, G.	21	FRENCH TUNE (see Scottish)
Gamble	37	AVON (see Scottish, Wilson)
Gamble	37	DRUMCLOG (see Scottish, Wilson)
Gamble	37	FENWICK (see Scottish, Wilson)
Gamble	37	**MARTYRDOM** (see Scottish, Wilson)
German	40	**NUREMBURG** (see Ahle)
Giardini, F. da	63	ITALIAN HYMN
Giardini, F. da	63	**TRINITY**
Gould, N.	75	**WOODLAND** (see National Church Harmony)
Green, J.	5	**AYLESBURY** (see Greene, Miller)
Greene, M.	5	**AYLESBURY** (see Green, Miller)
Handel	53	**ST. MICHAEL'S** (see Rippon)
Handel	54	**ST. THOMAS** (see Williams, A., Williams' Collection)
Handel	62	DAVID
Handel	62	GERMANY
Handel	62	HALLAM
Handel	62	HANDEL
Handel	62	THACHER
Handel	62	**THATCHER**
Handel, G.	14	**CHRISTMAS**
Harrison, R.	45	**PETERBOROUGH**
Hastings, T.	76	**ZION**
Hatton, J.	20	**DUKE STREET**
Hatton, J.	20	NEWRY
Haydn, F. J.	18	**CREATION** (see also Haydn, M.)
Haydn, F. J.	35	**LYONS** (see Haydn, J. M.)
Haydn, J. M.	35	**LYONS** (see Haydn, F. J.)
Haydn, M.	18	**CREATION** (see also Haydn, F. J .)
Hille, J. G.	2	**AMSTERDAM**
Holdroyd	50	**ROCHESTER** (see English, Williams)
Holdroyd, I. (or Holdrad, Holdrayd, Holroyd)	70	**WELLS**
Ingalls	28	**KENTUCKY** (see Western Air; Chapin, A.)
Jones	59	**STEPHEN'S**
Kirbye, G.	74	OLD WINDSOR (see Ravenscroft, Scottish)
Kirbye, G.	74	**WINDSOR** (see Ravenscroft, Scottish)
Klug, J.	33	JUDGMENT (see Luther, M.)
Klug, J.	33	**LUTHER'S HYMN** (see Luther, M.)

Klug, J.	33	MONMOUTH (see Luther, M.)
Law, A.	31	ADISHAM
Law, A.	31	**LITCHFIELD**
Law, A.	48	**PLYMOUTH DOCK**
Leach, J.	69	**WATCHMAN** (see Read)
Lucas, J.	61	**SWANWICK**
Luther	38	**MEAR** (see Williams; Williams, C.)
Luther	38	NEW MEAR (see Williams; Williams, C.)
Luther	41	**OLD HUNDRED** (see Franc)
Luther	41	**OLD HUNDREDTH** (see Franc)
Luther, M.	33	JUDGMENT (see Klug, J.)
Luther, M.	33	**LUTHER'S HYMN** (see Klug, J.)
Luther, M.	33	MONMOUTH (see Klug, J.)
Mason	57	**SICILIAN HYMN** (see Mozart)
Mason, L.	10	**BRIGHTON** (see English)
Mason, L.	66	**UXBRIDGE**
Miller	5	**AYLESBURY** (see Green, J. Greene, M.)
Miller	43	**PECKHAM** (see Smith, I.)
Miller	58	FALCON (see Smith, I.)
Miller	43	NEWTON (see Smith, I.)
Miller	58	**SILVER STREET** (see Smith, I.)
Mozart	57	**SICILIAN HYMN** (see Mason)
Nares, J.	2	**AMSTERDAM**
National Church Harmony	75	**WOODLAND** (see Gould, N.)
Oakley, W.	44	**PENITENCE**
Pleyel, I.	8	**BRATTLE STREET**
Pleyel, I.	8	DEVOTION
Pleyel, I.	47	**PLEYEL'S HYMN** (see Rippon)
Randall, J.	12	**CAMBRIDGE** (see Clark, T.)
Randall, J.	12	RANDALL (see Clark, T.)
Ravenscroft	74	OLD WINDSOR (see Kirbye, G., Scottish)
Ravenscroft	74	**WINDSOR** (see Kirbye, G., Scottish)
Read	69	**WATCHMAN** (see Leach, J.)
Read, D.	30	**LISBON**
Read, D./J.	73	**WINDHAM**
Rippon	19	**DEVIZES** (see Cuzens, Tucker, I.)
Rippon	47	**PLEYEL'S HYMN** (see Pleyel, I.)
Rippon	53	**ST. MICHAEL'S** (see Handel)
Rousseau, J.-J.	27	ABSENCE
Rousseau, J.-J.	27	**GREENVILLE**
Scottish	21	**DUNDEE** (see Franc, G.)
Scottish	21	FRENCH TUNE (see Franc, G.)
Scottish	37	AVON (see Gamble, Wilson, H.)
Scottish	37	DRUMCLOG (see Gamble, Wilson, H.)
Scottish	37	FENWICK (see Gamble, Wilson, H.)
Scottish	37	**MARTYRDOM** (see Gamble, Wilson, H.)
Scottish	74	OLD WINDSOR (see Kirbye, G., Ravenscroft)

Scottish	74	**WINDSOR** (see Kirbye, G., Ravenscroft)
Smith	52	**ST. MARTIN'S** (see Tans'ur, W.)
Smith, I.	39	**NEW SABBATH**
Smith, I.	43	**PECKHAM** (see Miller)
Smith, I.	43	**RIPPON**
Smith, I.	58	**FALCON** (see Miller)
Smith, I.	58	**NEWTON** (see Miller)
Smith, I.	58	**SILVER STREET** (see Miller)
Stanley, S.	56	**SHIRLAND**
Stanley, S.	60	**DOVERSDALE**
Stanley, S.	60	**STONEFIELD**
Stanley, S.	68	**WARWICK**
Swan, T.	13	**CHINA**
Tans'ur, W.	15	**COLCHESTER** (see Williams)
Tans'ur, W.	52	**ST. MARTIN'S** (see Smith)
Thorley, T.	48	**PORTUGAL**
Tucker, I.	19	**DEVIZES** (see Cuzens, Rippon)
Venua	42	**PARK STREET**
Webbe, S.	7	**BENEVENTO**
Webbe, S.	16	**ALMA** (see Bridgewater)
Webbe, S.	16	**COME YE DISCONSOLATE** (see Bridge-water)
Webbe, S.	16	**CONSOLATION** (see Bridgewater)
Webbe, S.	16	**GILFORD** (see Bridgewater)
Webbe, S.	16	**MERCY SEAT** (see Bridgewater)
Weber, C. M. von	72	**WILMOT**
Wells	3	**ANTIGUA** (see English Tune)
Western Air	28	**KENTUCKY** (see Chapin, A.; Ingalls)
Whitfield-Clark, J.	55	**SCOTLAND**
Williams	15	**COLCHESTER** (see Tans'ur, W.)
Williams	38	**MEAR** (see Luther)
Williams	38	**NEW MEAR** (see Luther)
Williams	50	**ROCHESTER** (see English, Holdroyd)
Williams, A.	32	**LITTLE MARLBOROUGH**
Williams, A.	54	**ST. THOMAS** (see Handel, Williams' Collection)
Williams, C.	38	**MEAR** (see Luther, Williams)
Williams, C.	38	**NEW MEAR** (see Luther, Williams)
Williams, Collection	32	**LITTLE MARLBOROUGH**
Williams, Collection	54	**ST. THOMAS** (see Handel; Williams, A.)
Wilson, H.	37	**AVON** (see Gamble, Scottish)
Wilson, H.	37	**DRUMCLOG** (see Gamble, Scottish)
Wilson, H.	37	**FENWICK** (see Gamble, Scottish)
Wilson, H.	37	**MARTYRDOM** (see Gamble, Scottish)
Wyvill, Z.	22	**EATON**

Appendix F
Chronological List of Tune Appearances

DATE	TUNE NAME	NUMBER	COMPOSER/EDITOR
n.d.	**SCOTLAND**	55	Clarke-Whitfield
1529	**LUTHER'S HYMN**	33	Luther, Klug
1561	**OLD HUNDRED**	41	G. Franc, Luther
1591	**WINDSOR**	74	Kirbye, Scottish Psalter, Ravenscroft
1615	**DUNDEE**	21	Scottish, G. Franc
1708	**ST. ANN'S**	51	Croft
1720	**NUREMBURG**	40	German, Ahle
1722	**ROCHESTER**	50	Holdroyd, English, Williams
1722	**ST. MICHAEL'S**	53	Handel, Rippon
1722	**WELLS**	70	Holdroyd
1724	**AYLESBURY**	5	Miller, Green, Greene
1734–1737	**MEAR**	38	Luther, Welsh Air, A. Williams
1735	**COLCHESTER**	15	Tans'ur
1742	**AMSTERDAM**	2	Hille
1748	**ST. MARTIN'S**	52	Tans'ur, Smith

1760–1763	**TRINITY**	63	Giardini
1763	**LITTLE MARLBOROUGH**	32	A. Williams
Ca. 1769	**ST. THOMAS**	54	Williams, Handel
1777	**LUTON**	34	Burder
1778	**MAJESTY**	36	Billings
1778	**PORTUGAL**	49	Thorley
1778	**TRURO**	65	Burney
1779–1780	**PECKHAM**	43	Smith, Miller
1779–1780	**SILVER STREET**	58	Smith, Miller
1782	**BRIDGEWATER**	9	Edson
1782	**LENOX**	29	Edson
1784	**ARLINGTON**	4	Arne
1785	**LISBON**	30	Read
1785	**WINDHAM**	73	Read
1786	**CAMBRIDGE**	12	Randall
1788	**ANTIGUA**	3	Addington
1788	**NEW SABBATH**	39	Smith
1788	**WILLOWBY**	71	Crane
1789	**STEPHEN'S**	59	Jones
1789	**SWANWICK**	61	Lucas
1789–1798	**WATCHMAN**	69	Leach, Read
1790	**WARWICK**	68	Stanley
1791	**CHRISTMAS**	14	Arnold, Handel
1791	**PLEYEL'S HYMN**	47	Pleyel, Rippon
1792	**BANISTER**	6	Banister
1792	**COME YE DISCONSOLATE**	16	Webbe
1792	**DEVIZES**	19	Tucker
1792	**SICILIAN HYMN**	57	Mozart, Mason

1793	**DUKE STREET**	20	Hatton
1793	**LITCHFIELD**	31	Law
1797	**GENEVA**	25	Cole
1800	**STONEFIELD**	60	Stanley
1801	**CHINA**	13	Swan
1801	**GOD OF ABRAHAM**	26	Beaumont
1802	**EATON**	22	Wyvill, Walker
1802	**SHIRLAND**	56	Stanley
1803	**PETERBOROUGH**	45	Harrison
1803	**PLYMOUTH DOCK**	48	Law
1805	**BRATTLE STREET**	8	Pleyel
1805	**BURNHAM**	11	Clark
1805	**CRANBROOK**	17	Clark
1806	**CREATION**	18	Gardiner/Haydn
1806	**THATCHER**	62	Handel
1807	**WARSAW**	67	Clark
1808	**GANGES**	24	Chandler
1811	**PIETY**	46	Clark
1813	**FOREST**	23	Chapin
1813	**KENTUCKY**	28	Chapin, Ingalls, Western Air
1813	**TRIUMPH**	64	Clark
1814	**ALFRETON**	1	Beastall
1815	**LYONS**	35	Haydn, Gardiner
1815	**PARK STREET**	42	Venua, Gardiner, Mason
1819	**BENEVENTO**	7	Webbe
1819	**GREENVILLE**	27	Rousseau
1823	**BRIGHTON**	10	English, Mason

1825	**MARTYRDOM**	37	Scottish, Wilson, Gamble
1830	**UXBRIDGE**	66	Mason
1831–1832	**ZION**	76	Hastings
1832	**WILMOT**	72	von Weber
1833–1835	**WOODLAND**	75	Gould
1837?	**PENITENCE**	44	Oakley

Selected Bibliography

Books

Baeumker, Wilhelm. *Das katholische deutsche Kirchenlied in seinem Singweisen von den fruehsten Zeiten bis gegen Ende des siebzehnted Jahrhunderts.* Hildesheim: G. Olms, 1962.

Brown, Theron, and Hezekiah Butterworth. *The Story of the Hymns and Tunes.* New York: G. H. Doran, 1906.

Chase, Gilbert. *America's Music.* 2nd ed. rev. New York: McGraw Hill, 1966.

Crawford, Richard A. *Andrew Law, American Psalmodist.* Evanston: Northwestern University Press, 1968.

———, ed. *The Core Repertory of Early American Psalmody.* Recent Researches in American Music, Vol. 11/12. Madison, WI: A-R Editions, 1984.

Creamer, David. *Methodist Hymnology.* New York: Longking, 1848.

Diehl, Katharine Smith. *Hymns and Tunes—an Index.* New York: Scarecrow Press, 1966.

Eskew, Harry, and Hugh T. McElrath. *Sing with Understanding.* Nashville, TN: Broadman Press, 1980.

Frost, Maurice. *English and Scottish Psalm and Hymn Tunes c. 1543–1677.* New York: Oxford University Press, 1953.

———, ed. *Historical Companion to Hymns Ancient and Modern.* London: William Clowes and Sons, 1962.

Gealy, Fred, Austin Lovelace, Carlton R. Young, and Emory S. Bucke, eds. *Companion to the Hymnal: A Handbook to the 1964 Methodist Hymnal.* New York: Abingdon, 1970.

Heydt, Johann Daniel von der. *Geschichte der Evangelischen Kirchenmusik in Deutschland.* Berlin: Trowitzsch, 1926.

Hildebrandt, Franz, and Oliver Beckerlegge, eds. *The Works of John Wesley*, Vol. 7. Oxford: Clarendon Press, 1983.

Hughes, Charles W. *American Hymns, Old and New: Notes on the Hymns and Biographies of the Authors and Composers.* New York: Columbia University Press, 1980.

The Hymnal 1940 Companion. The Church Pension Fund, New York. 3rd rev. ed. Worcester, MA: Heffernan Press, 1949, 1951.

Jackson, George Pullen, ed. *White Spirituals in Southern Uplands.* Chapel Hill: University of North Carolina Press, 1933.

———. *Another Sheaf of White Spirituals.* Gainesville, FL: University of Florida Press, 1952.

———. *Down-East Spirituals and Others.* 2nd ed. Locust Valley, NY: J. J. Augustin, 1953.

Julian, John, ed. *A Dictionary of Hymnology.* New York: Charles Scribners Sons, 1892. 1616 pp.

Leaver, Robin A. *Goostly Psalmes and Spirituall Songes: English and Dutch Metrical Psalms from Coverdale to Utenhove, 1535–1566.* Oxford: Clarendon Press, 1991.

Lightwood, James T. *Hymn Tunes and Their Story.* London: Charles H. Kelly, 1905.

———. *Methodist Music in the Eighteenth Century.* London: Epworth Press, 1927.

———. *The Music of the Methodist Hymnbook.* London: Epworth Press, 1935.

Lowens, Irving. *Music and Musicians in Early America.* New York: W. W. Norton, 1964.

Mason, Henry L. *Hymn Tunes of Lowell Mason: A Bibliography.* Cambridge, MA: University Press, 1944.

McCutchan, Robert G. *Our Hymnody: A Manual of the Methodist Hymnal.* 2nd ed. Nashville: Abingdon-Cokesbury Press, 1937.

————. *Hymn Tune Names: Their Sources and Significance.* New York: Abingdon, 1957.

Metcalf, Frank J. *Stories of Hymn Tunes.* New York: Abingdon, 1928.

Moffatt, James, and Millar Patrick, eds. *Handbook to the Church Hymnary.* London: H. Milford, Oxford University Press, 1935.

Pemberton, Carol A. *Lowell Mason: A Bio-Bibliography.* New York, CT: Greenwood Press, 1988.

Reynolds, William J. *A Survey of Christian Hymnody.* New York: Holt, Rinehart, and Winston, 1963.

Rogal, Samuel J. *Guide to the Hymns and Tunes of American Methodism.* Music Reference Collection, no. 7. New York: Greenwood Press, 1986.

Routley, Erik. *The Music of Christian Hymns.* Chicago: GIA Publications, 1981.

Sadie, Stanley, ed., and John Tyrell, executive director. *The New Grove Dictionary of Music and Musicians,* 2nd ed., 29 vols. New York: Grove, 2001.

Stevenson, Robert. *Protestant Church Music in America.* New York: W. W. Norton, 1966.

Temperley, Nicholas. *The Music of the English Parish Church,* 2 vols. Cambridge: Cambridge University Press, 1979.

————. *The Hymn Tune Index: A Census of English Language Hymn Tunes in Printed Sources, 1535–1820,* 4 vols. Oxford: Clarendon Press, 1998.

Temperley, Nicholas, and Charles G. Manns. *Fuging Tunes in the Eighteenth Century.* Detroit Studies in Music Bibliography, no. 49. Detroit: Information Coordinators, 1983.

Wasson, D. DeWitt. *Hymntune Index and Related Hymn Materials,* 3 vols. Lanham, MD and London: Scarecrow Press, 1998.

Watson, Richard, and Kenneth Trickett, eds. *Companion to Hymns and Psalms.* Peterborough, England: Methodist Publishing House, 1988.

Young, Carlton R. *Companion to the United Methodist Hymnal.* Nashville: Abingdon Press, 1993.

————. *Music of the Heart.* Carol Stream, IL: Hope Publishing, 1995.

Dissertations

Adams, Nelson Falls. "The Musical Sources for John Wesley's Tunebooks: the Genealogy of 148 Tunes." S.M.D. dissertation, Union Theological Seminary, New York, 1973.

Baldridge, Terry L. "Evolving Tastes in Hymntunes of the Methodist Episcopal Church in the Nineteenth Century." Ph.D. dissertation, University of Kansas, 1982.

Bickley, Thomas Frank. "David's Harp (1813). A Methodist Tunebook from Baltimore: An Analysis and Facsimile." M.A. thesis, American University, 1983.

Hill, Double E. "A Study in Tastes in American Church Music as Reflected in the Music of the Methodist Episcopal Church to 1900." Ph.D. dissertation, University of Illinois, 1962.

Ingles, Faith Petra. "The Role of Wesleyan Hymnody in the Development of Congregational Song." D.M.A. dissertation, Combs College, 1986.

Kroeger, Karl. "The Worcester Collection of Sacred Harmony and Sacred Music in America, 1786–1803." Ph.D. dissertation, Brown University, 1975.

Murrell, Irvin Henry. "An Examination of Southern Ante-Bellum Baptist Hymnals and Tunebooks as Indicators of the Congregational Hymn and Tune Repertories of the Period." D.M.A. thesis, New Orleans Theological Seminary, 1984.

Wade, William Nash. "A History of Public Worship in the Methodist Episcopal Church and Methodist Episcopal Church, South, from 1784 to 1905." Ph.D. dissertation, University of Notre Dame, 1981.

Articles

Brandon, George. "Some Classic Tunes in Lowell Mason's Collections." *The Hymn* 18 (July 1967): 78–79.

"Church Music Again—the New Tune Book, etc." *Christian Advocate and Journal* 19 (New York, January 1848).

Hammond, Paul. "The Hymnody of the Second Great Awakening." *The Hymn* 29 (January 1978): 19–28.

Higginson, J. Vincent. "Notes on Lowell Mason's Tunes." *The Hymn* 18 (April 1967): 37–42.

Leaver, Robin A. Review of *The Core Repertory of Early American Psalmody* (Recent Researches in American Music, Vol. 11/12), edited by Richard Crawford (Madison, WI: A-R Editions, 1984). *News of Hymnody*, no. 17 (January 1986).

Lowens, Irving. "The Origins of the American Fuging Tune," *Journal of the American Musicological Society* 6 (Spring 1953).

Schalk, Carl. "Hymnody, American Lutheran." Pp. 222–231 in *Key Words in Church Music*, edited by Carl Schalk. St. Louis: Concordia Publishing House, 1978.

"Singing—Social meetings." *Zion's Herald and Wesleyan Journal* 17 (January 1849): 10.

Strauss, Barbara J. "The Methodist/Moravian Legacy of Hymns," *Methodist History* 24, no. 3 (April 1986).

Temperley, Nicholas. "The Old Way of Singing." *Journal of the American Musicological Society* 34, no. 3 (Fall 1981).

Van Burkalow, Anastasia. "Expanding Horizons: Two Hundred Years of American Methodist Hymnody." *The Hymn* 17 (July 1966): 74–84, 90.

Wentworth, Erastus. "Methodists and Music." *Methodist Quarterly Review* 47 (July 1865).

Young, Carlton R. "A Survey of American Methodist Hymnbooks." Pp. 54–61 in *Companion to the Hymnal: A Handbook to the 1964 Methodist Hymnal*, edited by Emory Stevens Bucke. Nashville: Abingdon Press, 1970.

———. "John Wesley's 1737 Charlestown Collection of Psalms and Hymns." *The Hymn* 41, no. 4 (1990): 19–27.

About the Author

Fred Kimball Graham is currently assistant professor of church music, university organist, and director of basic degree studies at Emmanuel College of Victoria University and the Toronto School of Theology, University of Toronto. Educated at the University of Toronto (Mus. Bac.), the Eastman School of Music (M.M.), and Drew University, Madison, NJ (M.Phil., Ph.D.), he held music leadership positions in Ottawa, Ontario; Rothesay, New Brunswick; and Halifax, Nova Scotia prior to his appointment as music and worship officer for The United Church of Canada in 1988. During his tenure, he made editorial contributions to all editions of *Voices United: The Hymn- and Worship-Book of the United Church* (1996), and was supervising editor for *Celebrate God's Presence* (2000), a book of services for the denomination. In tandem with his academic duties, he acts as music director at Humbercrest United Church, Toronto. In 2002, he was elected to a three-year term as chairperson of the Consultation on Common Texts, an ecumenical forum of eighteen denominations from across North America. He is a charter member of the Charles Wesley Society (1990) and a member of the North American Academy of Liturgy, of Societas Liturgica, The Hymn Society in the United States and Canada, and the Royal Canadian College of Organists. He has presented lectures, recitals, and workshops across Canada, in Britain, and in Germany. His published hymn tune, LIFE RESTORED, appears in *Voices United.*